FBP
FEDERAL BUREAU OF PHYSICS

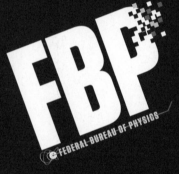

VOLUME 4
THE END TIMES

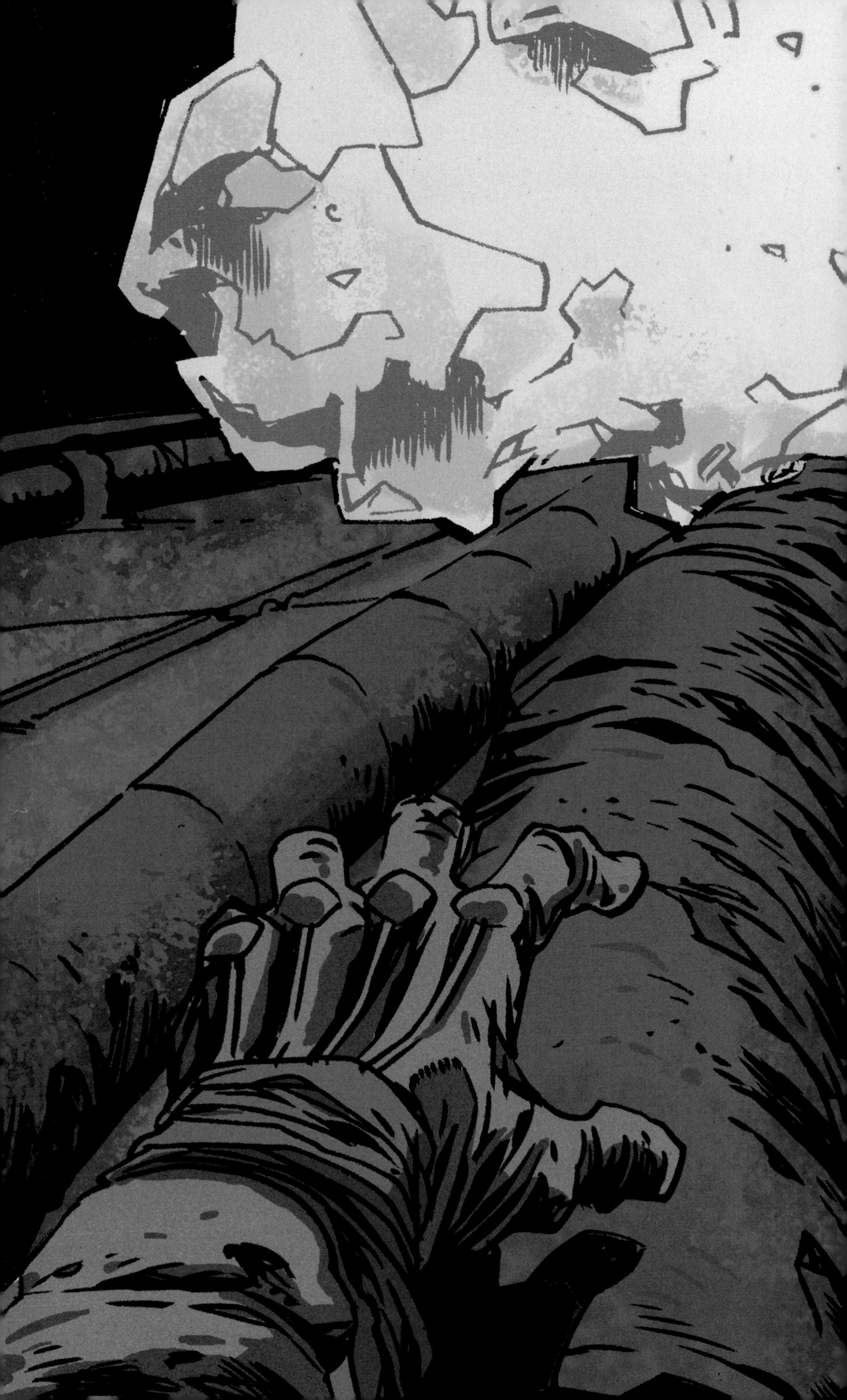

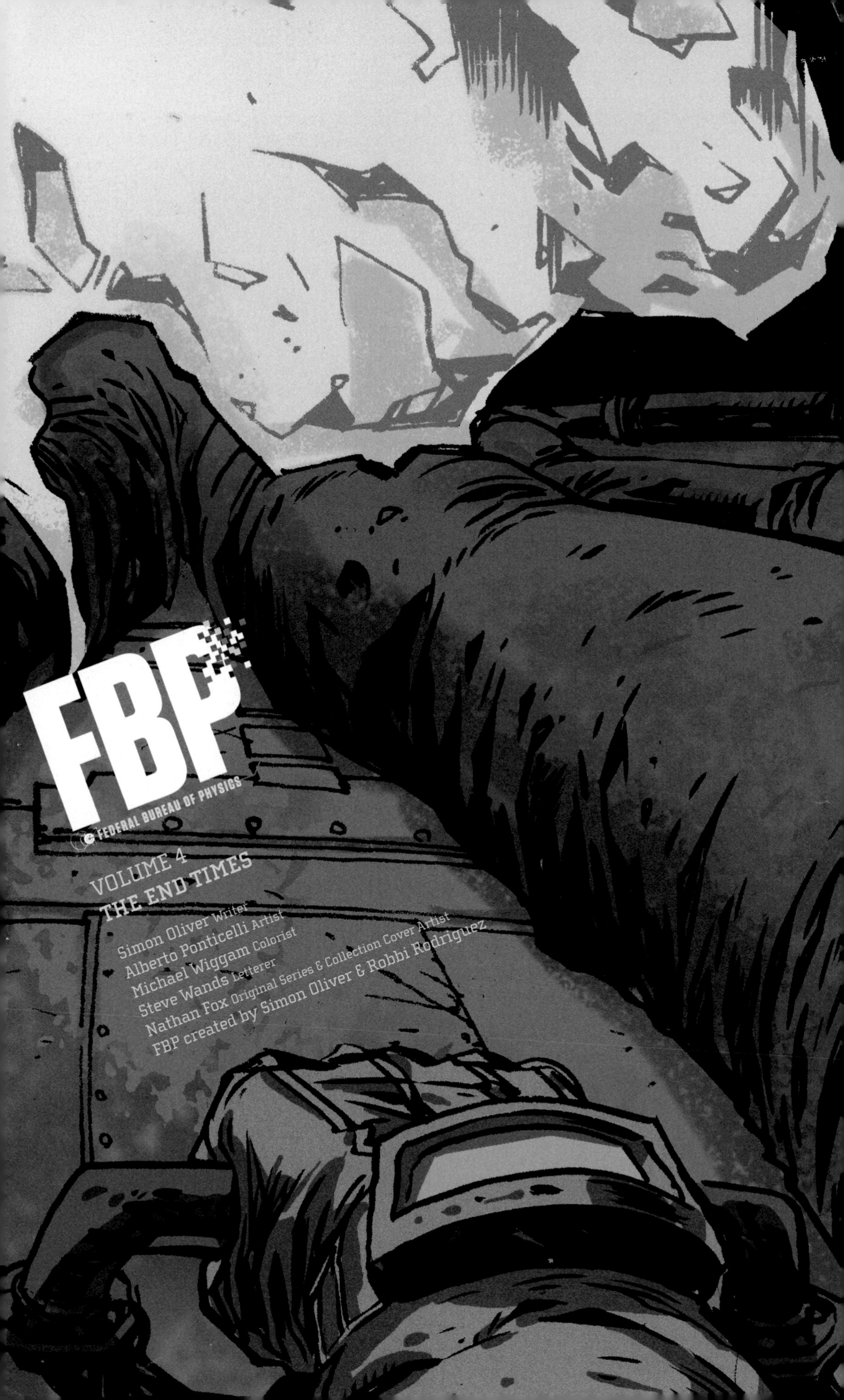

FBP
Federal Bureau of Physics

Volume 4
The End Times

Simon Oliver Writer
Alberto Ponticelli Artist
Michael Wiggam Colorist
Steve Wands Letterer
Nathan Fox Original Series & Collection Cover Artist
FBP created by Simon Oliver & Robbi Rodriguez

Molly Mahan Jamie S. Rich Greg Lockard Editors – Original Series
Sara Miller Assistant Editor – Original Series
Jeb Woodard Group Editor – Collected Editions
Liz Erickson Editor – Collected Edition
Louis Prandi Publication Design

Shelly Bond VP & Executive Editor – Vertigo

Diane Nelson President
Dan DiDio and Jim Lee Co-Publishers
Geoff Johns Chief Creative Officer
Amit Desai Senior VP – Marketing & Global Franchise Management
Nairi Gardiner Senior VP – Finance
Sam Ades VP – Digital Marketing
Bobbie Chase VP – Talent Development
Mark Chiarello Senior VP – Art, Design & Collected Editions
John Cunningham VP – Content Strategy
Anne DePies VP – Strategy Planning & Reporting
Don Falletti VP – Manufacturing Operations
Lawrence Ganem VP – Editorial Administration & Talent Relations
Alison Gill Senior VP – Manufacturing & Operations
Hank Kanalz Senior VP – Editorial Strategy & Administration
Jay Kogan VP – Legal Affairs
Derek Maddalena Senior VP – Sales & Business Development
Jack Mahan VP – Business Affairs
Dan Miron VP – Sales Planning & Trade Development
Nick Napolitano VP – Manufacturing Administration
Carol Roeder VP – Marketing
Eddie Scannell VP – Mass Account & Digital Sales
Courtney Simmons Senior VP – Publicity & Communications
Jim (Ski) Sokolowski VP – Comic Book Specialty & Newsstand Sales
Sandy Yi Senior VP – Global Franchise Management

FBP: FEDERAL BUREAU OF PHYSICS VOLUME 4: THE END TIMES

DC Comics, 2900 West Alameda Ave, Burbank, CA 91505
Printed by RR Donnelley, Owensville, MO, USA. 12/04/15. First Printing.
ISBN: 978-1-4012-5845-0

Oliver, Simon.
  FBP : Federal Bureau of Physics. Volume 4 / Simon Oliver, writer ;
Alberto Ponticelli, artist.
     pages cm
ISBN: 978-1-4012-5845-0
 1. Graphic novels. I. Ponticelli, Alberto, illustrator. II. Title.
 PN6727.05F4 2016
 741.5'973—dc23

                    2015034645

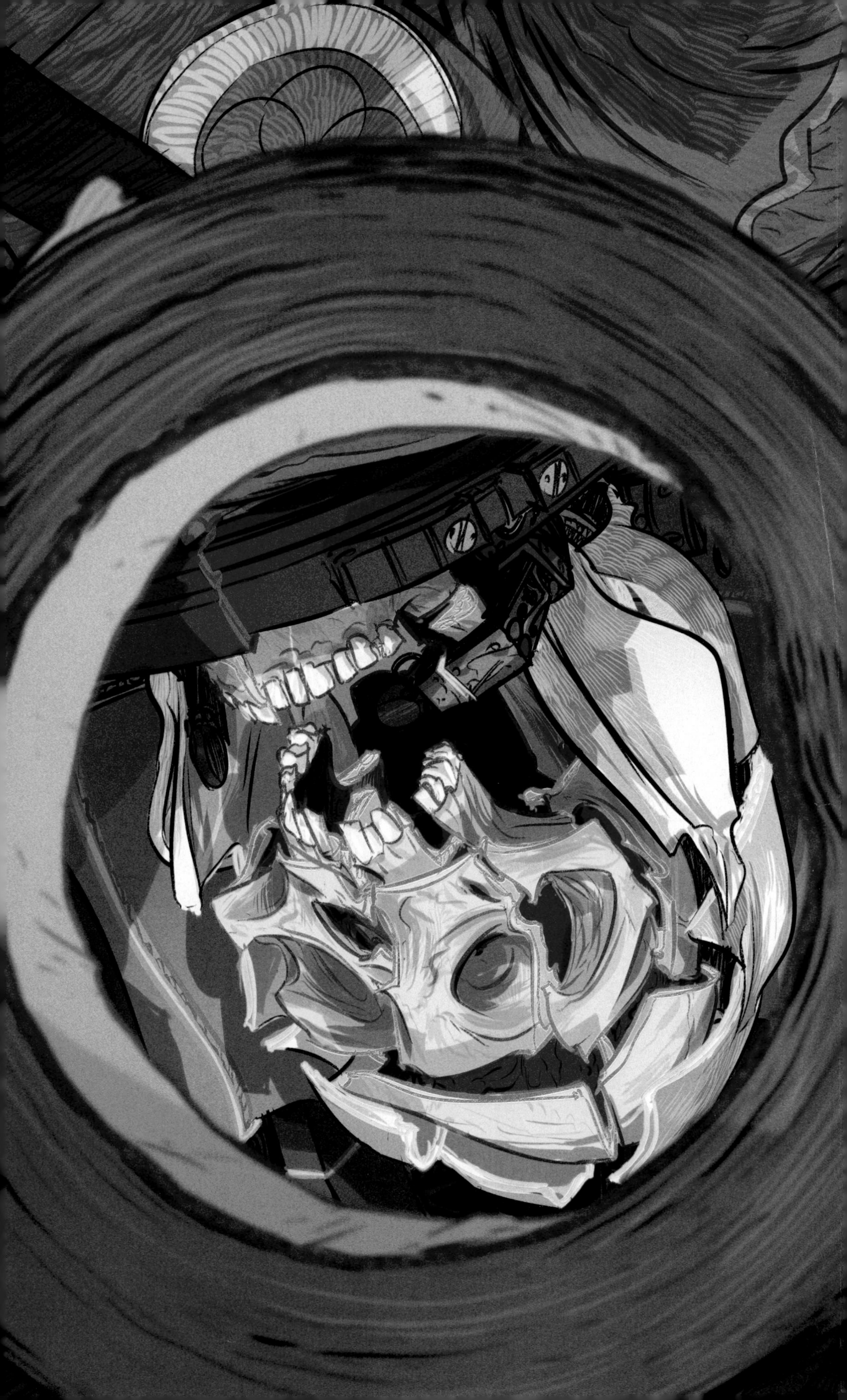

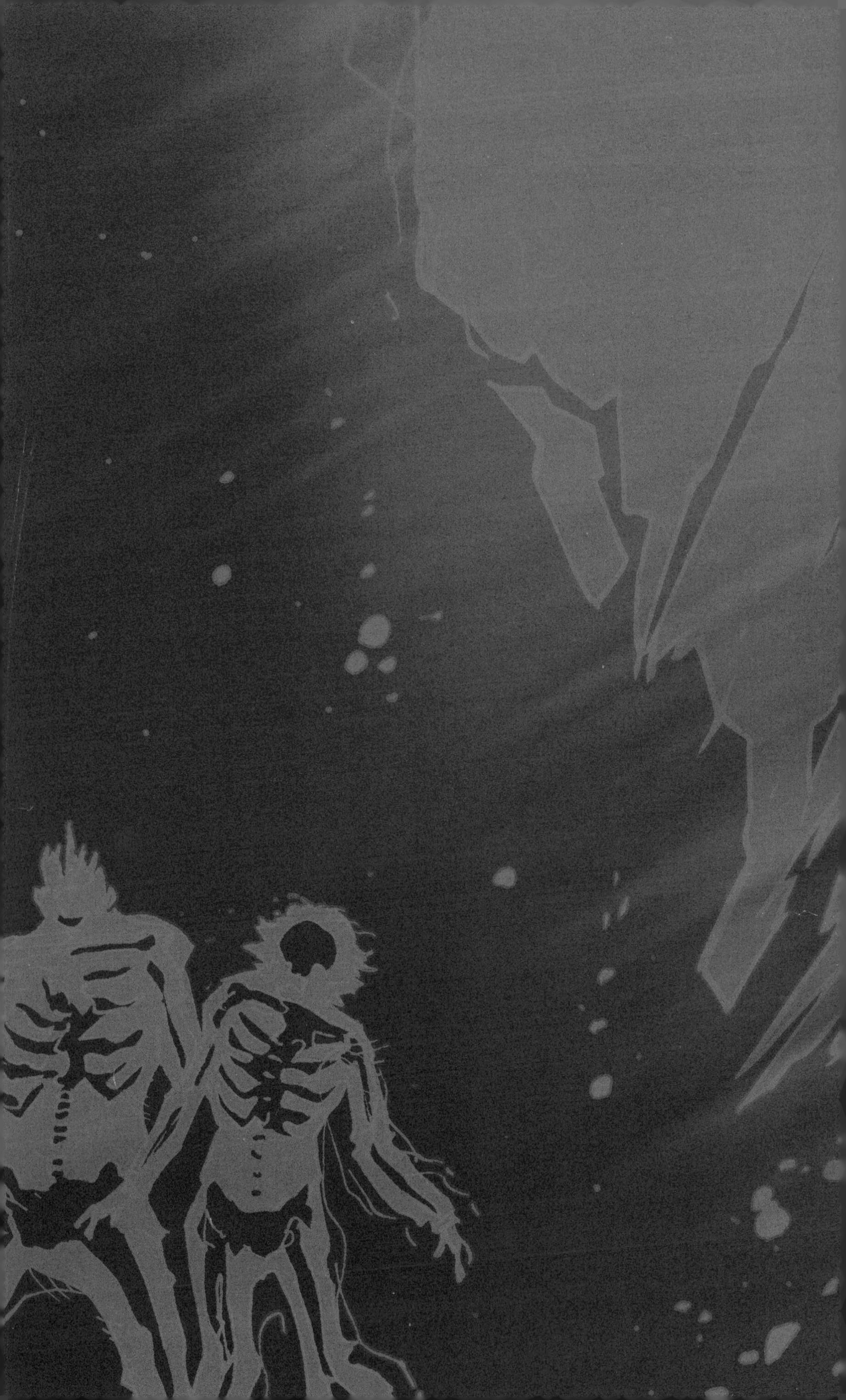

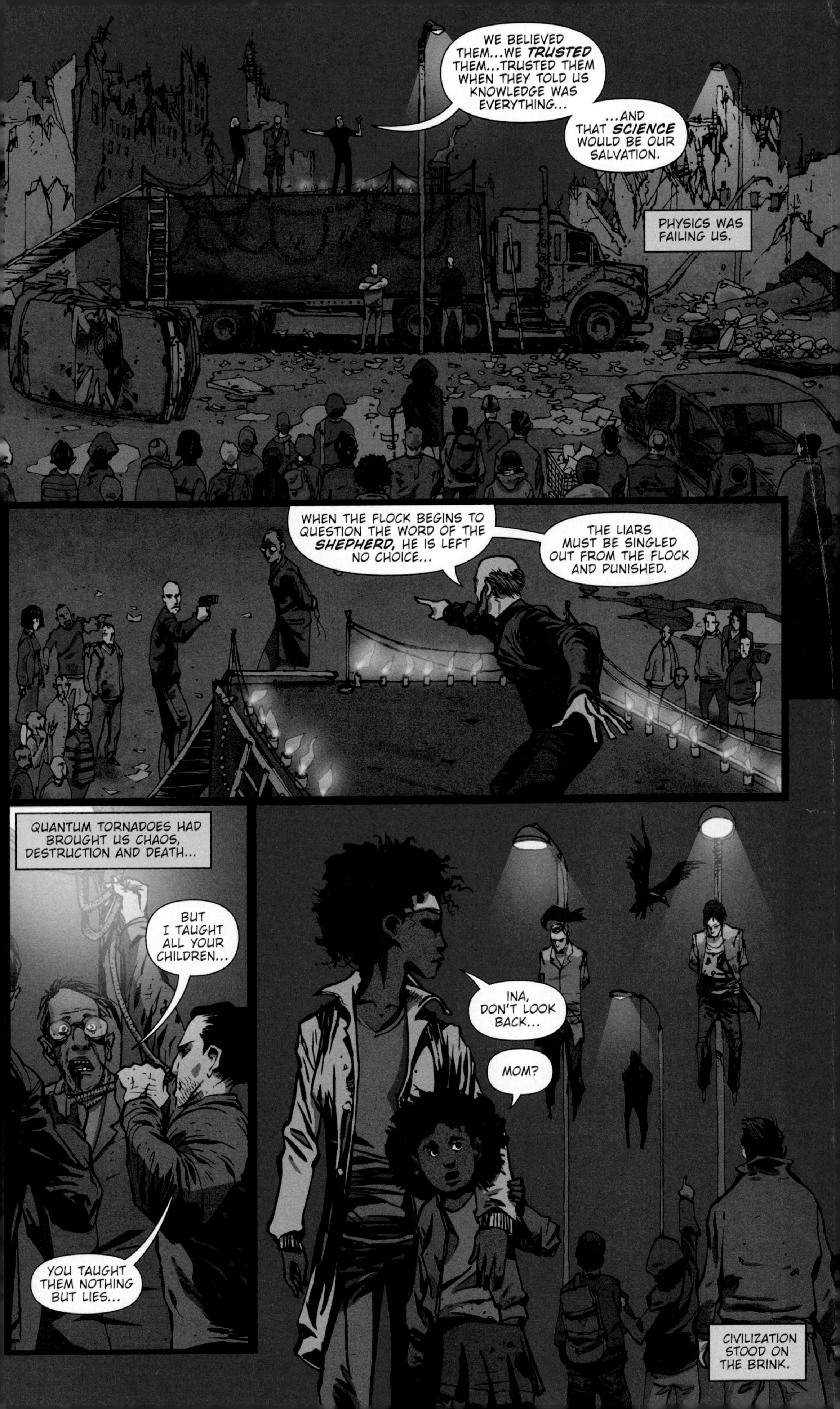
WE BELIEVED THEM...WE TRUSTED THEM...TRUSTED THEM WHEN THEY TOLD US KNOWLEDGE WAS EVERYTHING...
...AND THAT SCIENCE WOULD BE OUR SALVATION.
PHYSICS WAS FAILING US.
WHEN THE FLOCK BEGINS TO QUESTION THE WORD OF THE SHEPHERD, HE IS LEFT NO CHOICE...
THE LIARS MUST BE SINGLED OUT FROM THE FLOCK AND PUNISHED.
QUANTUM TORNADOES HAD BROUGHT US CHAOS, DESTRUCTION AND DEATH...
BUT I TAUGHT ALL YOUR CHILDREN...
YOU TAUGHT THEM NOTHING BUT LIES...
INA, DON'T LOOK BACK...
MOM?
CIVILIZATION STOOD ON THE BRINK.

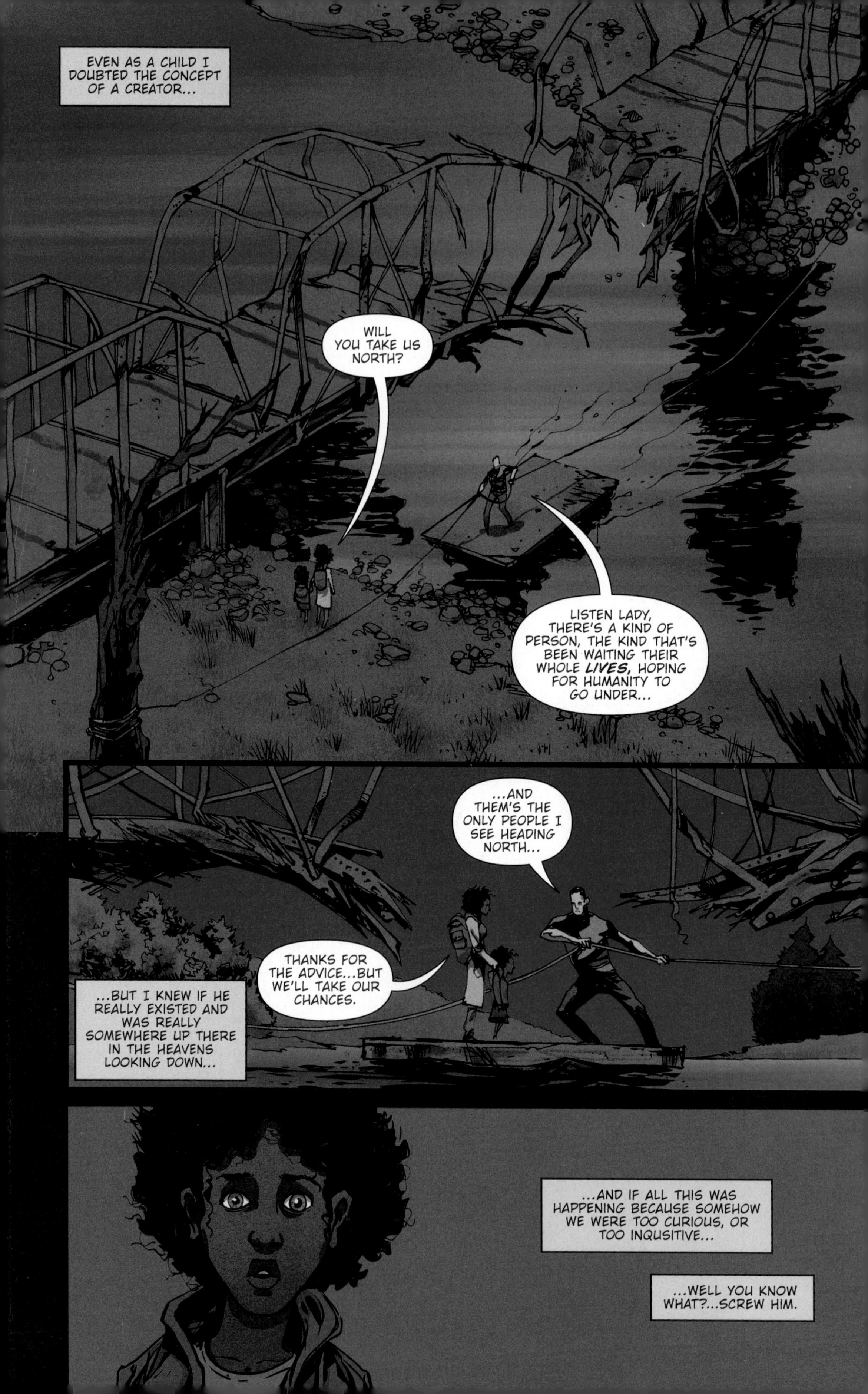
EVEN AS A CHILD I DOUBTED THE CONCEPT OF A CREATOR...
WILL YOU TAKE US NORTH?
LISTEN LADY, THERE'S A KIND OF PERSON, THE KIND THAT'S BEEN WAITING THEIR WHOLE *LIVES,* HOPING FOR HUMANITY TO GO UNDER...
...AND THEM'S THE ONLY PEOPLE I SEE HEADING NORTH...
THANKS FOR THE ADVICE...BUT WE'LL TAKE OUR CHANCES.
...BUT I KNEW IF HE REALLY EXISTED AND WAS REALLY SOMEWHERE UP THERE IN THE HEAVENS LOOKING DOWN...
...AND IF ALL THIS WAS HAPPENING BECAUSE SOMEHOW WE WERE TOO CURIOUS, OR TOO INQUISITIVE...
...WELL YOU KNOW WHAT?...SCREW HIM.

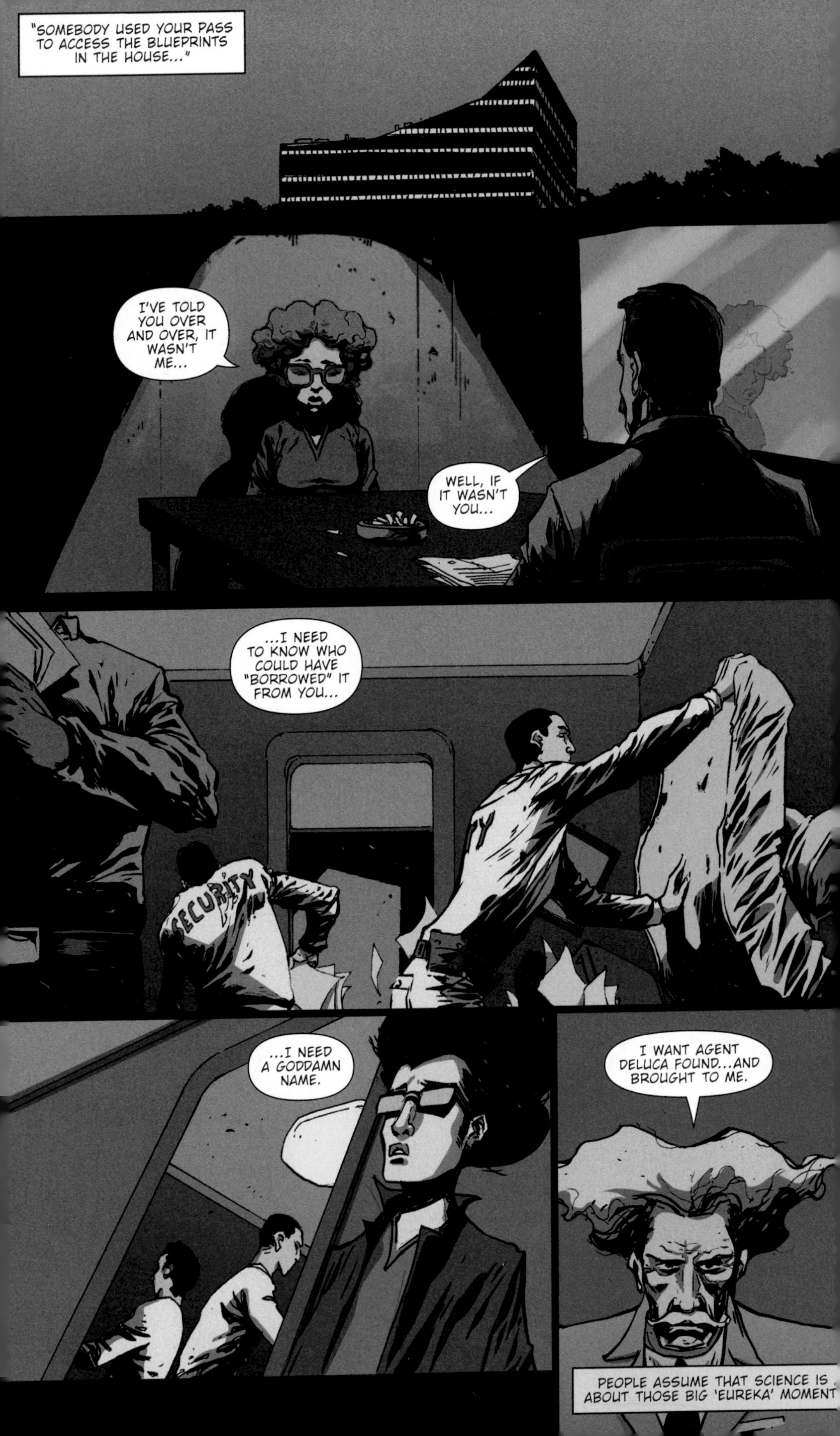
"SOMEBODY USED YOUR PASS TO ACCESS THE BLUEPRINTS IN THE HOUSE..."
I'VE TOLD YOU OVER AND OVER, IT WASN'T ME...
WELL, IF IT WASN'T YOU...
...I NEED TO KNOW WHO COULD HAVE "BORROWED" IT FROM YOU...
SECURITY
...I NEED A GODDAMN NAME.
I WANT AGENT DELUCA FOUND...AND BROUGHT TO ME.
PEOPLE ASSUME THAT SCIENCE IS ABOUT THOSE BIG 'EUREKA' MOMENT

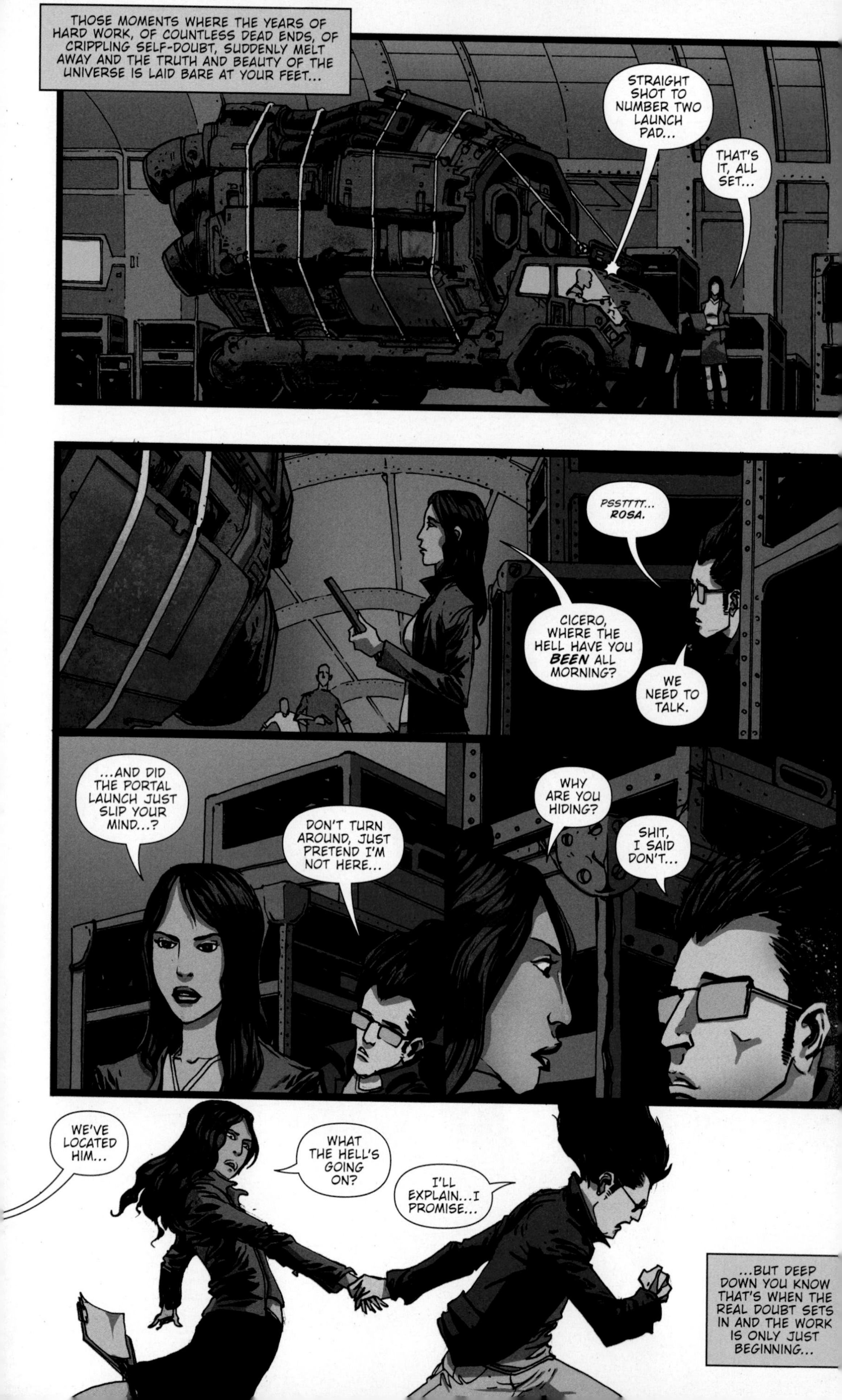

THOSE MOMENTS WHERE THE YEARS OF HARD WORK, OF COUNTLESS DEAD ENDS, OF CRIPPLING SELF-DOUBT, SUDDENLY MELT AWAY AND THE TRUTH AND BEAUTY OF THE UNIVERSE IS LAID BARE AT YOUR FEET...
STRAIGHT SHOT TO NUMBER TWO LAUNCH PAD...
THAT'S IT, ALL SET...
PSSTTTT... ROSA.
CICERO, WHERE THE HELL HAVE YOU BEEN ALL MORNING?
WE NEED TO TALK.
...AND DID THE PORTAL LAUNCH JUST SLIP YOUR MIND...?
DON'T TURN AROUND, JUST PRETEND I'M NOT HERE...
WHY ARE YOU HIDING?
SHIT, I SAID DON'T...
WE'VE LOCATED HIM...
WHAT THE HELL'S GOING ON?
I'LL EXPLAIN...I PROMISE...
...BUT DEEP DOWN YOU KNOW THAT'S WHEN THE REAL DOUBT SETS IN AND THE WORK IS ONLY JUST BEGINNING...

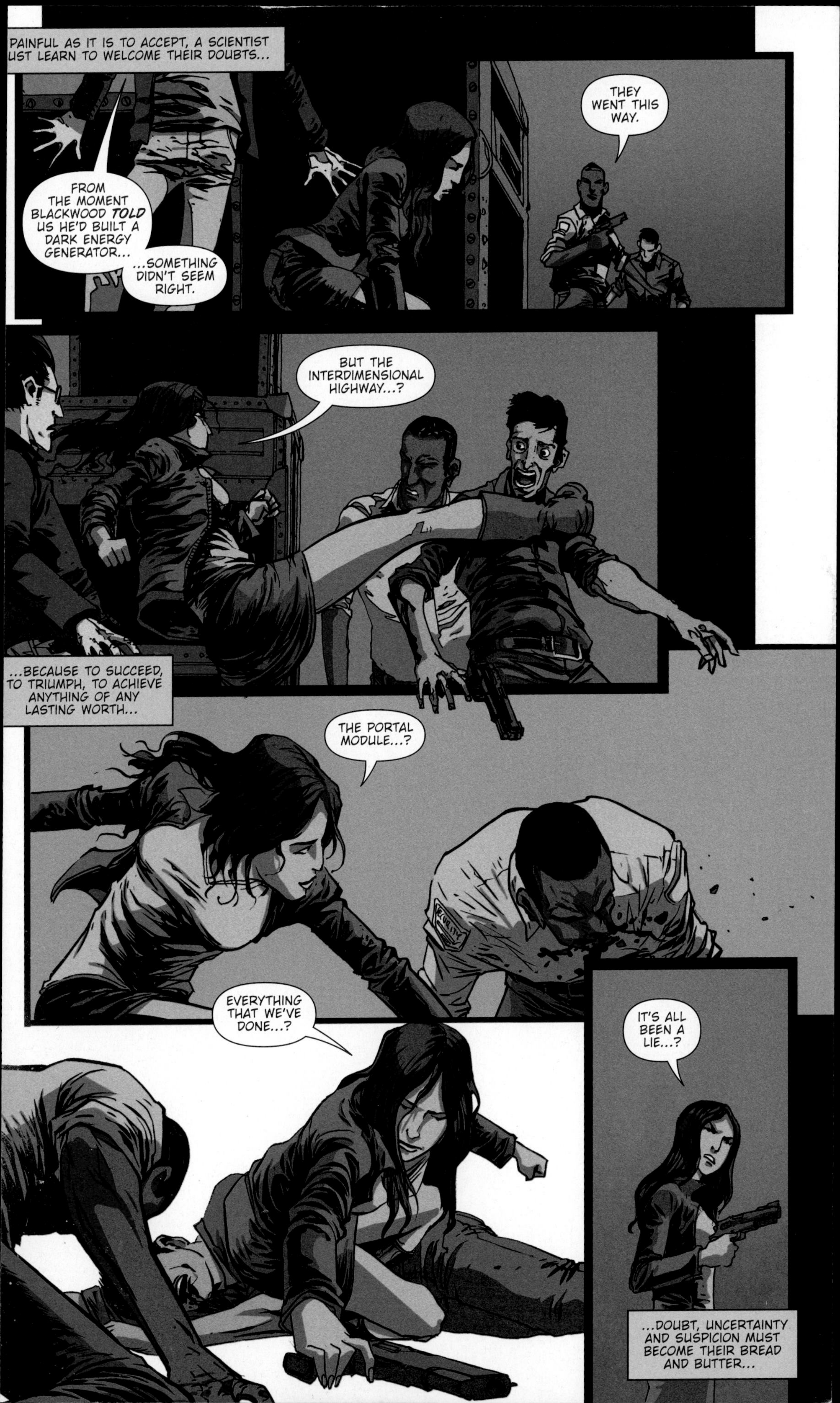

PAINFUL AS IT IS TO ACCEPT, A SCIENTIST UST LEARN TO WELCOME THEIR DOUBTS...
FROM THE MOMENT BLACKWOOD TOLD US HE'D BUILT A DARK ENERGY GENERATOR...
...SOMETHING DIDN'T SEEM RIGHT.
THEY WENT THIS WAY.
BUT THE INTERDIMENSIONAL HIGHWAY...?
...BECAUSE TO SUCCEED, TO TRIUMPH, TO ACHIEVE ANYTHING OF ANY LASTING WORTH...
THE PORTAL MODULE...?
EVERYTHING THAT WE'VE DONE...?
IT'S ALL BEEN A LIE...?
...DOUBT, UNCERTAINTY AND SUSPICION MUST BECOME THEIR BREAD AND BUTTER...

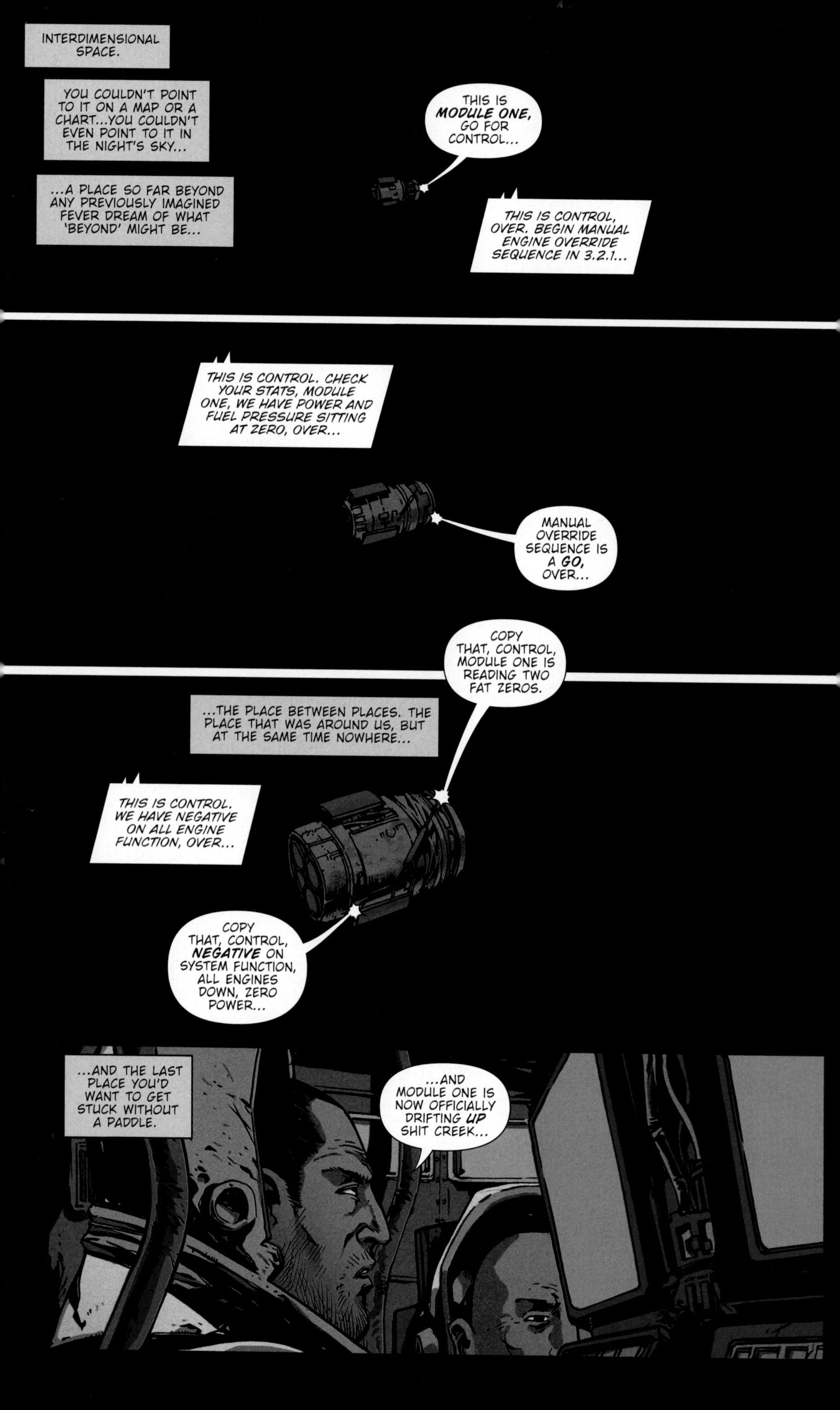

INTERDIMENSIONAL SPACE.
YOU COULDN'T POINT TO IT ON A MAP OR A CHART...YOU COULDN'T EVEN POINT TO IT IN THE NIGHT'S SKY...
...A PLACE SO FAR BEYOND ANY PREVIOUSLY IMAGINED FEVER DREAM OF WHAT 'BEYOND' MIGHT BE...
THIS IS MODULE ONE, GO FOR CONTROL...
THIS IS CONTROL, OVER. BEGIN MANUAL ENGINE OVERRIDE SEQUENCE IN 3.2.1...
THIS IS CONTROL. CHECK YOUR STATS, MODULE ONE, WE HAVE POWER AND FUEL PRESSURE SITTING AT ZERO, OVER...
MANUAL OVERRIDE SEQUENCE IS A GO, OVER...
...THE PLACE BETWEEN PLACES. THE PLACE THAT WAS AROUND US, BUT AT THE SAME TIME NOWHERE...
COPY THAT, CONTROL, MODULE ONE IS READING TWO FAT ZEROS.
THIS IS CONTROL. WE HAVE NEGATIVE ON ALL ENGINE FUNCTION, OVER...
COPY THAT, CONTROL, NEGATIVE ON SYSTEM FUNCTION, ALL ENGINES DOWN, ZERO POWER...
...AND THE LAST PLACE YOU'D WANT TO GET STUCK WITHOUT A PADDLE.
...AND MODULE ONE IS NOW OFFICIALLY DRIFTING UP SHIT CREEK...

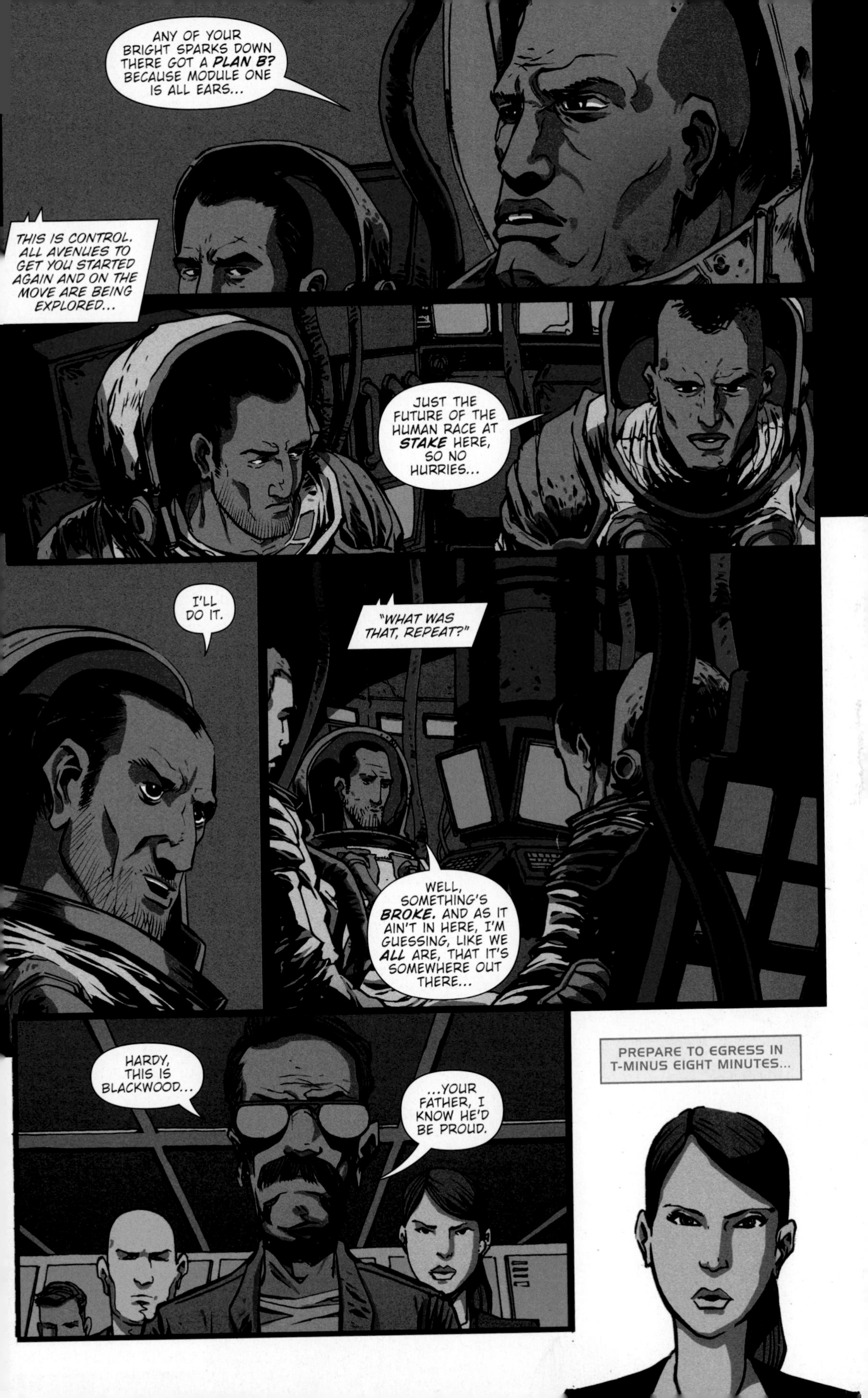
ANY OF YOUR BRIGHT SPARKS DOWN THERE GOT A PLAN B? BECAUSE MODULE ONE IS ALL EARS...
THIS IS CONTROL. ALL AVENUES TO GET YOU STARTED AGAIN AND ON THE MOVE ARE BEING EXPLORED...
JUST THE FUTURE OF THE HUMAN RACE AT STAKE HERE, SO NO HURRIES...
I'LL DO IT.
"WHAT WAS THAT, REPEAT?"
WELL, SOMETHING'S BROKE. AND AS IT AIN'T IN HERE, I'M GUESSING, LIKE WE ALL ARE, THAT IT'S SOMEWHERE OUT THERE...
HARDY, THIS IS BLACKWOOD...
...YOUR FATHER, I KNOW HE'D BE PROUD.
PREPARE TO EGRESS IN T-MINUS EIGHT MINUTES...

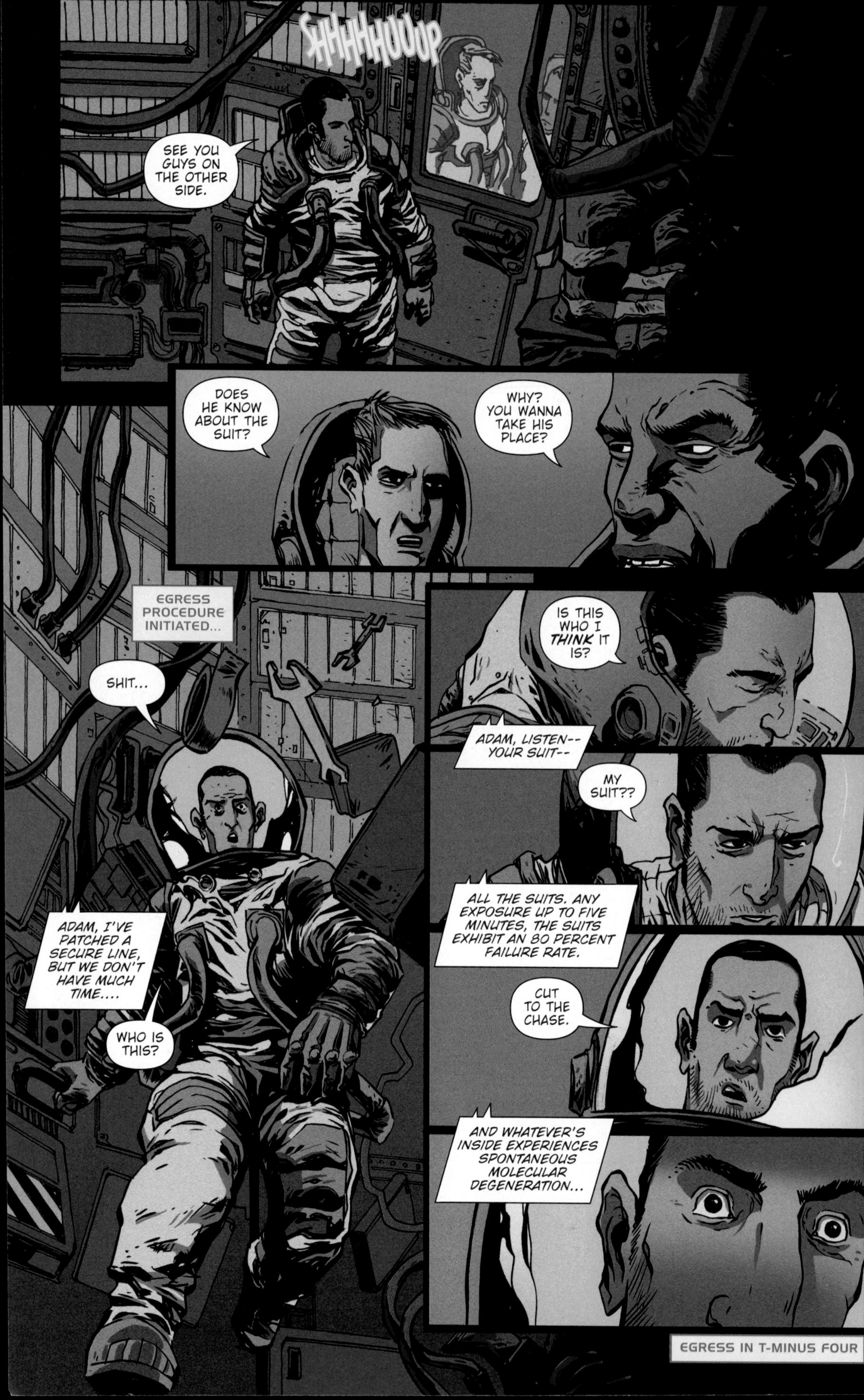
SHHHHHOOOP
SEE YOU GUYS ON THE OTHER SIDE.
DOES HE KNOW ABOUT THE SUIT?
WHY? YOU WANNA TAKE HIS PLACE?
EGRESS PROCEDURE INITIATED...
SHIT...
IS THIS WHO I *THINK* IT IS?
ADAM, LISTEN-- YOUR SUIT--
MY SUIT??
ALL THE SUITS. ANY EXPOSURE UP TO FIVE MINUTES, THE SUITS EXHIBIT AN 80 PERCENT FAILURE RATE.
ADAM, I'VE PATCHED A SECURE LINE, BUT WE DON'T HAVE MUCH TIME....
WHO IS THIS?
CUT TO THE CHASE.
AND WHATEVER'S INSIDE EXPERIENCES SPONTANEOUS MOLECULAR DEGENERATION...
EGRESS IN T-MINUS FOUR

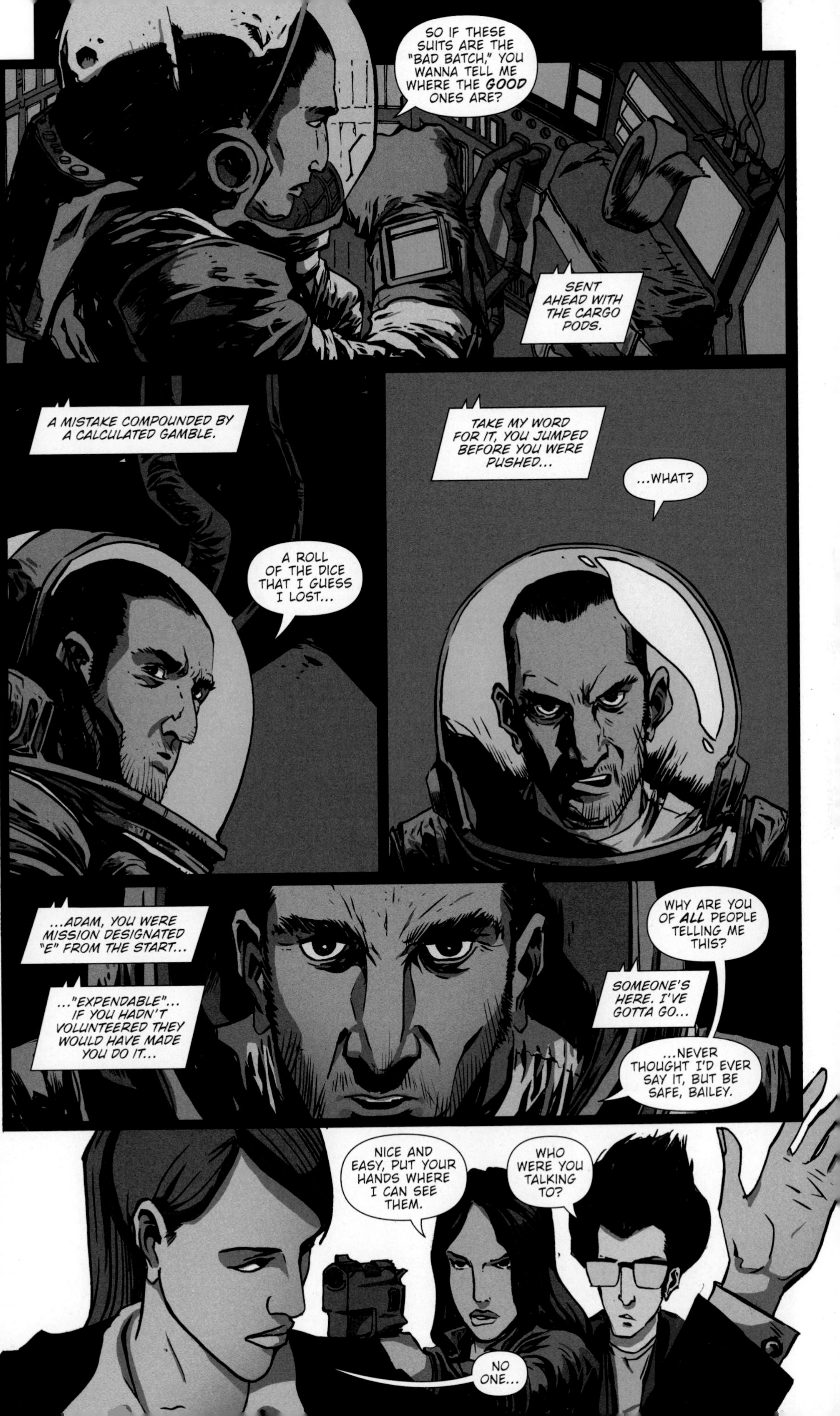
SO IF THESE SUITS ARE THE "BAD BATCH," YOU WANNA TELL ME WHERE THE GOOD ONES ARE?
SENT AHEAD WITH THE CARGO PODS.
A MISTAKE COMPOUNDED BY A CALCULATED GAMBLE.
A ROLL OF THE DICE THAT I GUESS I LOST...
TAKE MY WORD FOR IT, YOU JUMPED BEFORE YOU WERE PUSHED...
...WHAT?
...ADAM, YOU WERE MISSION DESIGNATED "E" FROM THE START...
..."EXPENDABLE"... IF YOU HADN'T VOLUNTEERED THEY WOULD HAVE MADE YOU DO IT...
WHY ARE YOU OF ALL PEOPLE TELLING ME THIS?
SOMEONE'S HERE. I'VE GOTTA GO...
...NEVER THOUGHT I'D EVER SAY IT, BUT BE SAFE, BAILEY.
NICE AND EASY, PUT YOUR HANDS WHERE I CAN SEE THEM.
WHO WERE YOU TALKING TO?
NO ONE...

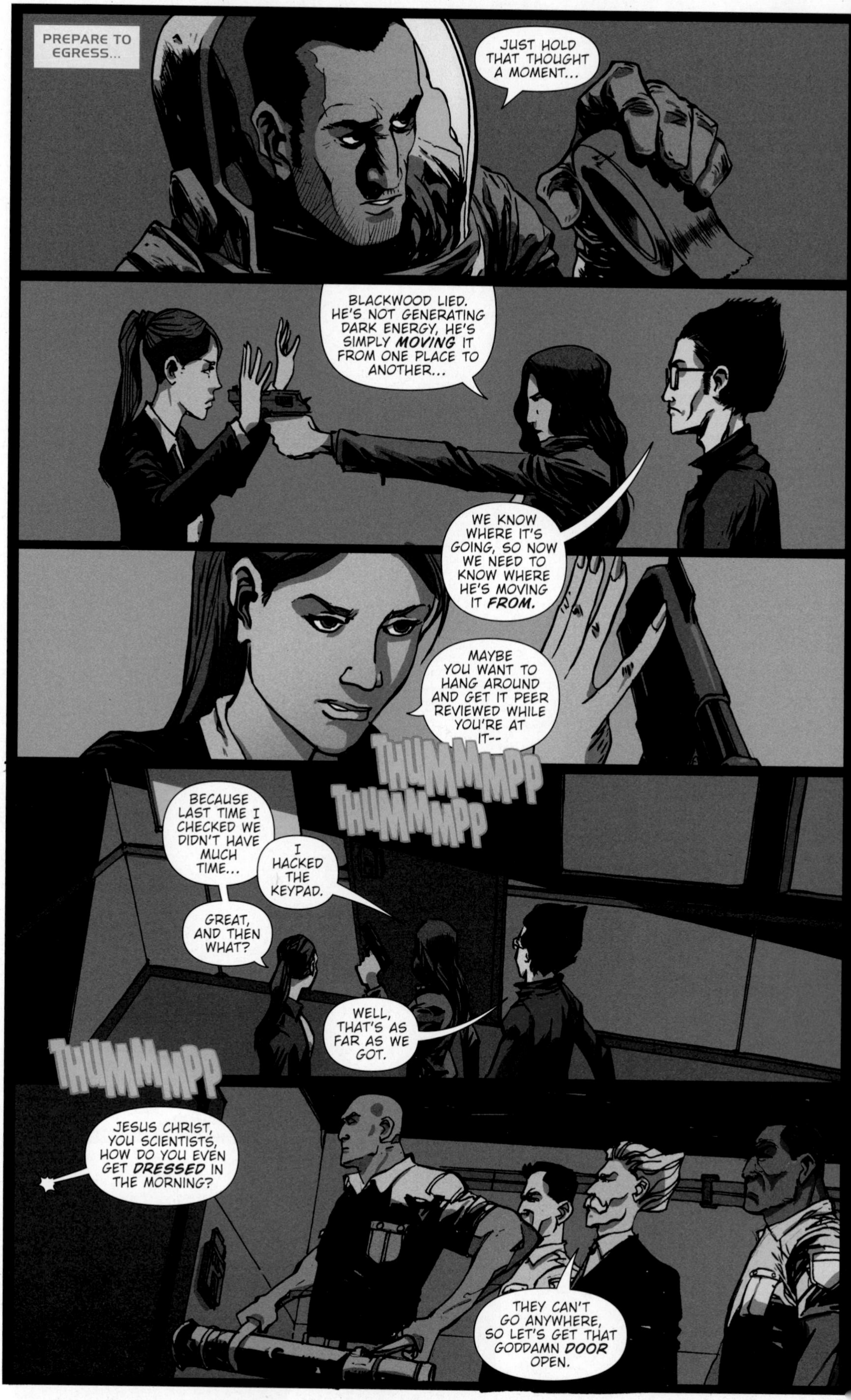
PREPARE TO EGRESS...
JUST HOLD THAT THOUGHT A MOMENT...
BLACKWOOD LIED. HE'S NOT GENERATING DARK ENERGY, HE'S SIMPLY MOVING IT FROM ONE PLACE TO ANOTHER...
WE KNOW WHERE IT'S GOING, SO NOW WE NEED TO KNOW WHERE HE'S MOVING IT FROM.
MAYBE YOU WANT TO HANG AROUND AND GET IT PEER REVIEWED WHILE YOU'RE AT IT--
THUMMMPP
THUMMMPP
BECAUSE LAST TIME I CHECKED WE DIDN'T HAVE MUCH TIME...
I HACKED THE KEYPAD.
GREAT, AND THEN WHAT?
WELL, THAT'S AS FAR AS WE GOT.
THUMMMPP
JESUS CHRIST, YOU SCIENTISTS, HOW DO YOU EVEN GET DRESSED IN THE MORNING?
THEY CAN'T GO ANYWHERE, SO LET'S GET THAT GODDAMN DOOR OPEN.

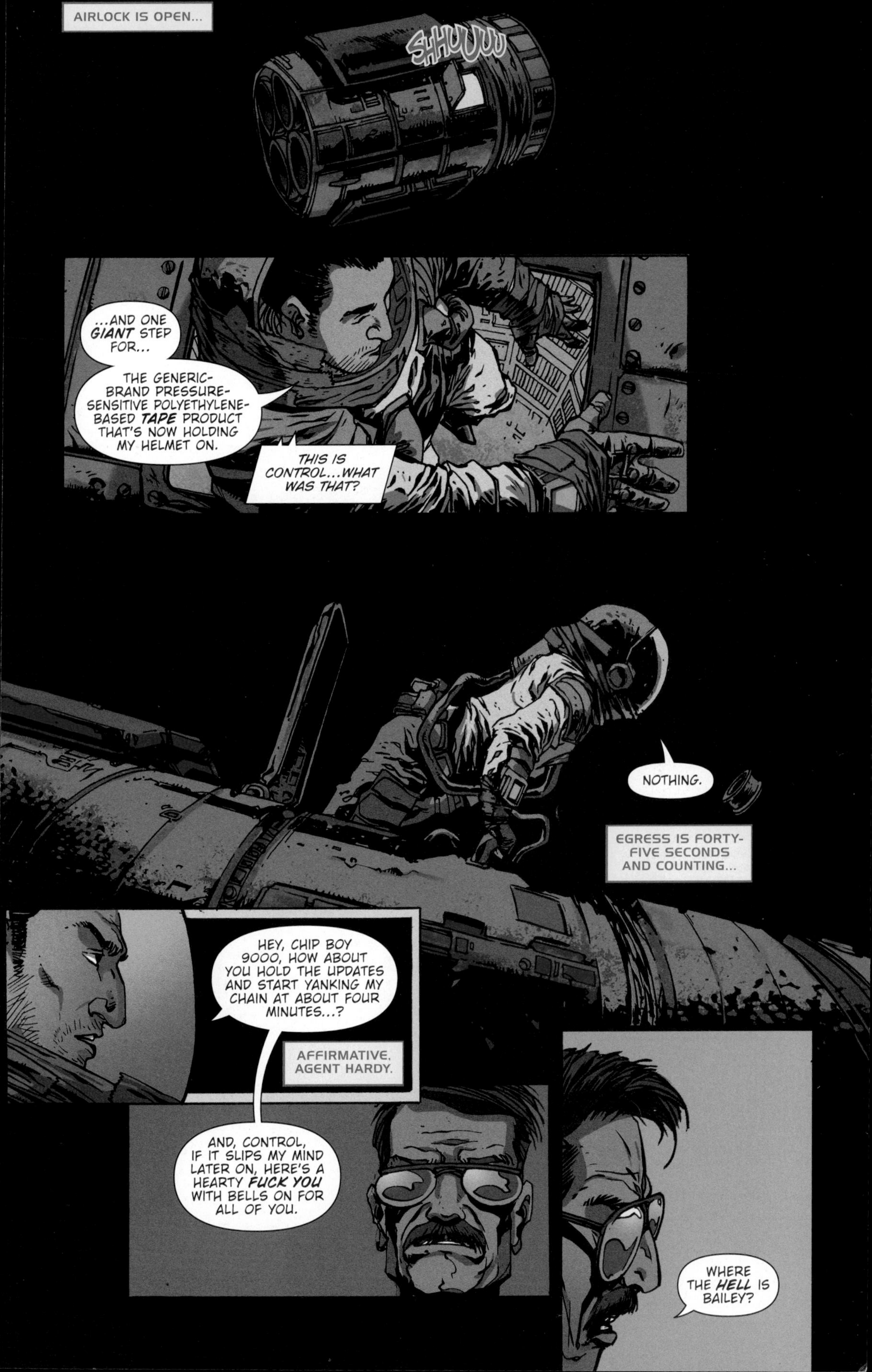
AIRLOCK IS OPEN...
SHHUUUU
...AND ONE GIANT STEP FOR...
THE GENERIC-BRAND PRESSURE-SENSITIVE POLYETHYLENE-BASED TAPE PRODUCT THAT'S NOW HOLDING MY HELMET ON.
THIS IS CONTROL...WHAT WAS THAT?
NOTHING.
EGRESS IS FORTY-FIVE SECONDS AND COUNTING...
HEY, CHIP BOY 9000, HOW ABOUT YOU HOLD THE UPDATES AND START YANKING MY CHAIN AT ABOUT FOUR MINUTES...?
AFFIRMATIVE. AGENT HARDY.
AND, CONTROL, IF IT SLIPS MY MIND LATER ON, HERE'S A HEARTY FUCK YOU WITH BELLS ON FOR ALL OF YOU.
WHERE THE HELL IS BAILEY?

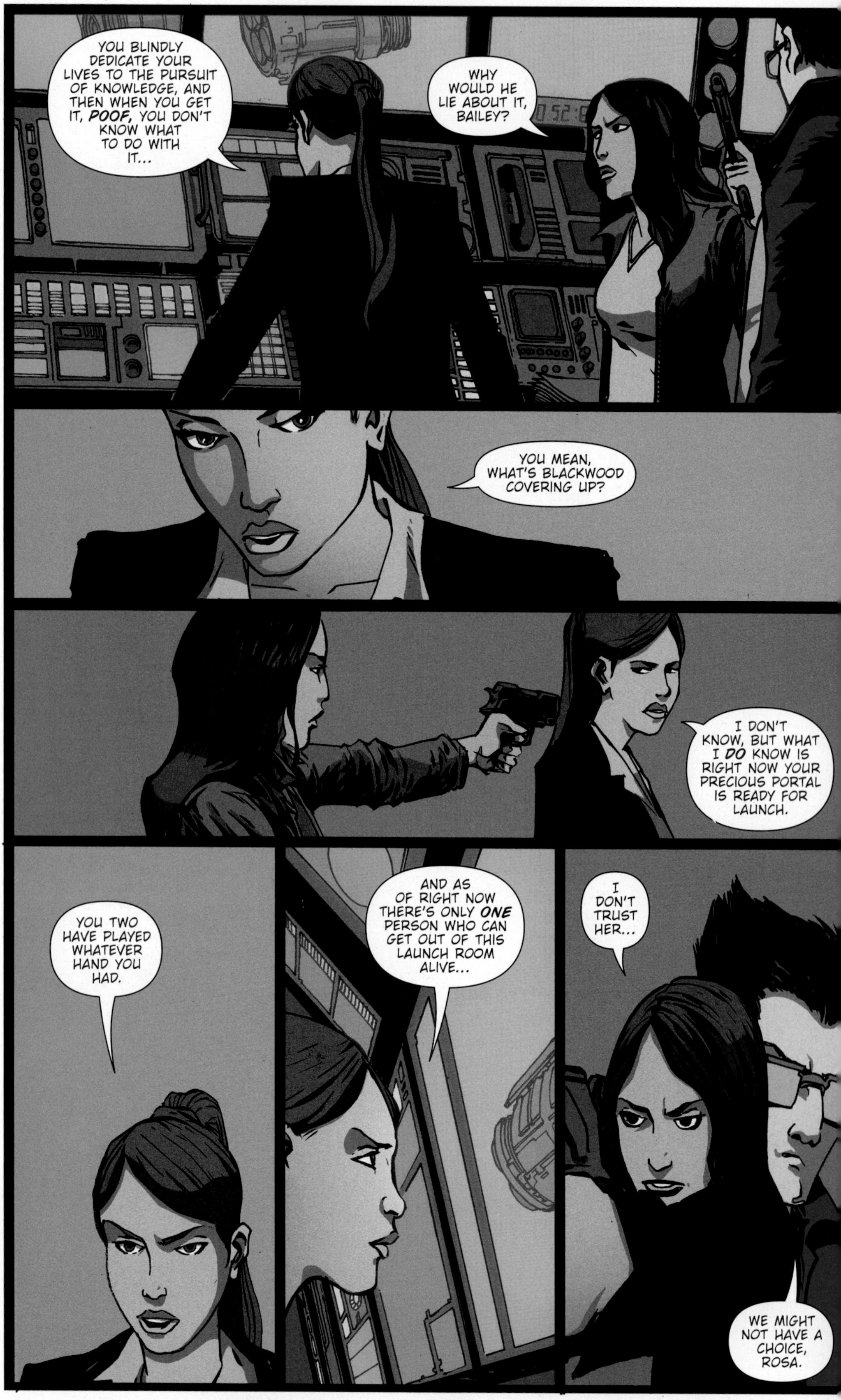

YOU BLINDLY DEDICATE YOUR LIVES TO THE PURSUIT OF KNOWLEDGE, AND THEN WHEN YOU GET IT, *POOF,* YOU DON'T KNOW WHAT TO DO WITH IT...
WHY WOULD HE LIE ABOUT IT, BAILEY?
YOU MEAN, WHAT'S BLACKWOOD COVERING UP?
I DON'T KNOW, BUT WHAT I *DO* KNOW IS RIGHT NOW YOUR PRECIOUS PORTAL IS READY FOR LAUNCH.
YOU TWO HAVE PLAYED WHATEVER HAND YOU HAD.
AND AS OF RIGHT NOW THERE'S ONLY *ONE* PERSON WHO CAN GET OUT OF THIS LAUNCH ROOM ALIVE...
I DON'T TRUST HER...
WE MIGHT NOT HAVE A CHOICE, ROSA.

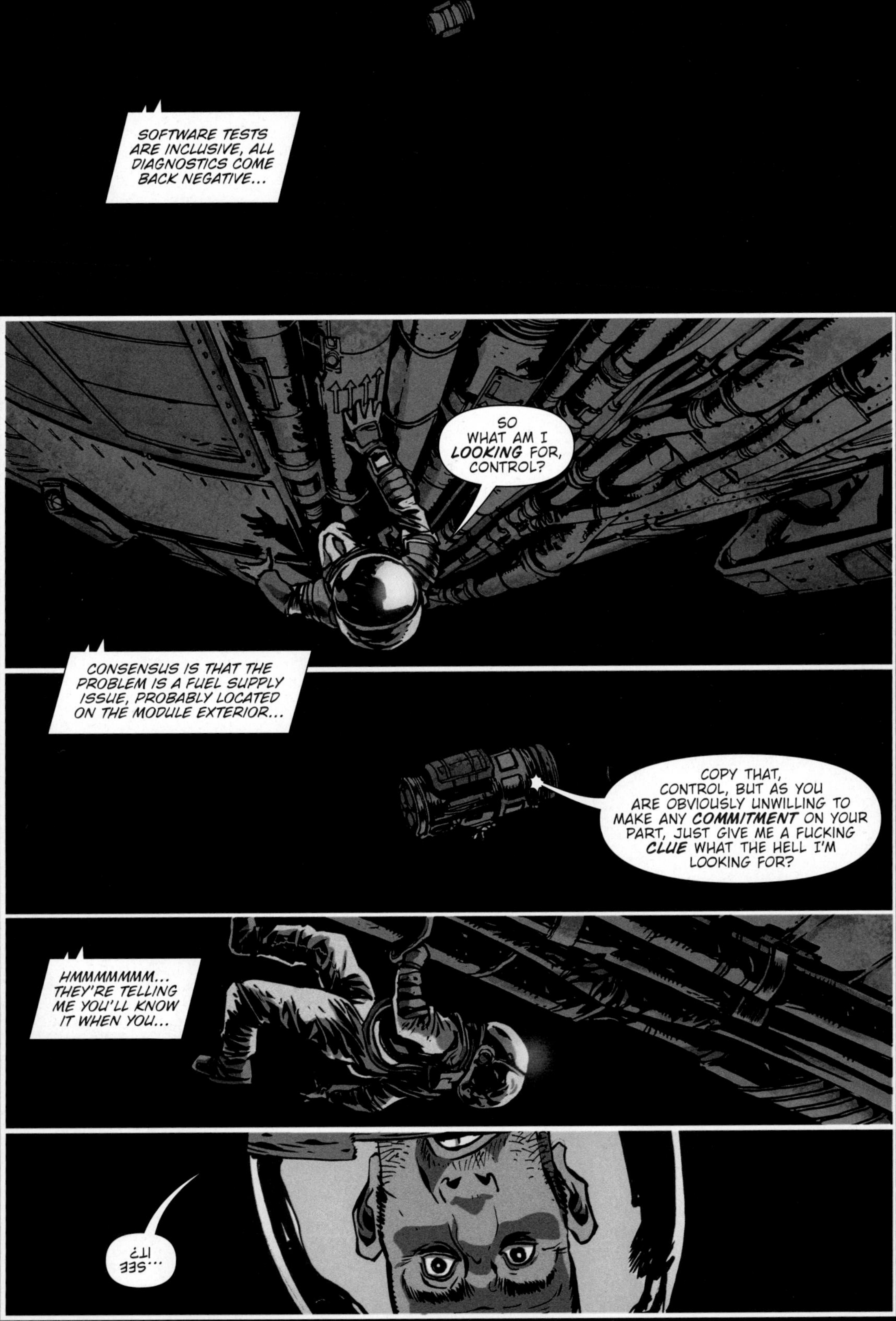
SOFTWARE TESTS ARE INCLUSIVE, ALL DIAGNOSTICS COME BACK NEGATIVE...
SO WHAT AM I LOOKING FOR, CONTROL?
CONSENSUS IS THAT THE PROBLEM IS A FUEL SUPPLY ISSUE, PROBABLY LOCATED ON THE MODULE EXTERIOR...
COPY THAT, CONTROL, BUT AS YOU ARE OBVIOUSLY UNWILLING TO MAKE ANY COMMITMENT ON YOUR PART, JUST GIVE ME A FUCKING CLUE WHAT THE HELL I'M LOOKING FOR?
HMMMMMMM... THEY'RE TELLING ME YOU'LL KNOW IT WHEN YOU...
...SEE IT?

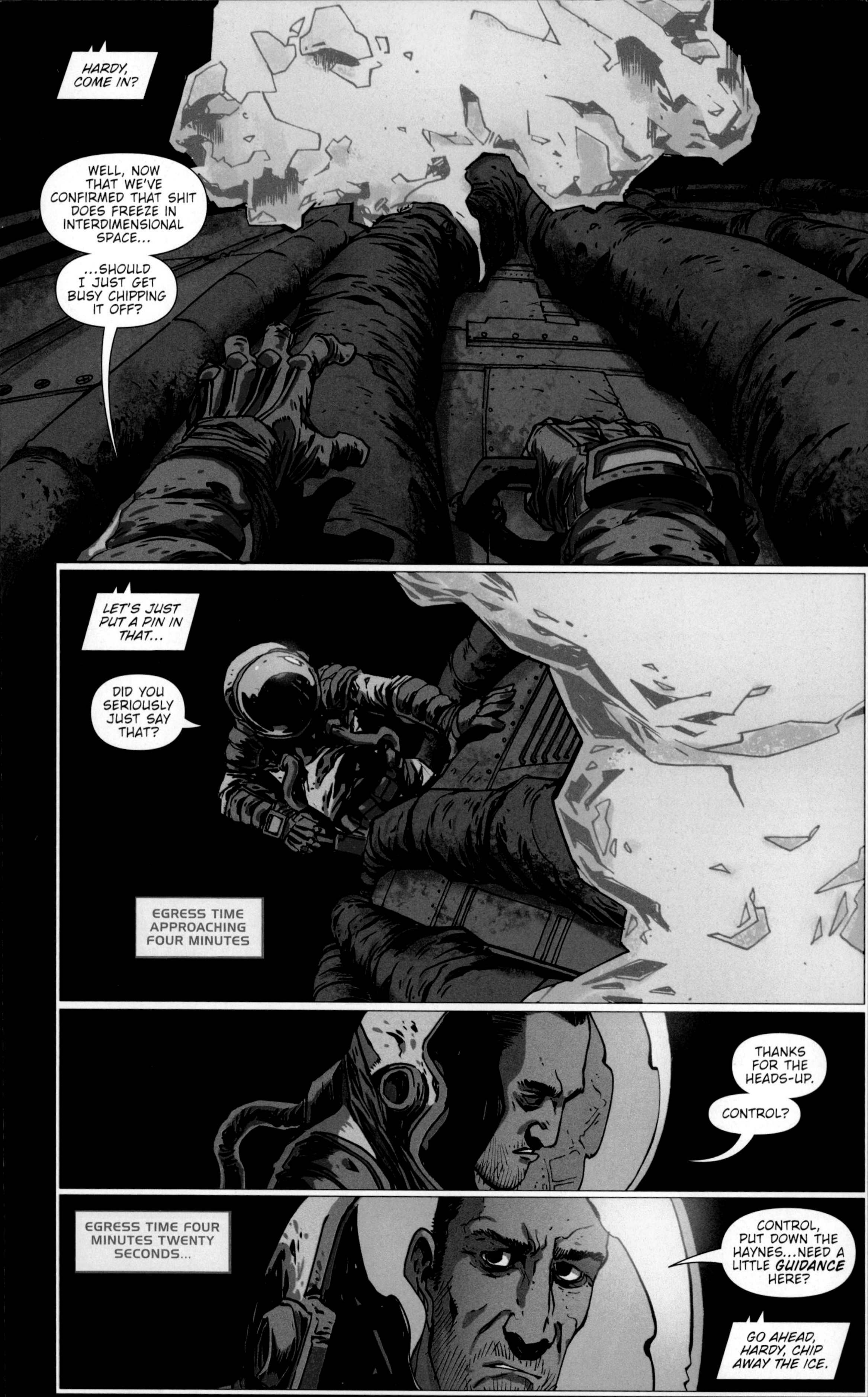
HARDY, COME IN?
WELL, NOW THAT WE'VE CONFIRMED THAT SHIT DOES FREEZE IN INTERDIMENSIONAL SPACE...
...SHOULD I JUST GET BUSY CHIPPING IT OFF?
LET'S JUST PUT A PIN IN THAT...
DID YOU SERIOUSLY JUST SAY THAT?
EGRESS TIME APPROACHING FOUR MINUTES
THANKS FOR THE HEADS-UP.
CONTROL?
EGRESS TIME FOUR MINUTES TWENTY SECONDS...
CONTROL, PUT DOWN THE HAYNES...NEED A LITTLE GUIDANCE HERE?
GO AHEAD, HARDY, CHIP AWAY THE ICE.

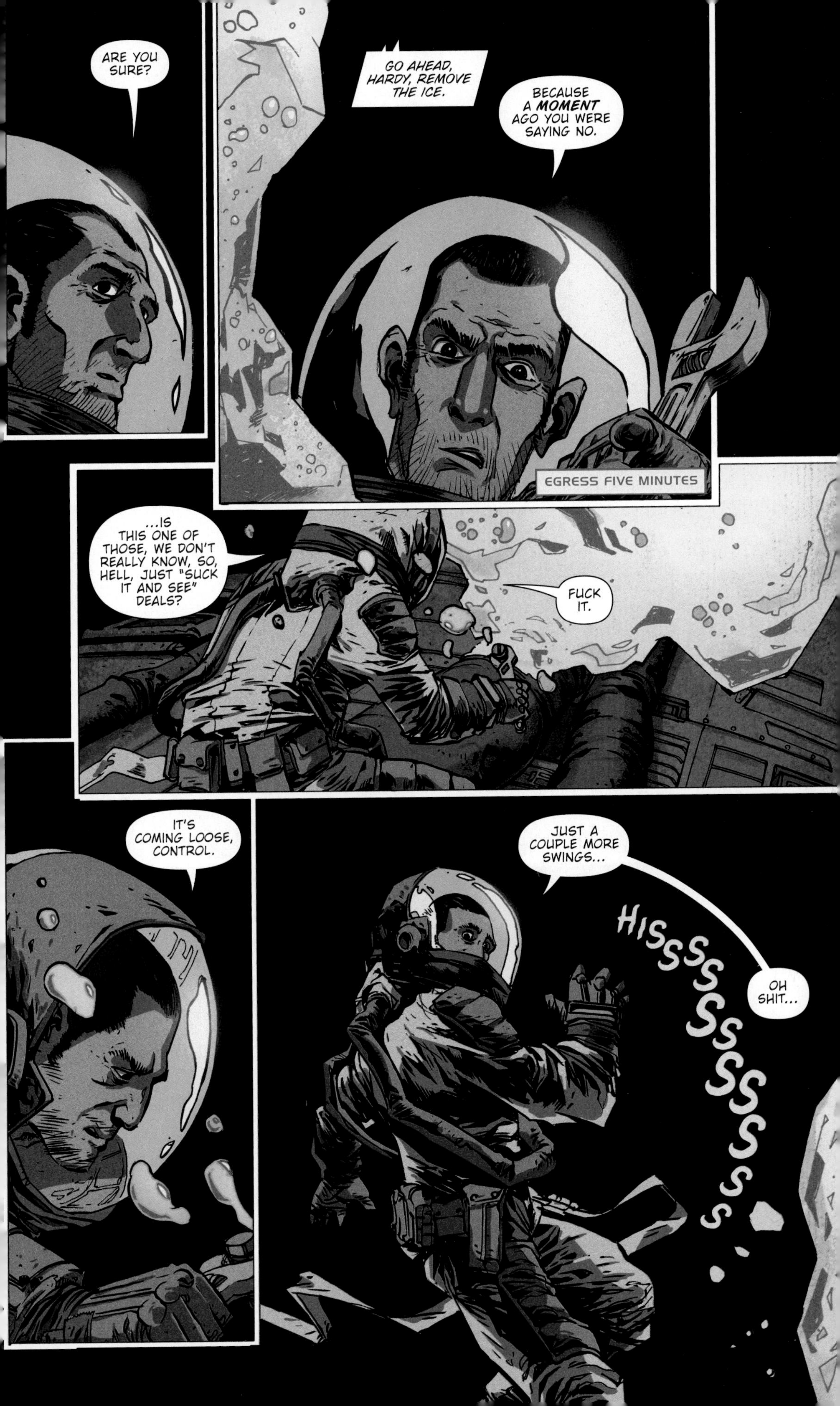
ARE YOU SURE?
GO AHEAD, HARDY, REMOVE THE ICE.
BECAUSE A **MOMENT** AGO YOU WERE SAYING NO.
EGRESS FIVE MINUTES
...IS THIS ONE OF THOSE, WE DON'T REALLY KNOW, SO, HELL, JUST "SUCK IT AND SEE" DEALS?
FUCK IT.
IT'S COMING LOOSE, CONTROL.
JUST A COUPLE MORE SWINGS...
HISSSSSSSSSSSSS
OH SHIT...

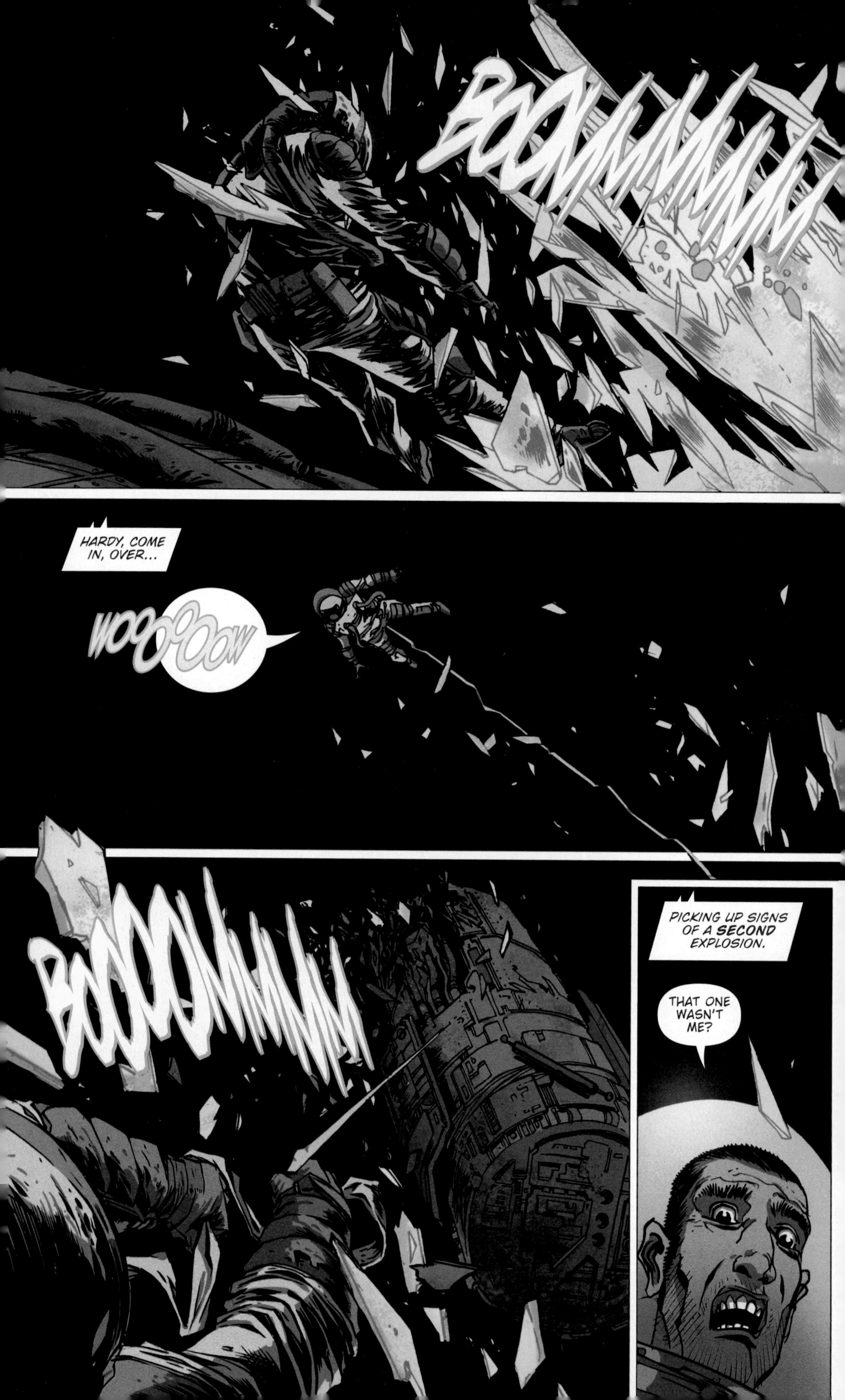
BOOMMMMMM
HARDY, COME IN, OVER...
WOOOOOOW
BOOOOMMMM
PICKING UP SIGNS OF A **SECOND** EXPLOSION.
THAT ONE WASN'T ME?

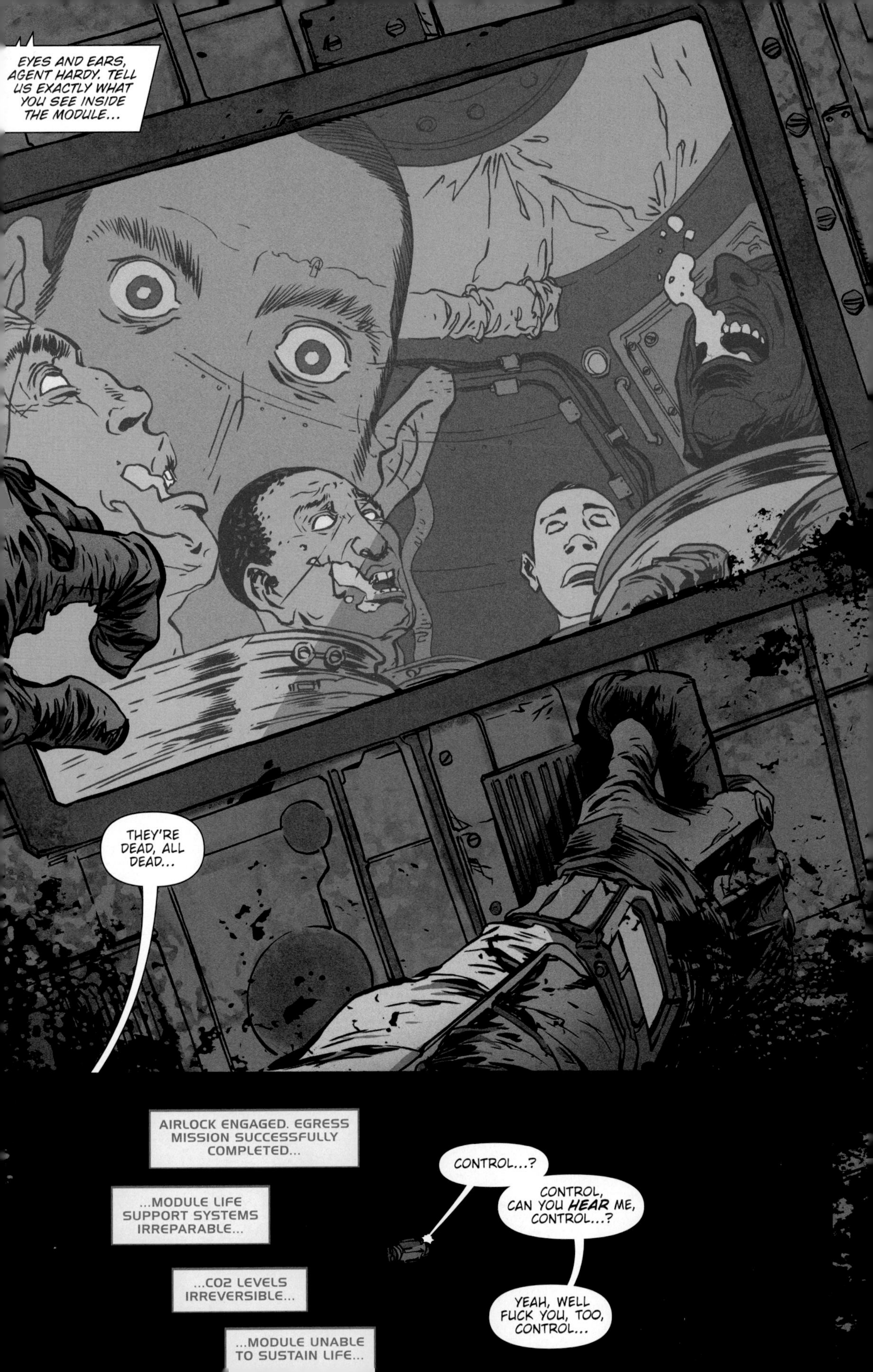
EYES AND EARS, AGENT HARDY. TELL US EXACTLY WHAT YOU SEE INSIDE THE MODULE...
THEY'RE DEAD, ALL DEAD...
AIRLOCK ENGAGED. EGRESS MISSION SUCCESSFULLY COMPLETED...
...MODULE LIFE SUPPORT SYSTEMS IRREPARABLE...
...CO2 LEVELS IRREVERSIBLE...
...MODULE UNABLE TO SUSTAIN LIFE...
CONTROL...?
CONTROL, CAN YOU HEAR ME, CONTROL...?
YEAH, WELL FUCK YOU, TOO, CONTROL...

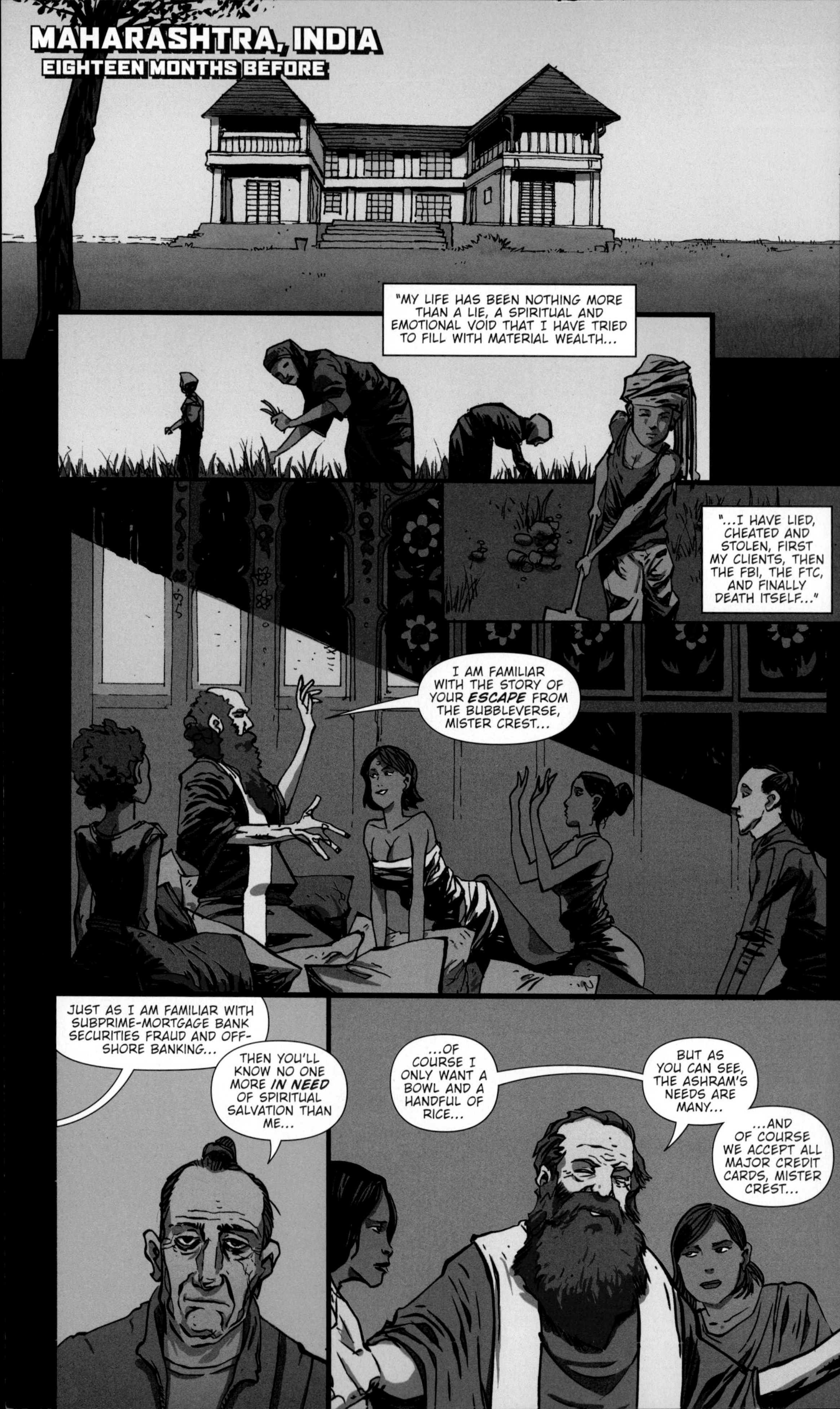
MAHARASHTRA, INDIA
EIGHTEEN MONTHS BEFORE
"MY LIFE HAS BEEN NOTHING MORE THAN A LIE, A SPIRITUAL AND EMOTIONAL VOID THAT I HAVE TRIED TO FILL WITH MATERIAL WEALTH...
"...I HAVE LIED, CHEATED AND STOLEN, FIRST MY CLIENTS, THEN THE FBI, THE FTC, AND FINALLY DEATH ITSELF..."
I AM FAMILIAR WITH THE STORY OF YOUR ESCAPE FROM THE BUBBLEVERSE, MISTER CREST...
JUST AS I AM FAMILIAR WITH SUBPRIME-MORTGAGE BANK SECURITIES FRAUD AND OFF-SHORE BANKING...
THEN YOU'LL KNOW NO ONE MORE IN NEED OF SPIRITUAL SALVATION THAN ME...
...OF COURSE I ONLY WANT A BOWL AND A HANDFUL OF RICE...
BUT AS YOU CAN SEE, THE ASHRAM'S NEEDS ARE MANY...
...AND OF COURSE WE ACCEPT ALL MAJOR CREDIT CARDS, MISTER CREST...

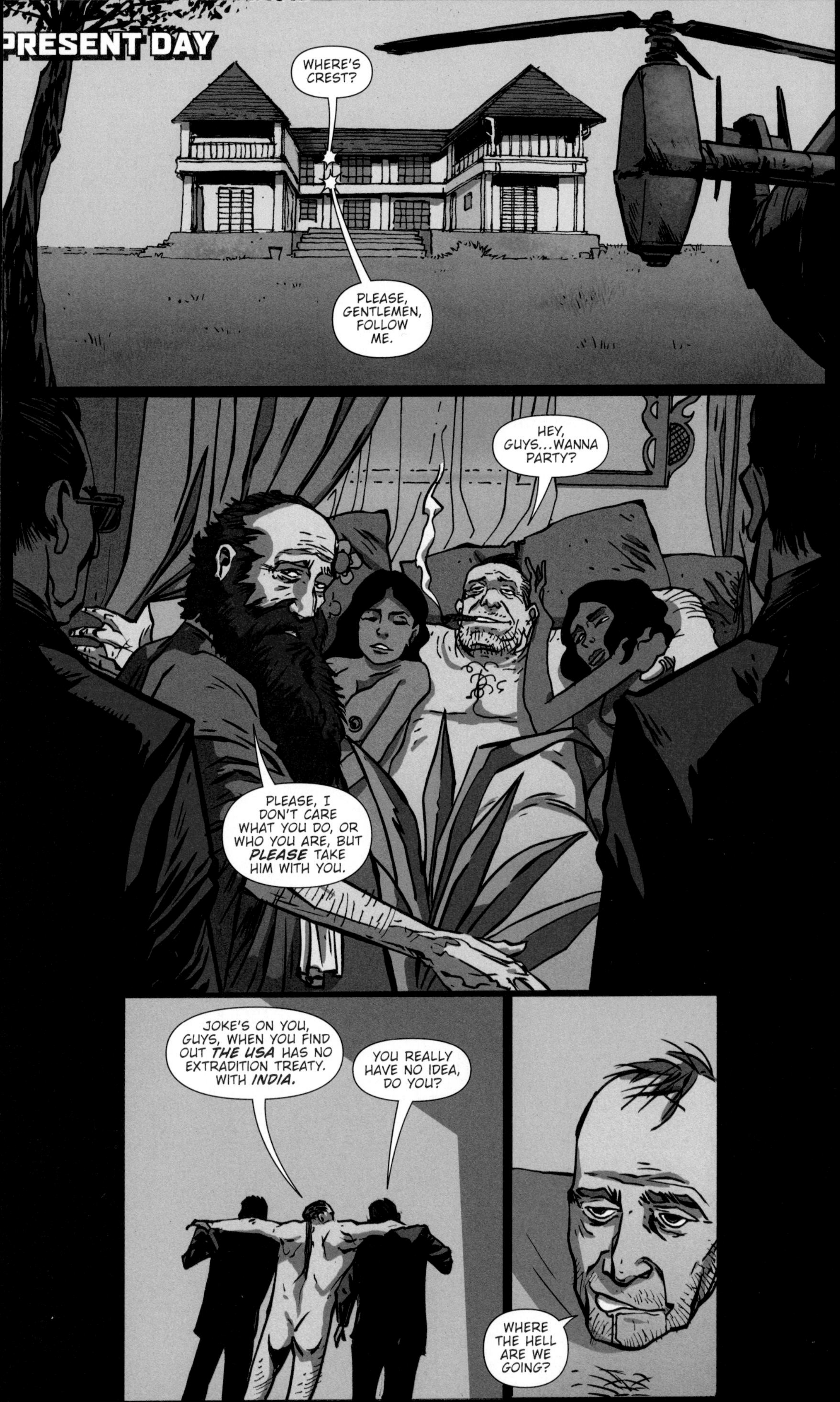
PRESENT DAY
WHERE'S CREST?
PLEASE, GENTLEMEN, FOLLOW ME.
HEY, GUYS...WANNA PARTY?
PLEASE, I DON'T CARE WHAT YOU DO, OR WHO YOU ARE, BUT PLEASE TAKE HIM WITH YOU.
JOKE'S ON YOU, GUYS, WHEN YOU FIND OUT THE USA HAS NO EXTRADITION TREATY. WITH INDIA.
YOU REALLY HAVE NO IDEA, DO YOU?
WHERE THE HELL ARE WE GOING?

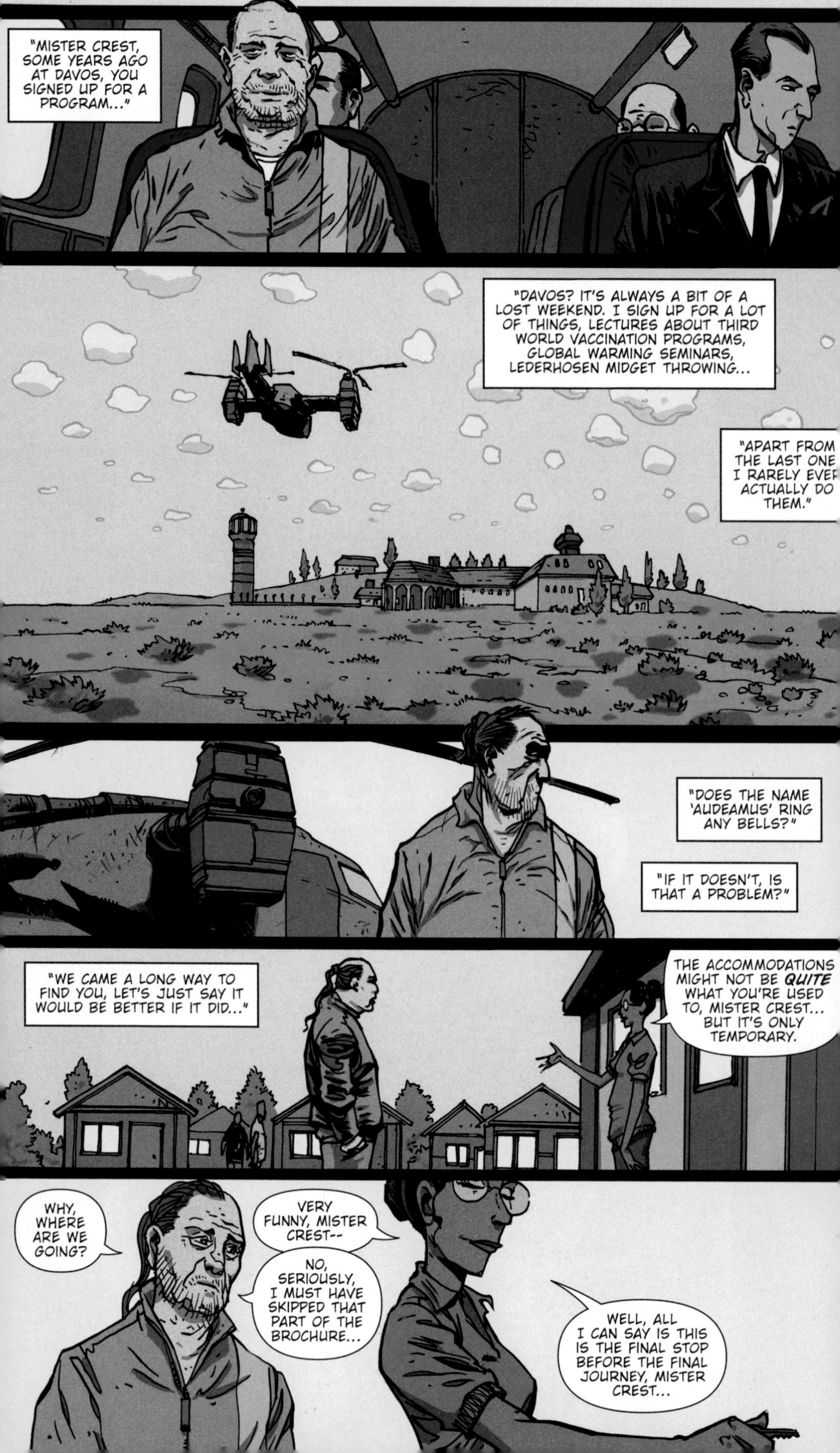
"MISTER CREST, SOME YEARS AGO AT DAVOS, YOU SIGNED UP FOR A PROGRAM..."
"DAVOS? IT'S ALWAYS A BIT OF A LOST WEEKEND. I SIGN UP FOR A LOT OF THINGS, LECTURES ABOUT THIRD WORLD VACCINATION PROGRAMS, GLOBAL WARMING SEMINARS, LEDERHOSEN MIDGET THROWING...
"APART FROM THE LAST ONE I RARELY EVER ACTUALLY DO THEM."
"DOES THE NAME 'AUDEAMUS' RING ANY BELLS?"
"IF IT DOESN'T, IS THAT A PROBLEM?"
"WE CAME A LONG WAY TO FIND YOU, LET'S JUST SAY IT WOULD BE BETTER IF IT DID..."
THE ACCOMMODATIONS MIGHT NOT BE QUITE WHAT YOU'RE USED TO, MISTER CREST... BUT IT'S ONLY TEMPORARY.
WHY, WHERE ARE WE GOING?
VERY FUNNY, MISTER CREST--
NO, SERIOUSLY, I MUST HAVE SKIPPED THAT PART OF THE BROCHURE...
WELL, ALL I CAN SAY IS THIS IS THE FINAL STOP BEFORE THE FINAL JOURNEY, MISTER CREST...

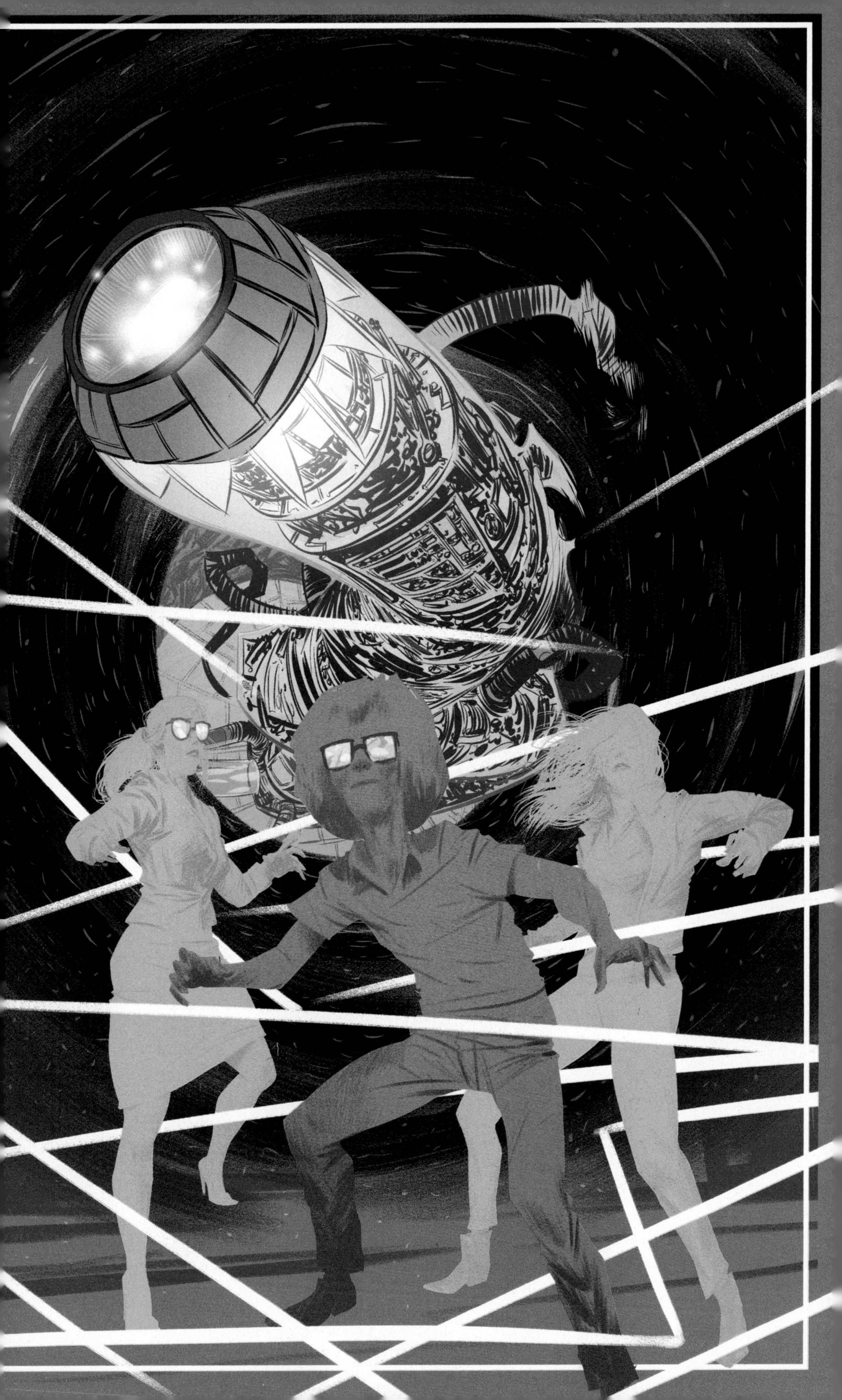

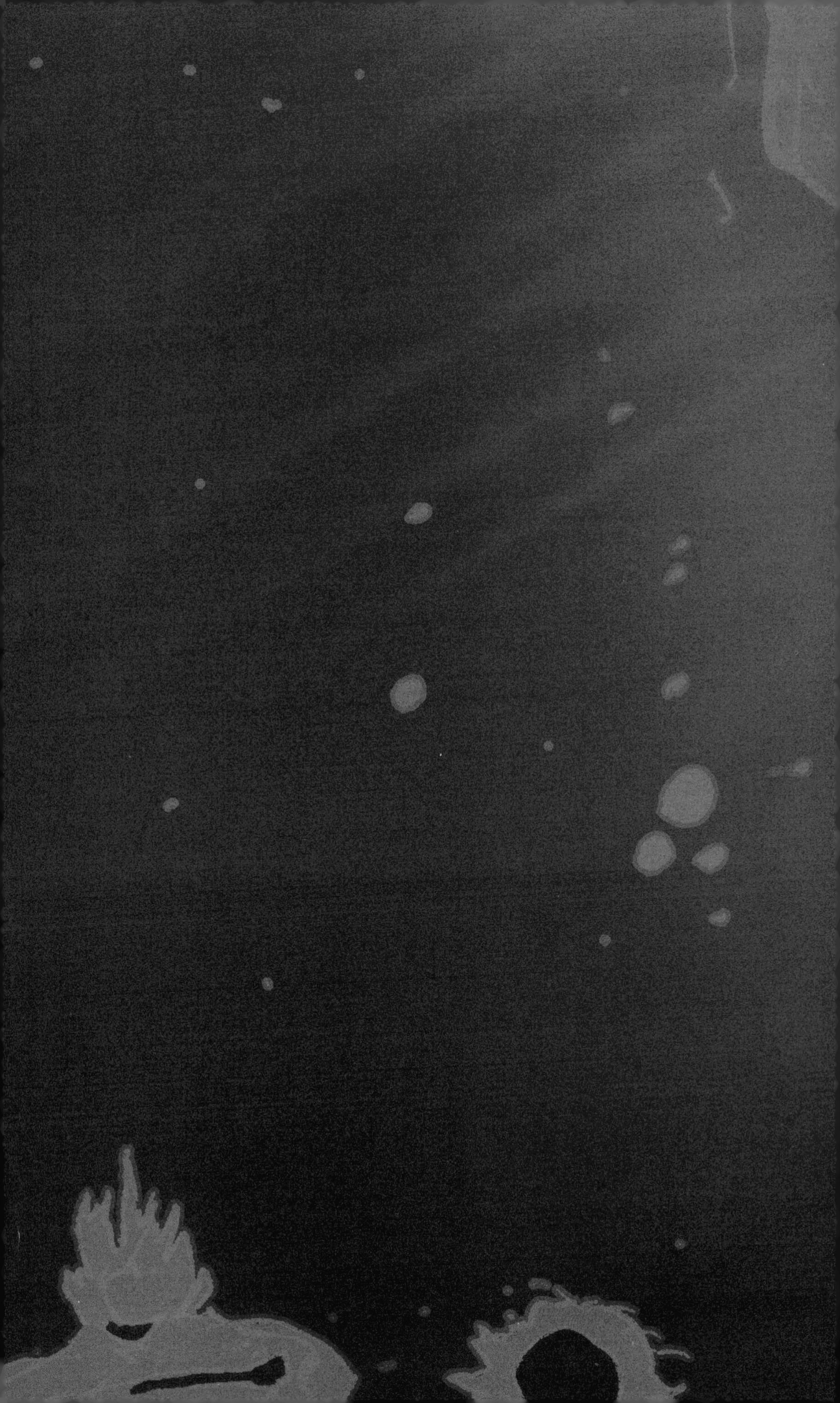

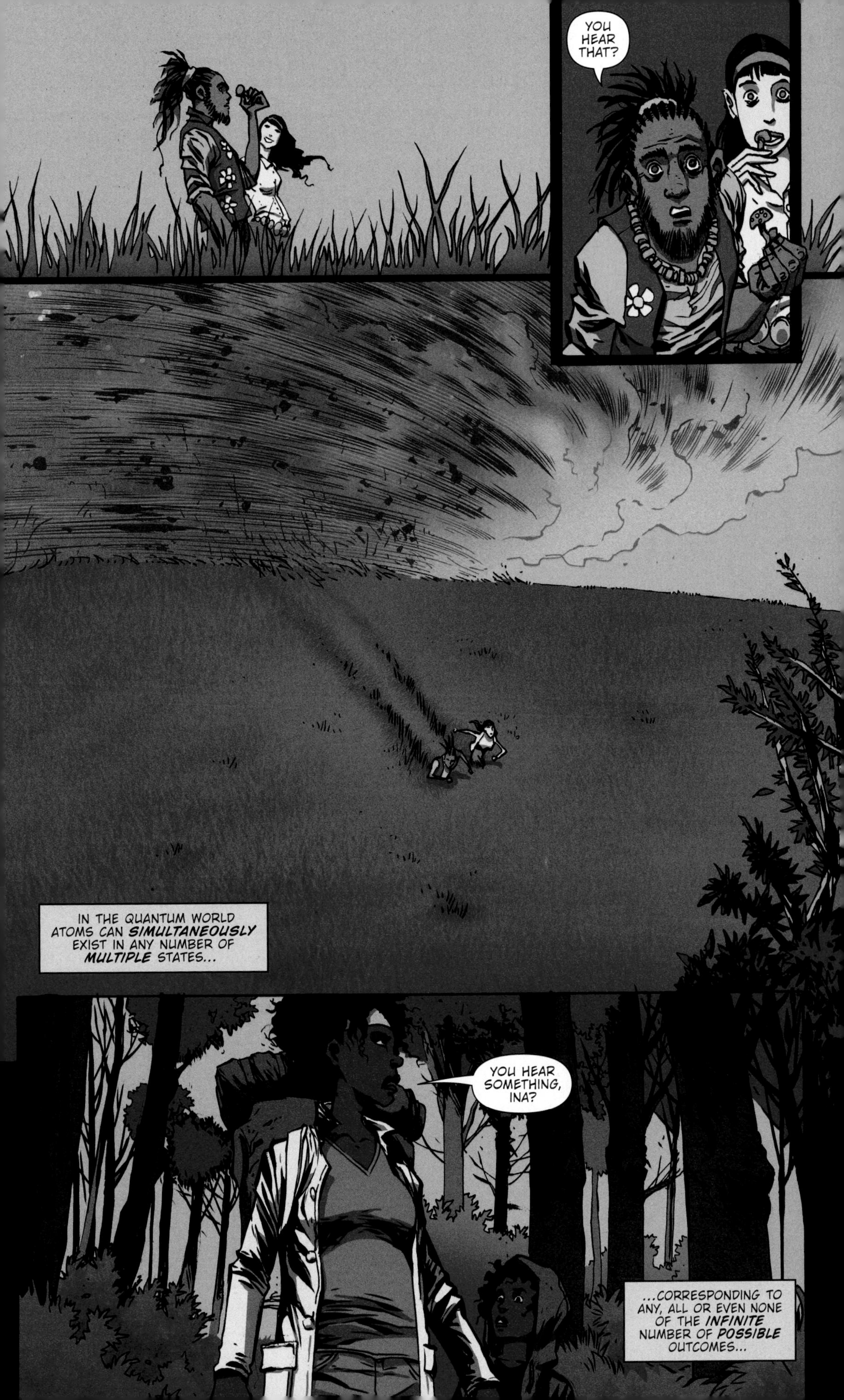
YOU HEAR THAT?
IN THE QUANTUM WORLD ATOMS CAN SIMULTANEOUSLY EXIST IN ANY NUMBER OF MULTIPLE STATES...
YOU HEAR SOMETHING, INA?
...CORRESPONDING TO ANY, ALL OR EVEN NONE OF THE INFINITE NUMBER OF POSSIBLE OUTCOMES...

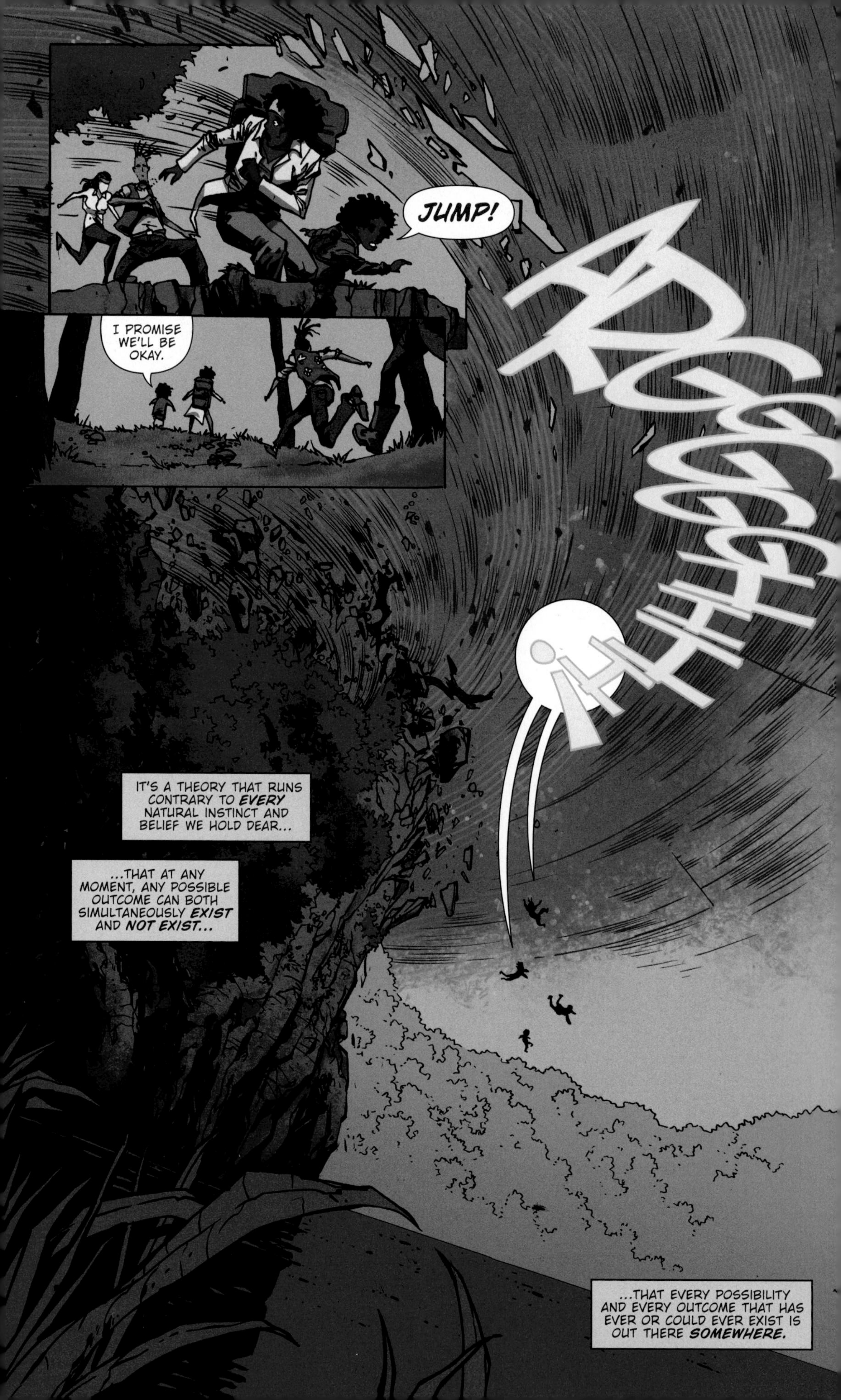
JUMP!
I PROMISE WE'LL BE OKAY.
AAAGGGHHH!
IT'S A THEORY THAT RUNS CONTRARY TO EVERY NATURAL INSTINCT AND BELIEF WE HOLD DEAR...
...THAT AT ANY MOMENT, ANY POSSIBLE OUTCOME CAN BOTH SIMULTANEOUSLY EXIST AND NOT EXIST...
...THAT EVERY POSSIBILITY AND EVERY OUTCOME THAT HAS EVER OR COULD EVER EXIST IS OUT THERE SOMEWHERE.

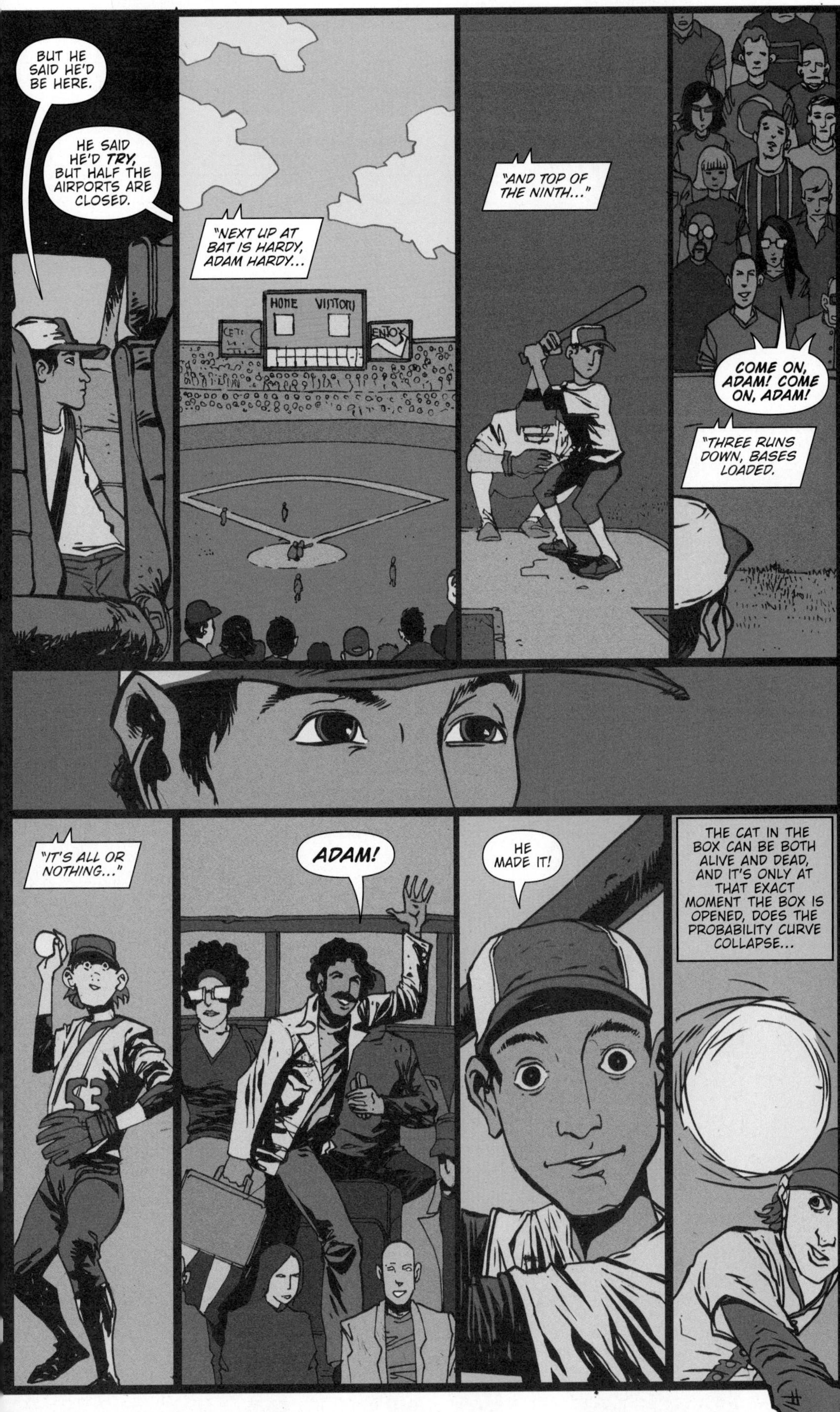

BUT HE SAID HE'D BE HERE.
HE SAID HE'D *TRY,* BUT HALF THE AIRPORTS ARE CLOSED.
"NEXT UP AT BAT IS HARDY, ADAM HARDY...
HOME VISITORS
"AND TOP OF THE NINTH..."
COME ON, ADAM! COME ON, ADAM!
"THREE RUNS DOWN, BASES LOADED.
"IT'S ALL OR NOTHING..."
ADAM!
HE MADE IT!
THE CAT IN THE BOX CAN BE BOTH ALIVE AND DEAD, AND IT'S ONLY AT THAT EXACT MOMENT THE BOX IS OPENED, DOES THE PROBABILITY CURVE COLLAPSE...

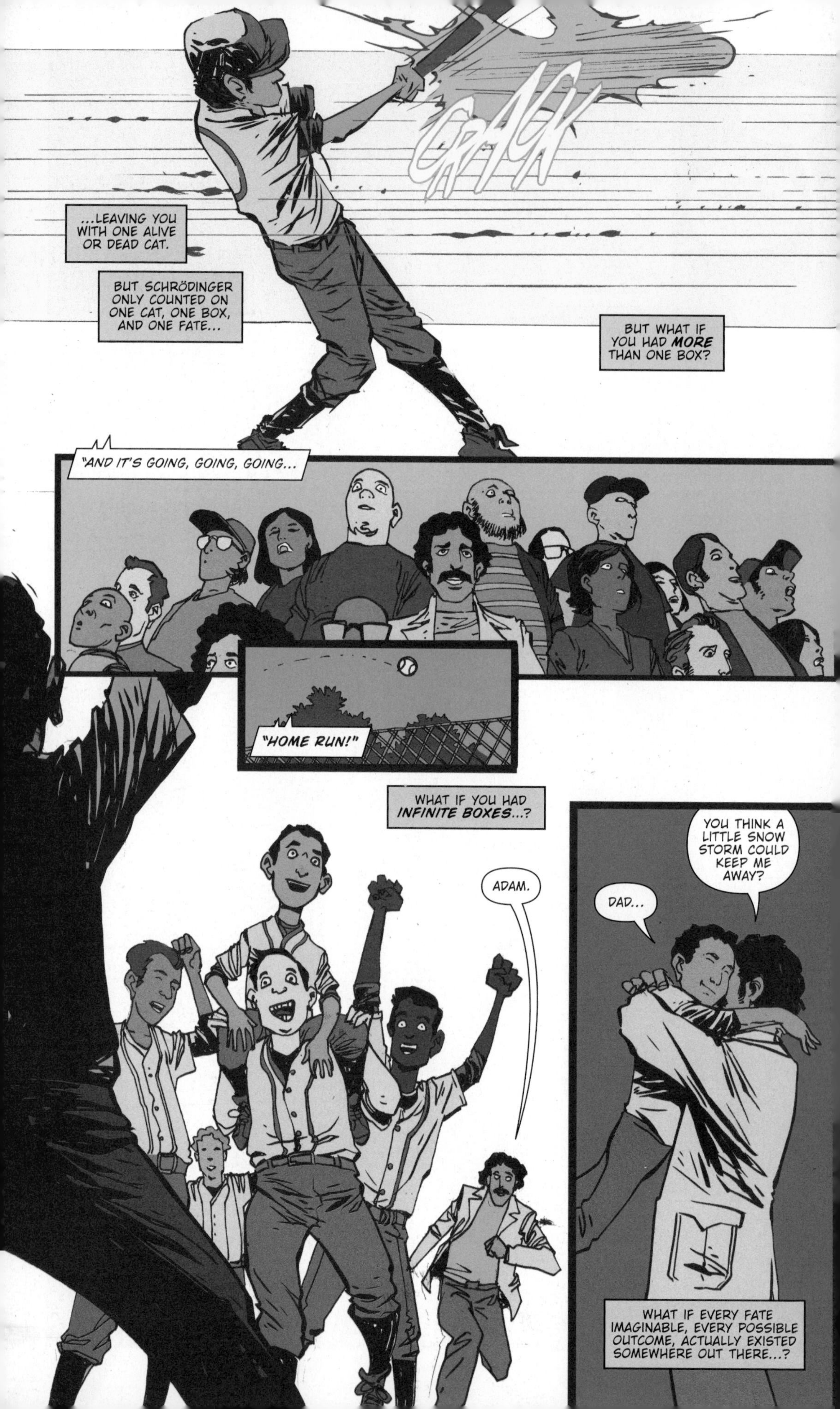

CRAAACK
...LEAVING YOU WITH ONE ALIVE OR DEAD CAT.
BUT SCHRÖDINGER ONLY COUNTED ON ONE CAT, ONE BOX, AND ONE FATE...
BUT WHAT IF YOU HAD MORE THAN ONE BOX?
"AND IT'S GOING, GOING, GOING...
"HOME RUN!"
WHAT IF YOU HAD INFINITE BOXES...?
ADAM.
DAD...
YOU THINK A LITTLE SNOW STORM COULD KEEP ME AWAY?
WHAT IF EVERY FATE IMAGINABLE, EVERY POSSIBLE OUTCOME, ACTUALLY EXISTED SOMEWHERE OUT THERE...?

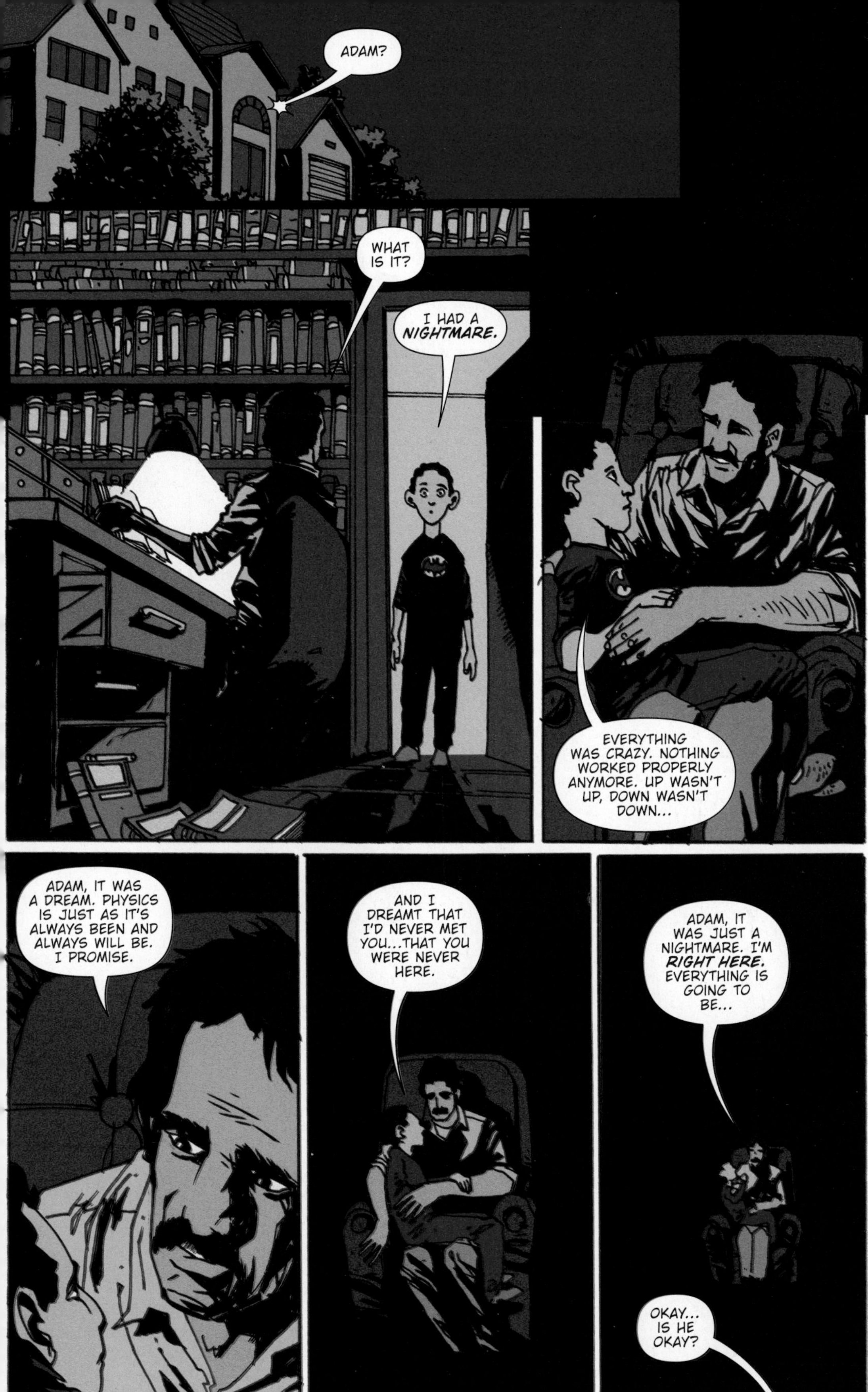
ADAM?
WHAT IS IT?
I HAD A NIGHTMARE.
EVERYTHING WAS CRAZY. NOTHING WORKED PROPERLY ANYMORE. UP WASN'T UP, DOWN WASN'T DOWN...
ADAM, IT WAS A DREAM. PHYSICS IS JUST AS IT'S ALWAYS BEEN AND ALWAYS WILL BE. I PROMISE.
AND I DREAMT THAT I'D NEVER MET YOU...THAT YOU WERE NEVER HERE.
ADAM, IT WAS JUST A NIGHTMARE. I'M RIGHT HERE. EVERYTHING IS GOING TO BE...
OKAY... IS HE OKAY?

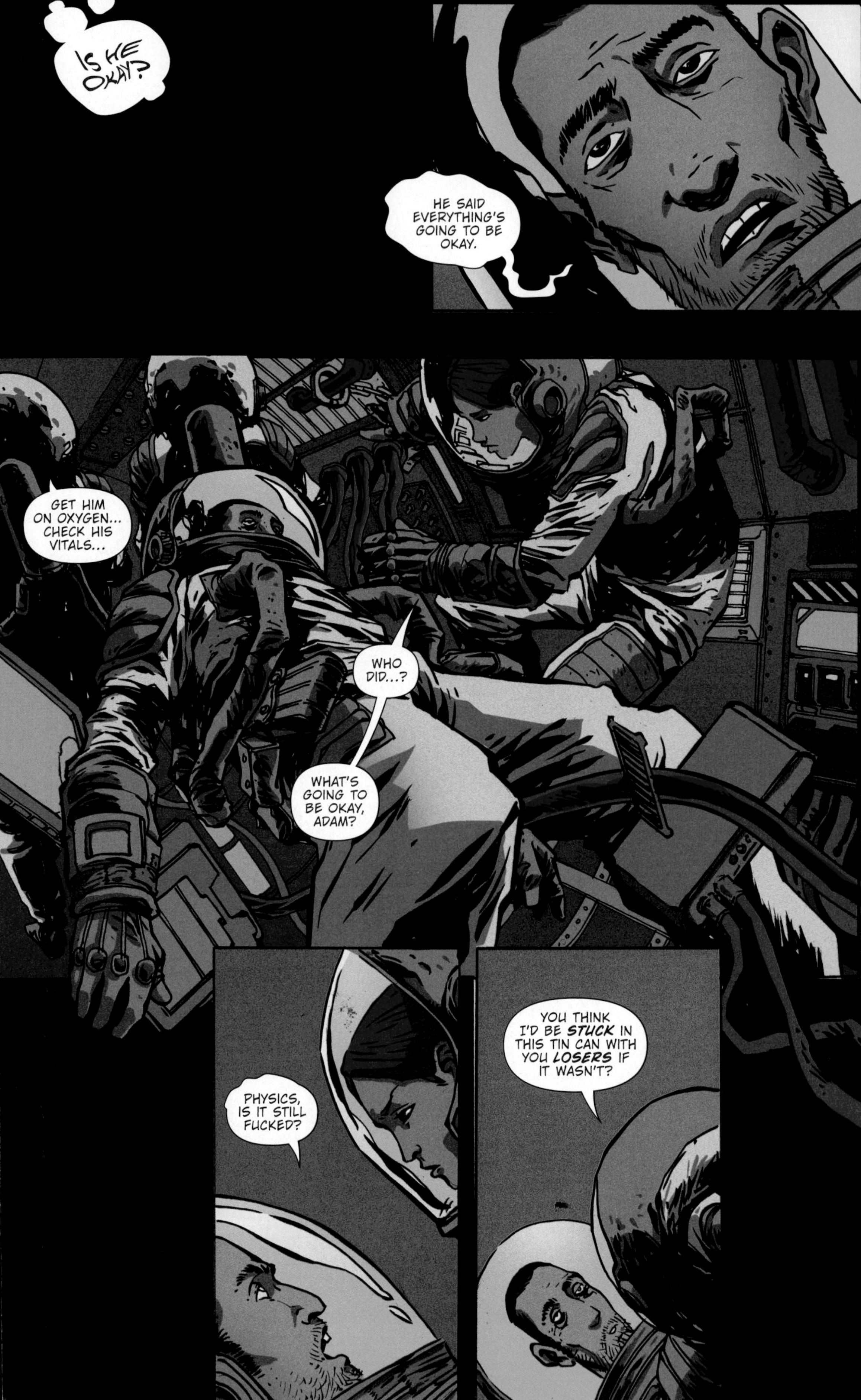
IS HE OKAY?
HE SAID EVERYTHING'S GOING TO BE OKAY.
GET HIM ON OXYGEN... CHECK HIS VITALS...
WHO DID...?
WHAT'S GOING TO BE OKAY, ADAM?
PHYSICS, IS IT STILL FUCKED?
YOU THINK I'D BE STUCK IN THIS TIN CAN WITH YOU LOSERS IF IT WASN'T?

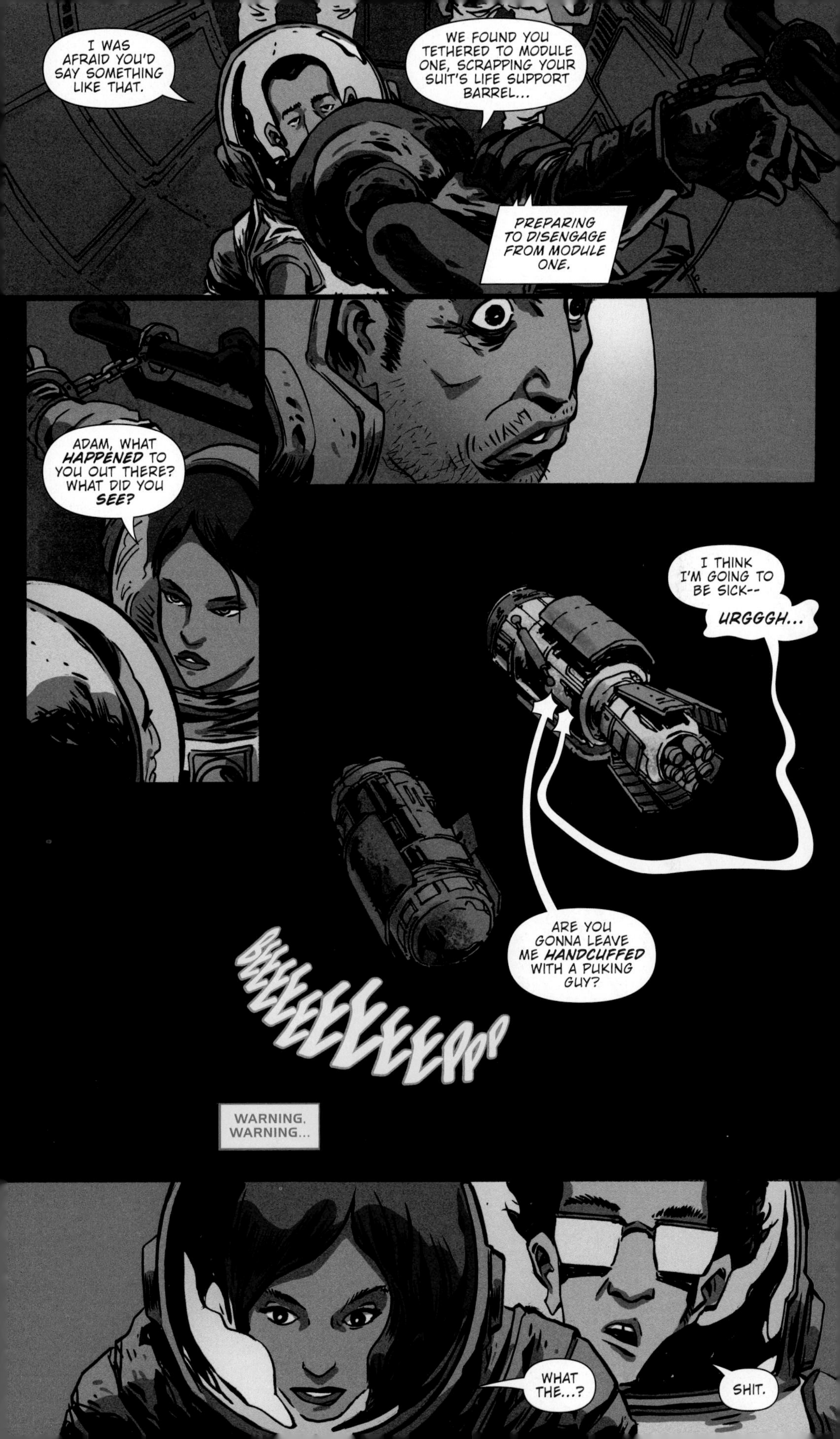
I WAS AFRAID YOU'D SAY SOMETHING LIKE THAT.
WE FOUND YOU TETHERED TO MODULE ONE, SCRAPPING YOUR SUIT'S LIFE SUPPORT BARREL...
PREPARING TO DISENGAGE FROM MODULE ONE.
ADAM, WHAT HAPPENED TO YOU OUT THERE? WHAT DID YOU SEE?
I THINK I'M GOING TO BE SICK--
URGGGH...
ARE YOU GONNA LEAVE ME HANDCUFFED WITH A PUKING GUY?
BEEEEEEEEEPPP
WARNING. WARNING...
WHAT THE...?
SHIT.

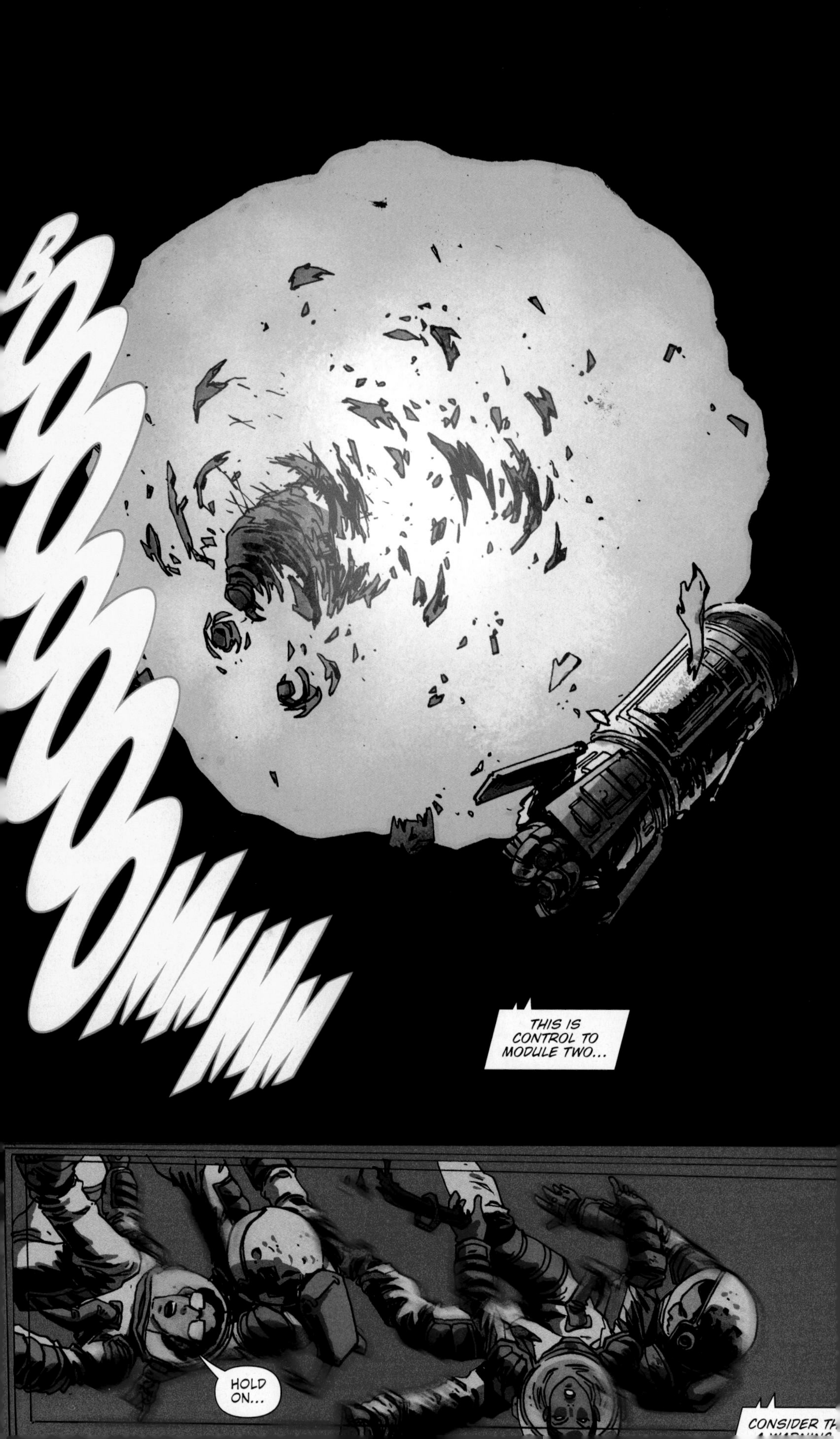
BOOOOOOOOMMMM
THIS IS CONTROL TO MODULE TWO...
HOLD ON...
CONSIDER

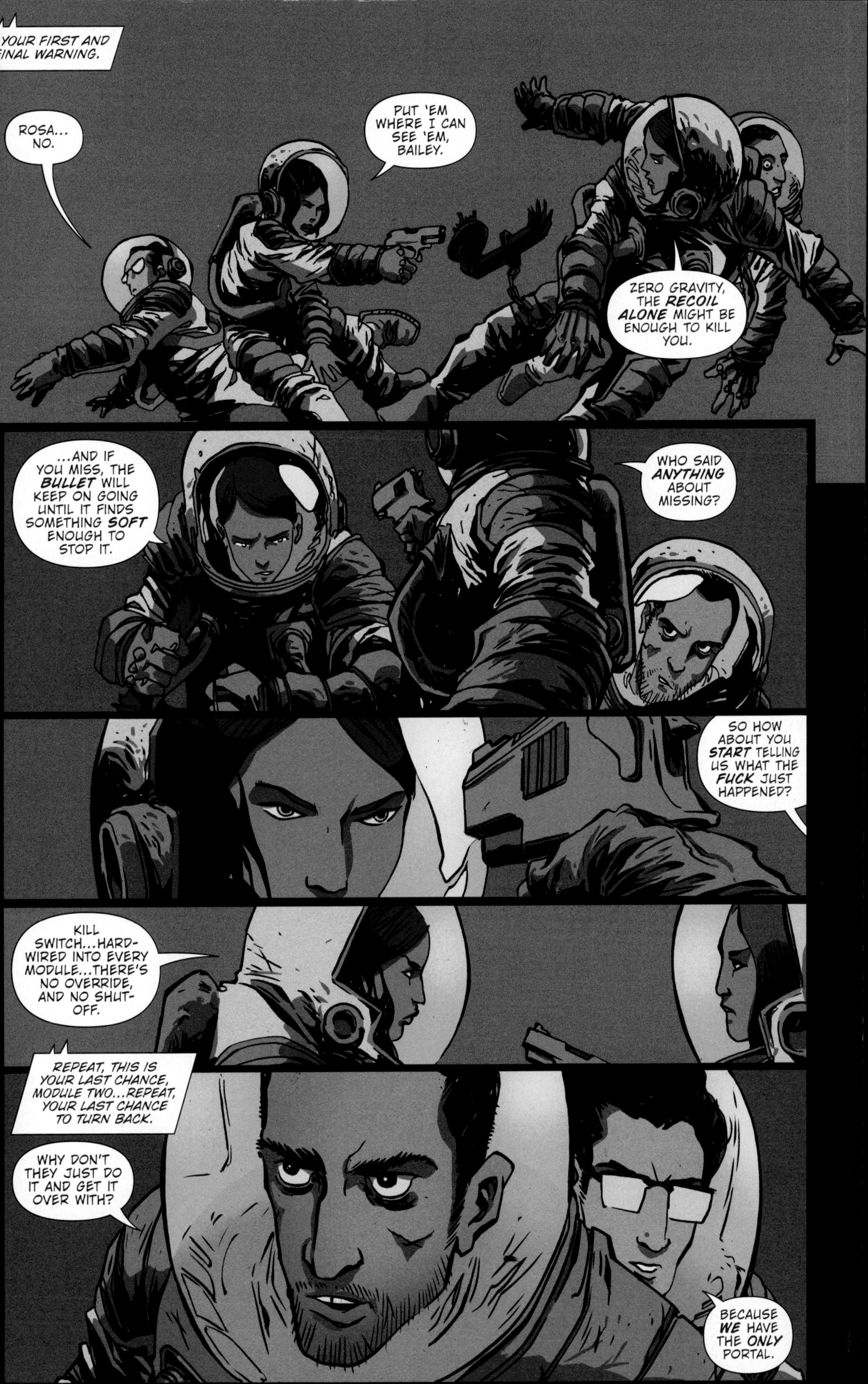
YOUR FIRST AND FINAL WARNING.
ROSA... NO.
PUT 'EM WHERE I CAN SEE 'EM, BAILEY.
ZERO GRAVITY, THE RECOIL ALONE MIGHT BE ENOUGH TO KILL YOU.
...AND IF YOU MISS, THE BULLET WILL KEEP ON GOING UNTIL IT FINDS SOMETHING SOFT ENOUGH TO STOP IT.
WHO SAID ANYTHING ABOUT MISSING?
SO HOW ABOUT YOU START TELLING US WHAT THE FUCK JUST HAPPENED?
KILL SWITCH...HARD-WIRED INTO EVERY MODULE...THERE'S NO OVERRIDE, AND NO SHUT-OFF.
REPEAT, THIS IS YOUR LAST CHANCE, MODULE TWO...REPEAT, YOUR LAST CHANCE TO TURN BACK.
WHY DON'T THEY JUST DO IT AND GET IT OVER WITH?
BECAUSE WE HAVE THE ONLY PORTAL.

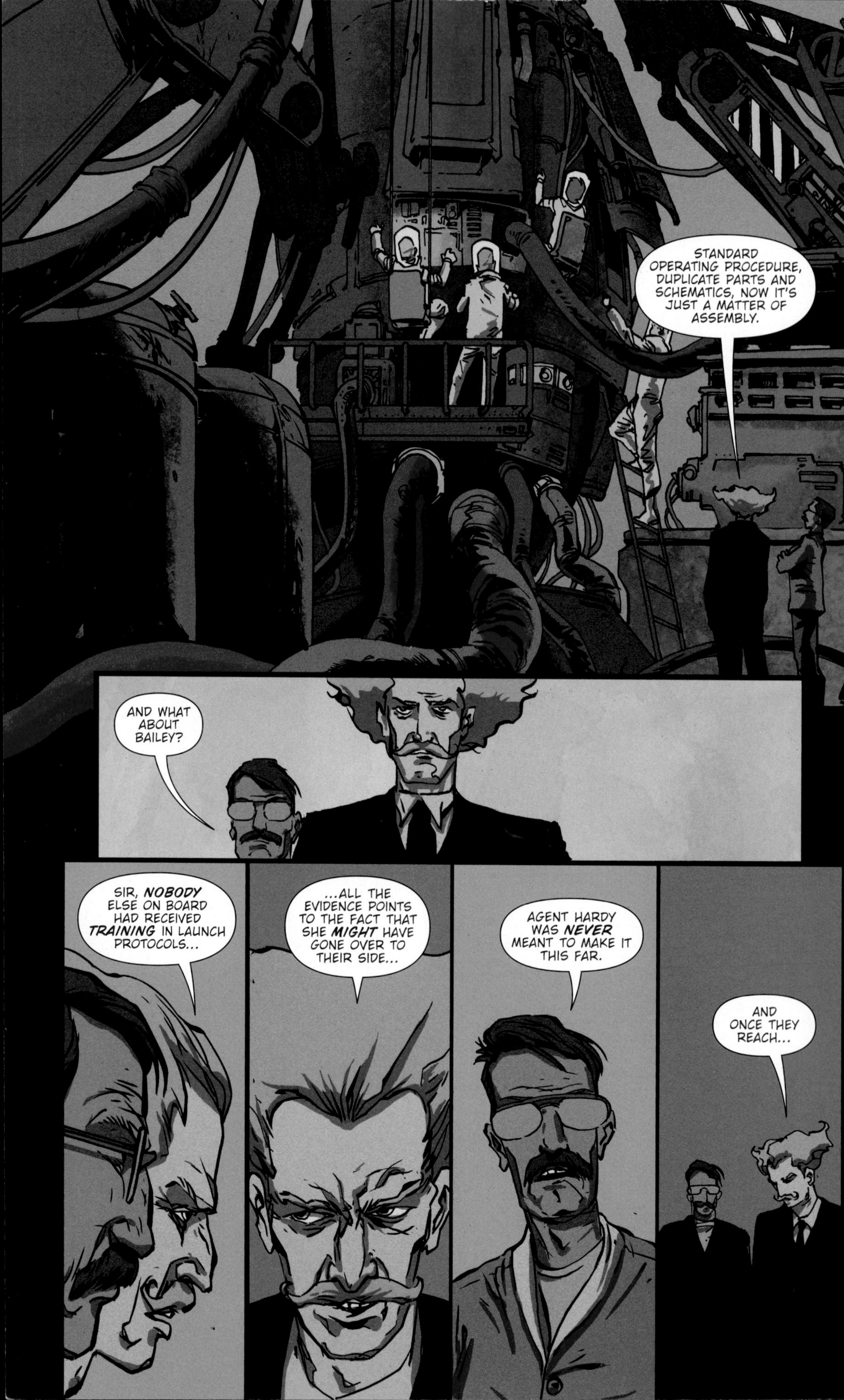
STANDARD OPERATING PROCEDURE, DUPLICATE PARTS AND SCHEMATICS, NOW IT'S JUST A MATTER OF ASSEMBLY.
AND WHAT ABOUT BAILEY?
SIR, NOBODY ELSE ON BOARD HAD RECEIVED TRAINING IN LAUNCH PROTOCOLS...
...ALL THE EVIDENCE POINTS TO THE FACT THAT SHE MIGHT HAVE GONE OVER TO THEIR SIDE...
AGENT HARDY WAS NEVER MEANT TO MAKE IT THIS FAR.
AND ONCE THEY REACH...

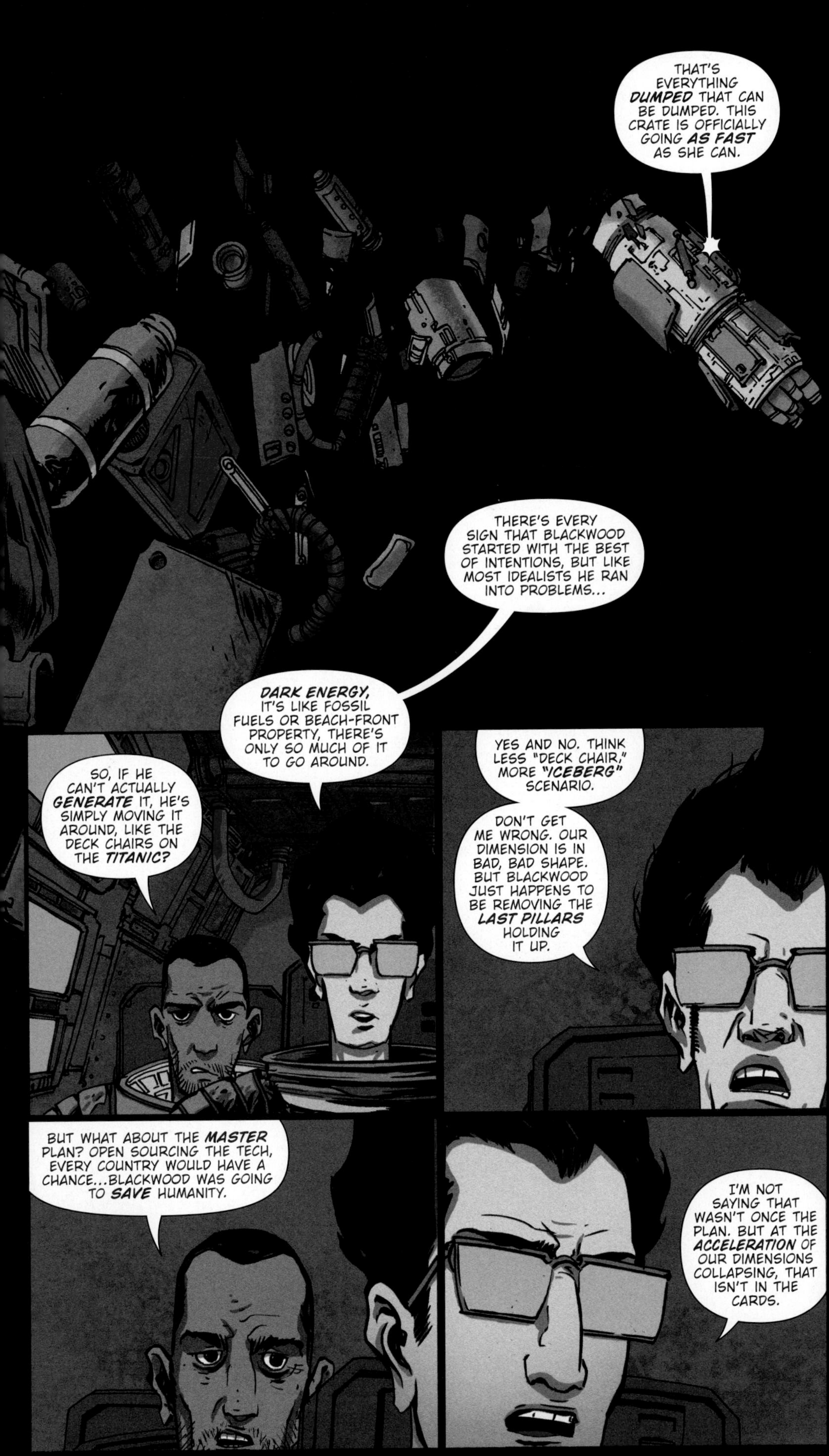
THAT'S EVERYTHING DUMPED THAT CAN BE DUMPED. THIS CRATE IS OFFICIALLY GOING AS FAST AS SHE CAN.
THERE'S EVERY SIGN THAT BLACKWOOD STARTED WITH THE BEST OF INTENTIONS, BUT LIKE MOST IDEALISTS HE RAN INTO PROBLEMS...
DARK ENERGY, IT'S LIKE FOSSIL FUELS OR BEACH-FRONT PROPERTY, THERE'S ONLY SO MUCH OF IT TO GO AROUND.
SO, IF HE CAN'T ACTUALLY GENERATE IT, HE'S SIMPLY MOVING IT AROUND, LIKE THE DECK CHAIRS ON THE TITANIC?
YES AND NO. THINK LESS "DECK CHAIR," MORE "ICEBERG" SCENARIO.
DON'T GET ME WRONG. OUR DIMENSION IS IN BAD, BAD SHAPE. BUT BLACKWOOD JUST HAPPENS TO BE REMOVING THE LAST PILLARS HOLDING IT UP.
BUT WHAT ABOUT THE MASTER PLAN? OPEN SOURCING THE TECH, EVERY COUNTRY WOULD HAVE A CHANCE...BLACKWOOD WAS GOING TO SAVE HUMANITY.
I'M NOT SAYING THAT WASN'T ONCE THE PLAN. BUT AT THE ACCELERATION OF OUR DIMENSIONS COLLAPSING, THAT ISN'T IN THE CARDS.

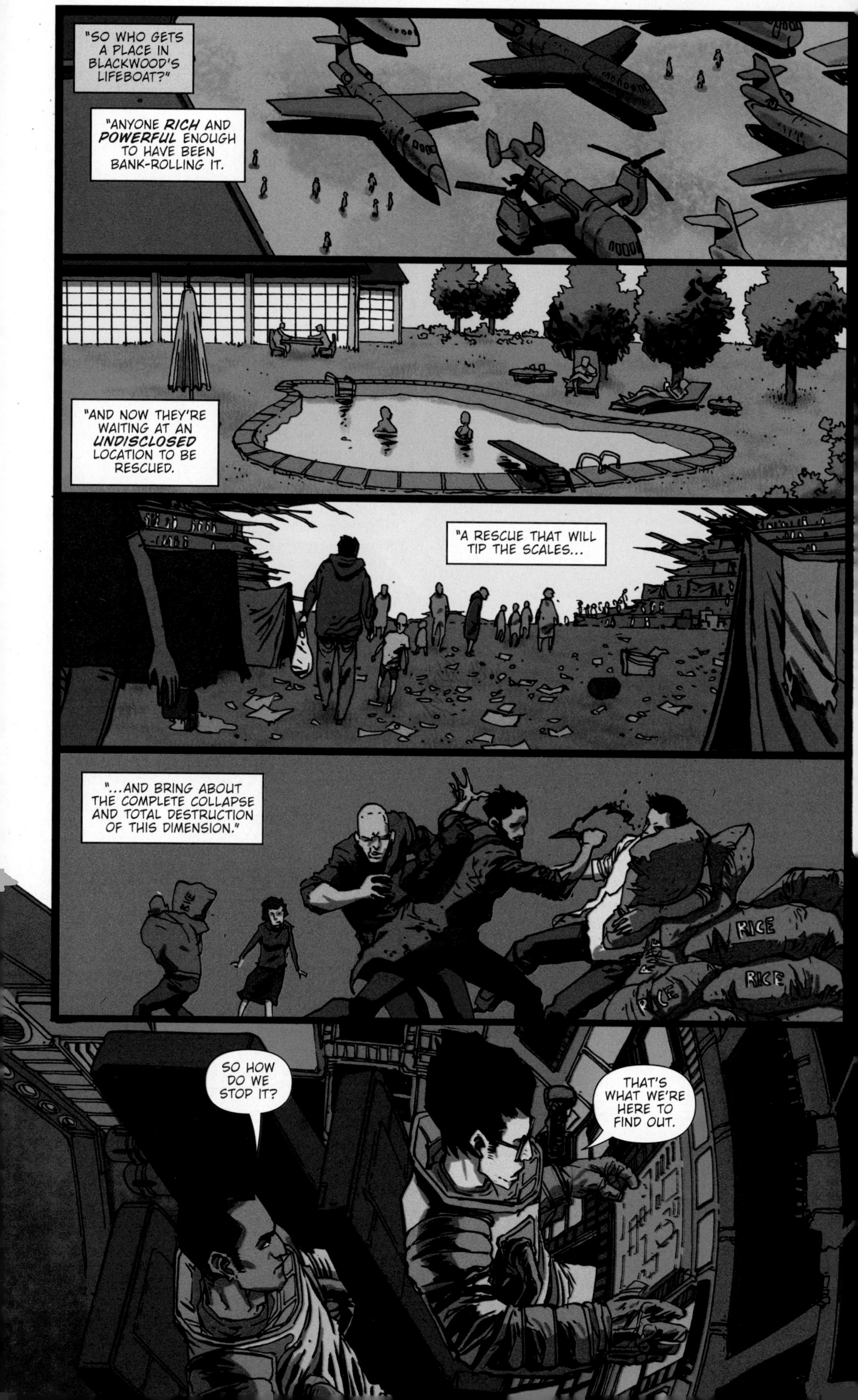
"SO WHO GETS A PLACE IN BLACKWOOD'S LIFEBOAT?"
"ANYONE RICH AND POWERFUL ENOUGH TO HAVE BEEN BANK-ROLLING IT.
"AND NOW THEY'RE WAITING AT AN UNDISCLOSED LOCATION TO BE RESCUED.
"A RESCUE THAT WILL TIP THE SCALES...
"...AND BRING ABOUT THE COMPLETE COLLAPSE AND TOTAL DESTRUCTION OF THIS DIMENSION."
RICE
RICE
SO HOW DO WE STOP IT?
THAT'S WHAT WE'RE HERE TO FIND OUT.

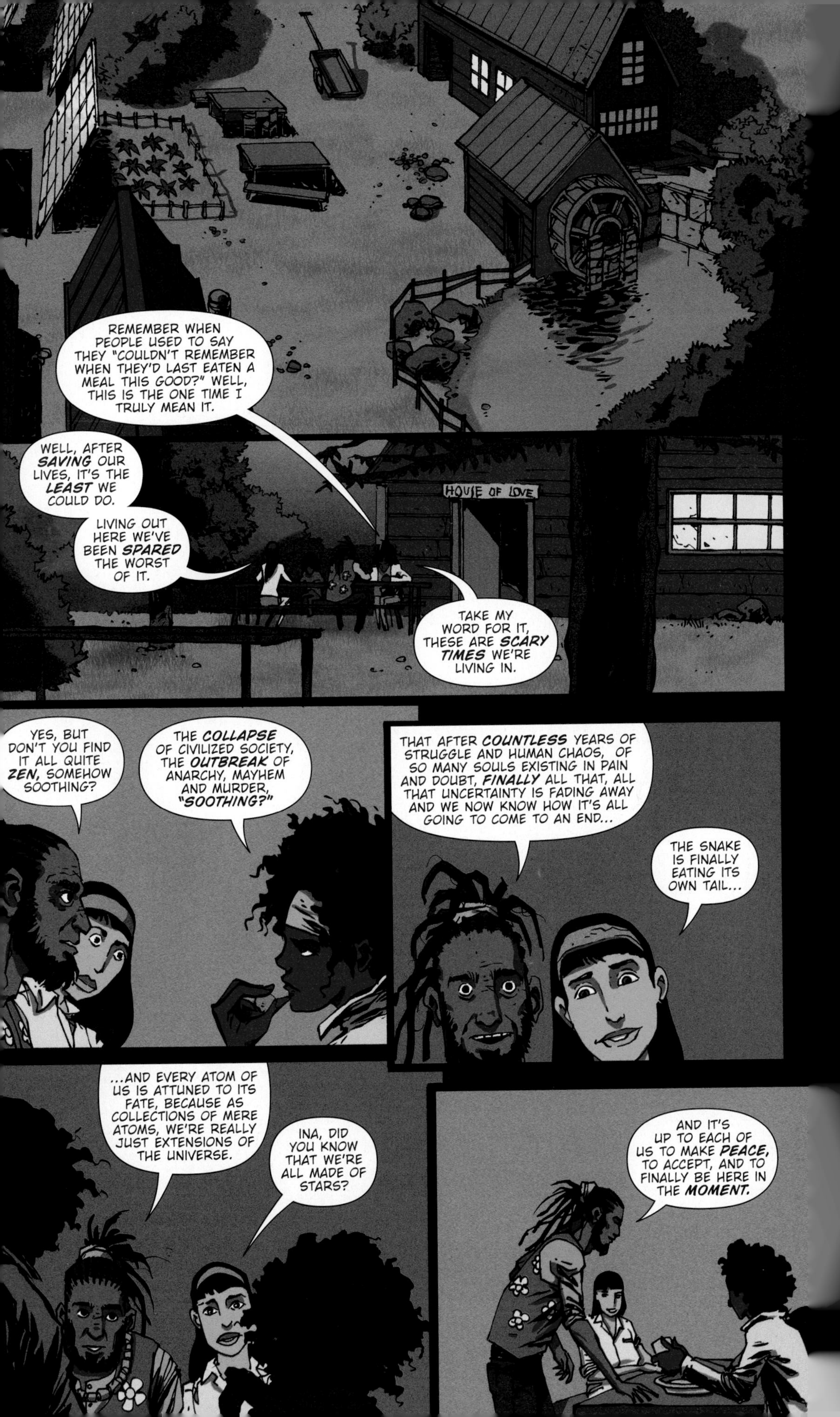
REMEMBER WHEN PEOPLE USED TO SAY THEY "COULDN'T REMEMBER WHEN THEY'D LAST EATEN A MEAL THIS GOOD?" WELL, THIS IS THE ONE TIME I TRULY MEAN IT.
WELL, AFTER SAVING OUR LIVES, IT'S THE LEAST WE COULD DO.
LIVING OUT HERE WE'VE BEEN SPARED THE WORST OF IT.
HOUSE OF LOVE
TAKE MY WORD FOR IT, THESE ARE SCARY TIMES WE'RE LIVING IN.
YES, BUT DON'T YOU FIND IT ALL QUITE ZEN, SOMEHOW SOOTHING?
THE COLLAPSE OF CIVILIZED SOCIETY, THE OUTBREAK OF ANARCHY, MAYHEM AND MURDER, "SOOTHING?"
THAT AFTER COUNTLESS YEARS OF STRUGGLE AND HUMAN CHAOS, OF SO MANY SOULS EXISTING IN PAIN AND DOUBT, FINALLY ALL THAT, ALL THAT UNCERTAINTY IS FADING AWAY AND WE NOW KNOW HOW IT'S ALL GOING TO COME TO AN END...
THE SNAKE IS FINALLY EATING ITS OWN TAIL...
...AND EVERY ATOM OF US IS ATTUNED TO ITS FATE, BECAUSE AS COLLECTIONS OF MERE ATOMS, WE'RE REALLY JUST EXTENSIONS OF THE UNIVERSE.
INA, DID YOU KNOW THAT WE'RE ALL MADE OF STARS?
AND IT'S UP TO EACH OF US TO MAKE PEACE, TO ACCEPT, AND TO FINALLY BE HERE IN THE MOMENT.

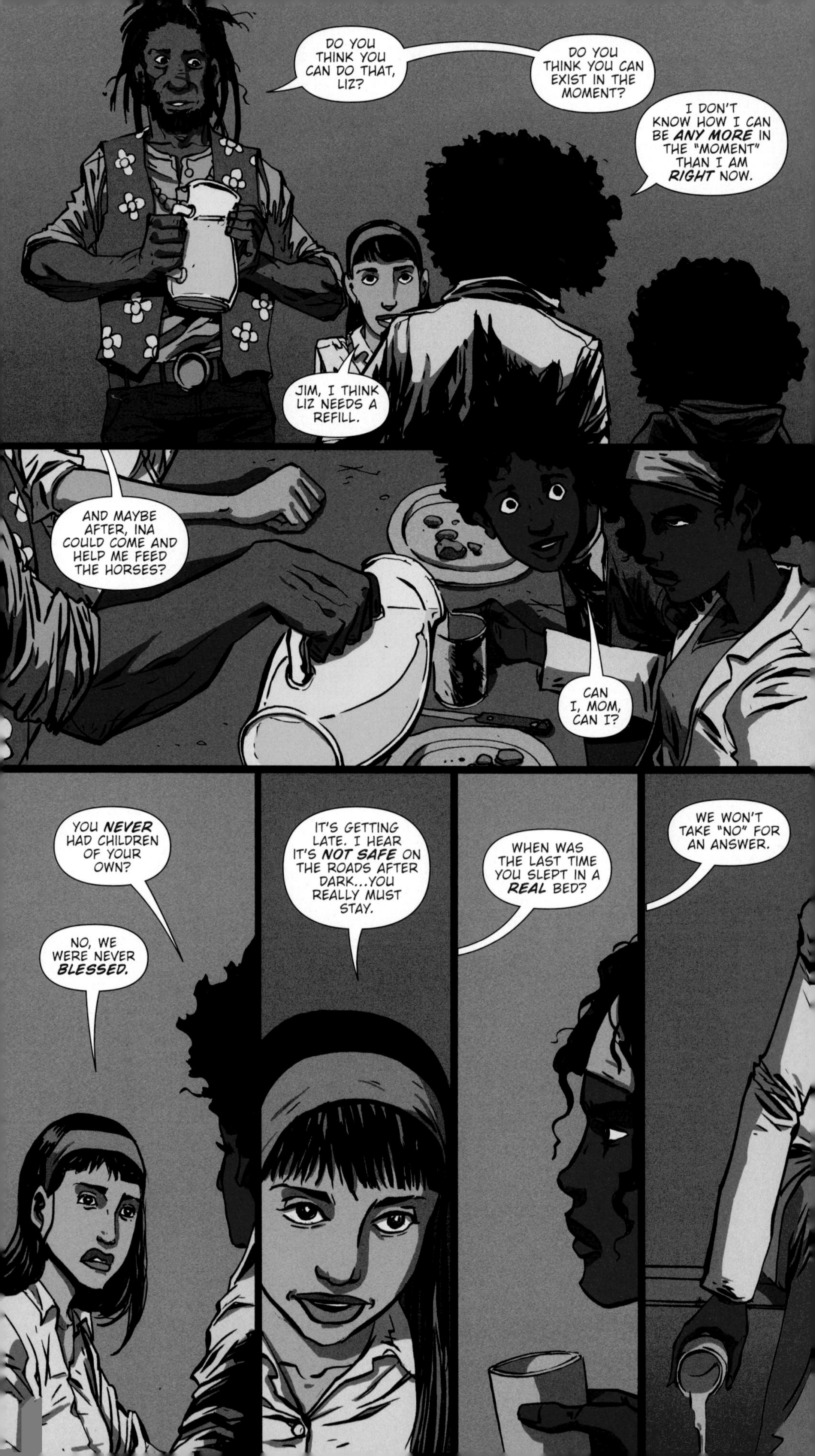
DO YOU THINK YOU CAN DO THAT, LIZ?
DO YOU THINK YOU CAN EXIST IN THE MOMENT?
I DON'T KNOW HOW I CAN BE ANY MORE IN THE "MOMENT" THAN I AM RIGHT NOW.
JIM, I THINK LIZ NEEDS A REFILL.
AND MAYBE AFTER, INA COULD COME AND HELP ME FEED THE HORSES?
CAN I, MOM, CAN I?
YOU NEVER HAD CHILDREN OF YOUR OWN?
NO, WE WERE NEVER BLESSED.
IT'S GETTING LATE. I HEAR IT'S NOT SAFE ON THE ROADS AFTER DARK...YOU REALLY MUST STAY.
WHEN WAS THE LAST TIME YOU SLEPT IN A REAL BED?
WE WON'T TAKE "NO" FOR AN ANSWER.

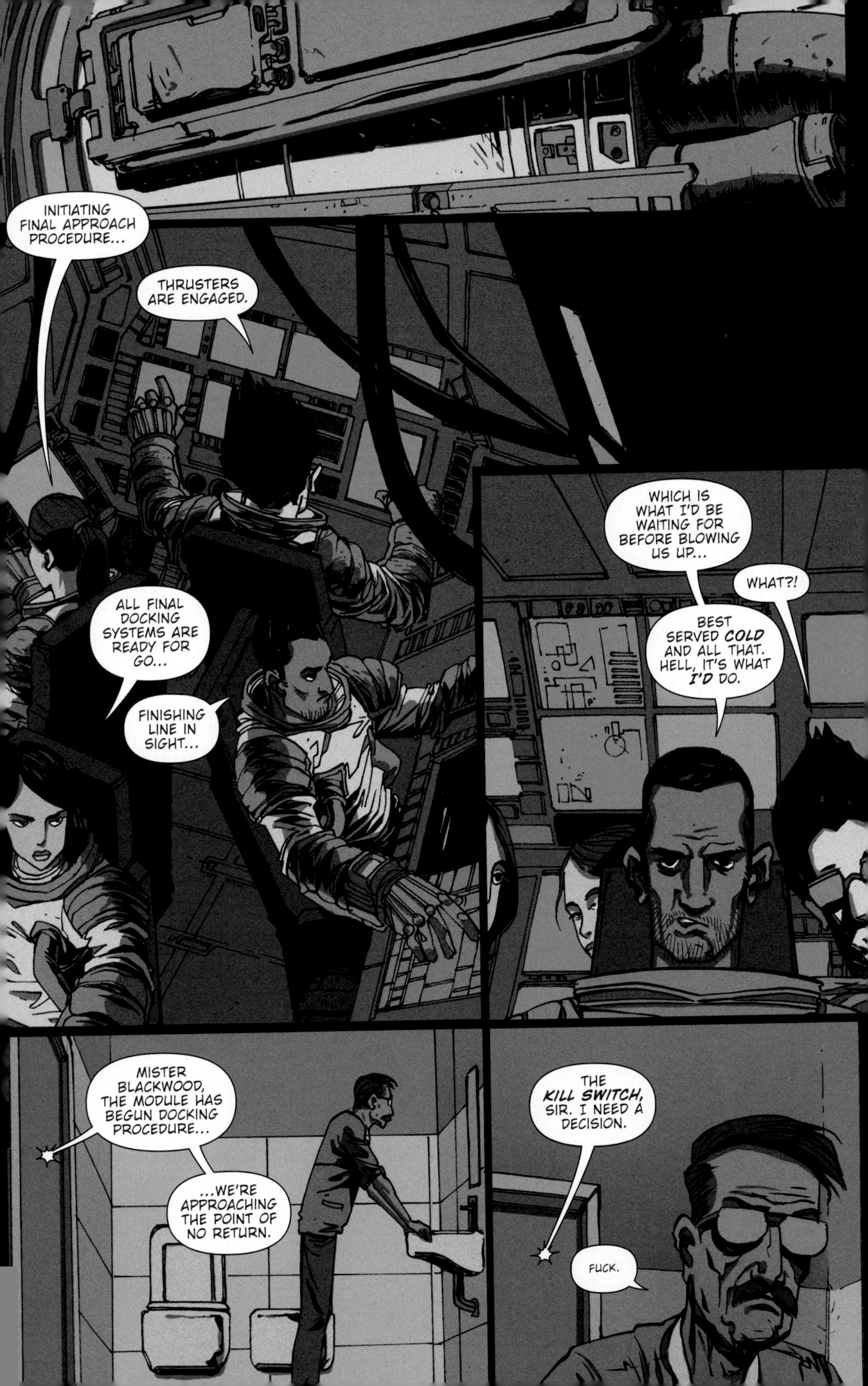
INITIATING FINAL APPROACH PROCEDURE...
THRUSTERS ARE ENGAGED.
ALL FINAL DOCKING SYSTEMS ARE READY FOR GO...
FINISHING LINE IN SIGHT...
WHICH IS WHAT I'D BE WAITING FOR BEFORE BLOWING US UP...
WHAT?!
BEST SERVED **COLD** AND ALL THAT. HELL, IT'S WHAT ***I'D*** DO.
MISTER BLACKWOOD, THE MODULE HAS BEGUN DOCKING PROCEDURE...
...WE'RE APPROACHING THE POINT OF NO RETURN.
THE ***KILL SWITCH,*** SIR. I NEED A DECISION.
FUCK.

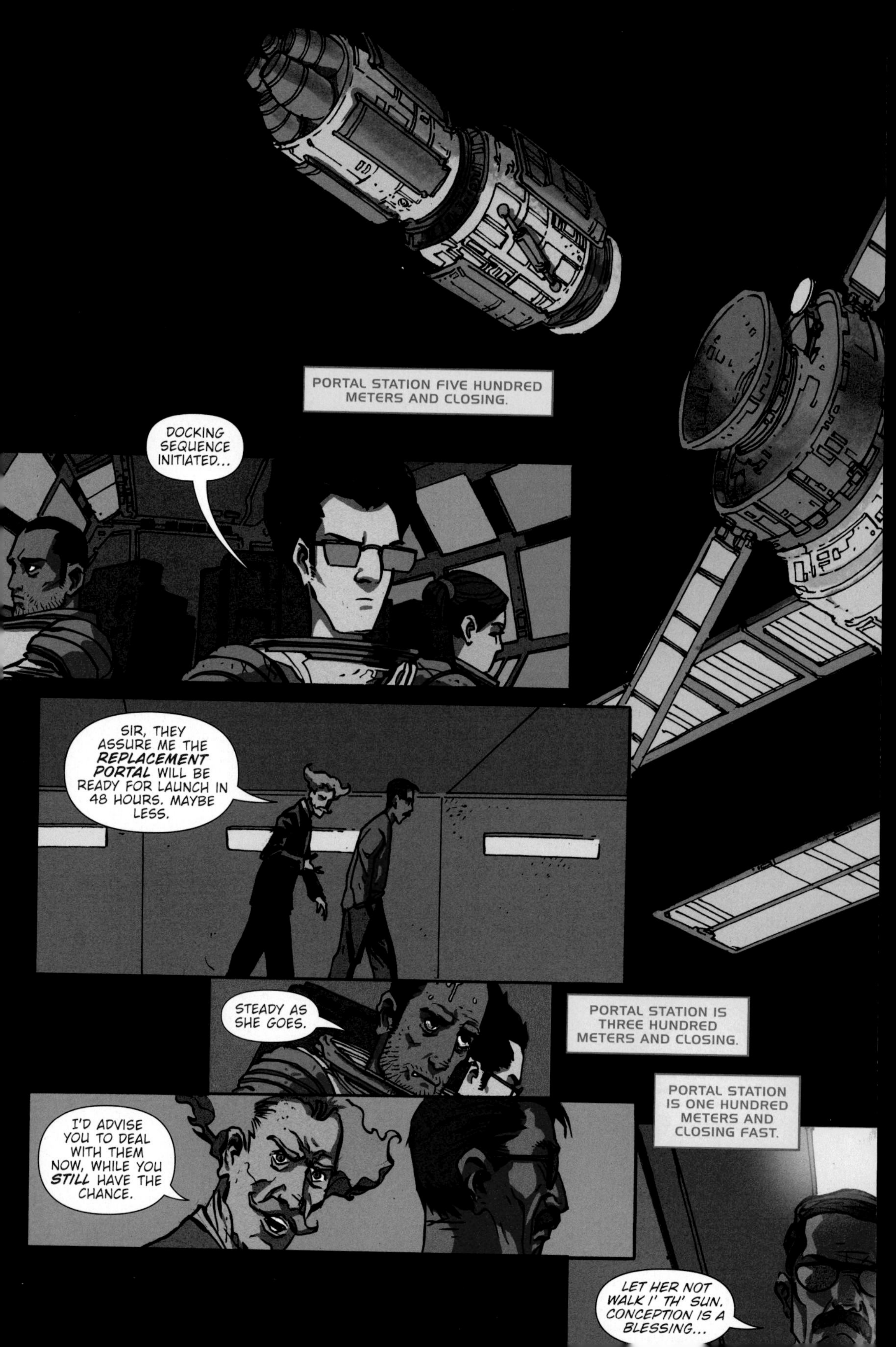
PORTAL STATION FIVE HUNDRED METERS AND CLOSING.
DOCKING SEQUENCE INITIATED...
SIR, THEY ASSURE ME THE **REPLACEMENT PORTAL** WILL BE READY FOR LAUNCH IN 48 HOURS. MAYBE LESS.
STEADY AS SHE GOES.
PORTAL STATION IS THREE HUNDRED METERS AND CLOSING.
I'D ADVISE YOU TO DEAL WITH THEM NOW, WHILE YOU **STILL** HAVE THE CHANCE.
PORTAL STATION IS ONE HUNDRED METERS AND CLOSING FAST.
LET HER NOT WALK I' TH' SUN. CONCEPTION IS A BLESSING...

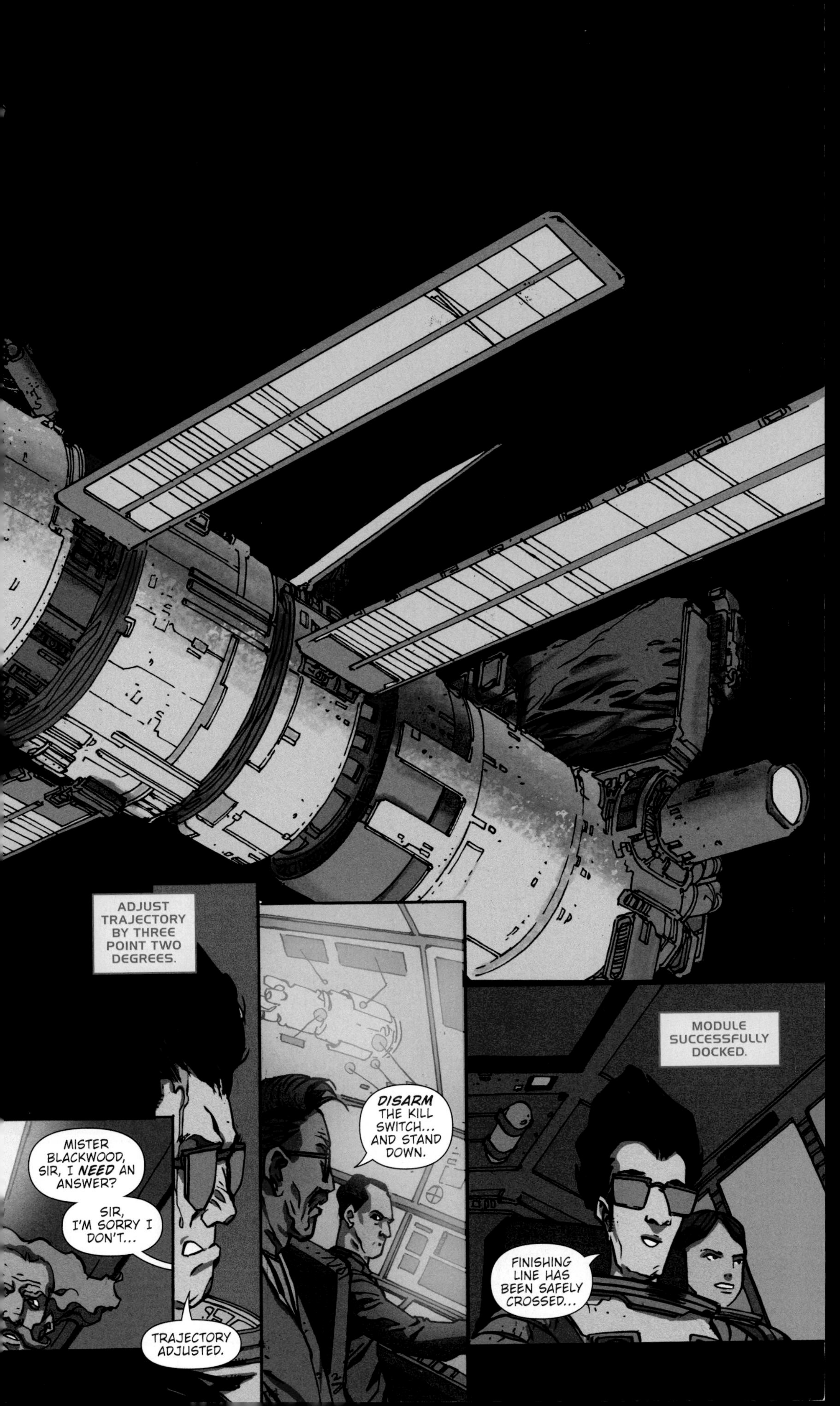
ADJUST TRAJECTORY BY THREE POINT TWO DEGREES.
MISTER BLACKWOOD, SIR, I NEED AN ANSWER?
SIR, I'M SORRY I DON'T...
TRAJECTORY ADJUSTED.
DISARM THE KILL SWITCH... AND STAND DOWN.
MODULE SUCCESSFULLY DOCKED.
FINISHING LINE HAS BEEN SAFELY CROSSED...

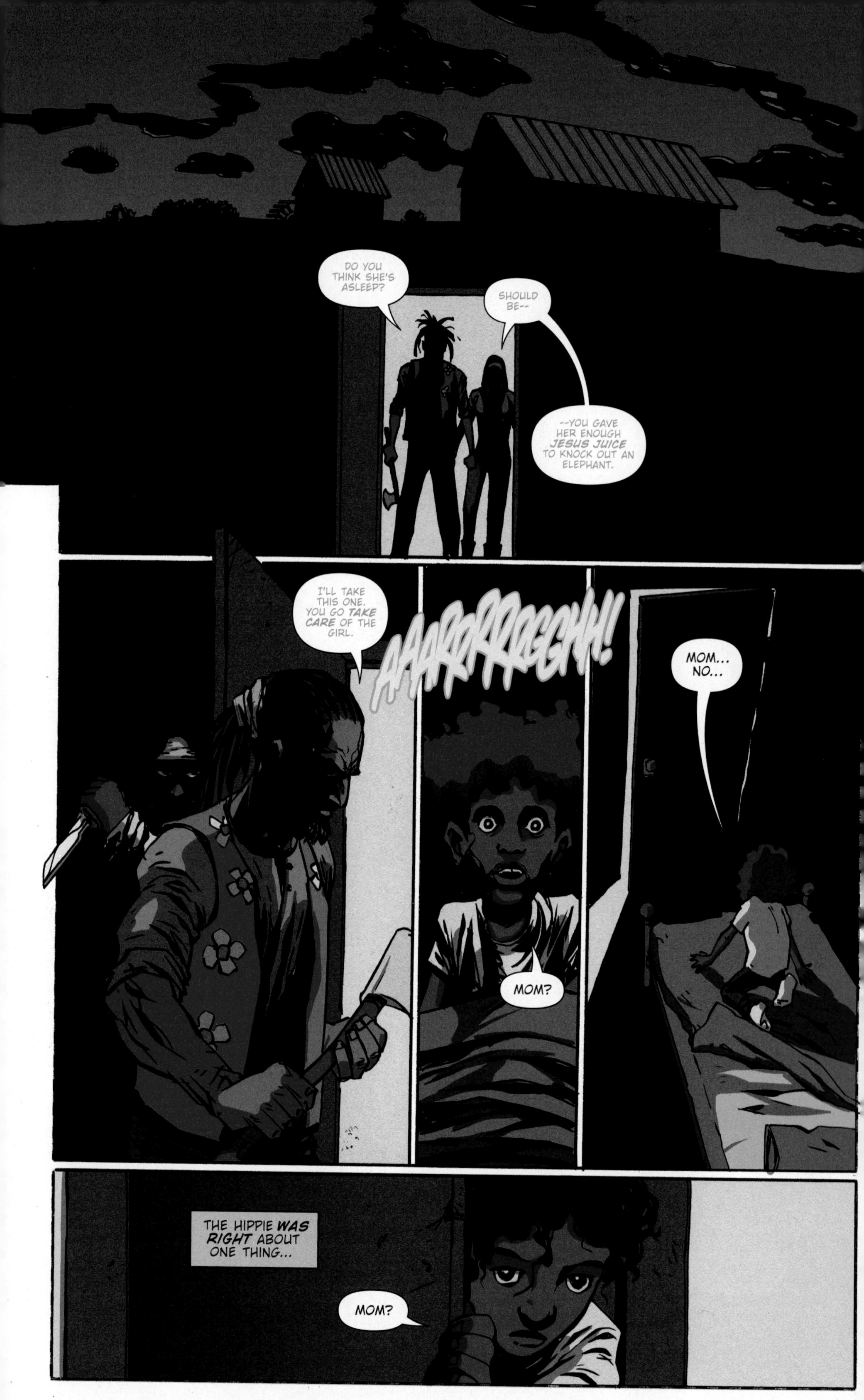
DO YOU THINK SHE'S ASLEEP?
SHOULD BE--
--YOU GAVE HER ENOUGH JESUS JUICE TO KNOCK OUT AN ELEPHANT.
I'LL TAKE THIS ONE. YOU GO TAKE CARE OF THE GIRL.
AAARRRRGGHH!
MOM?
MOM... NO...
THE HIPPIE WAS RIGHT ABOUT ONE THING...
MOM?

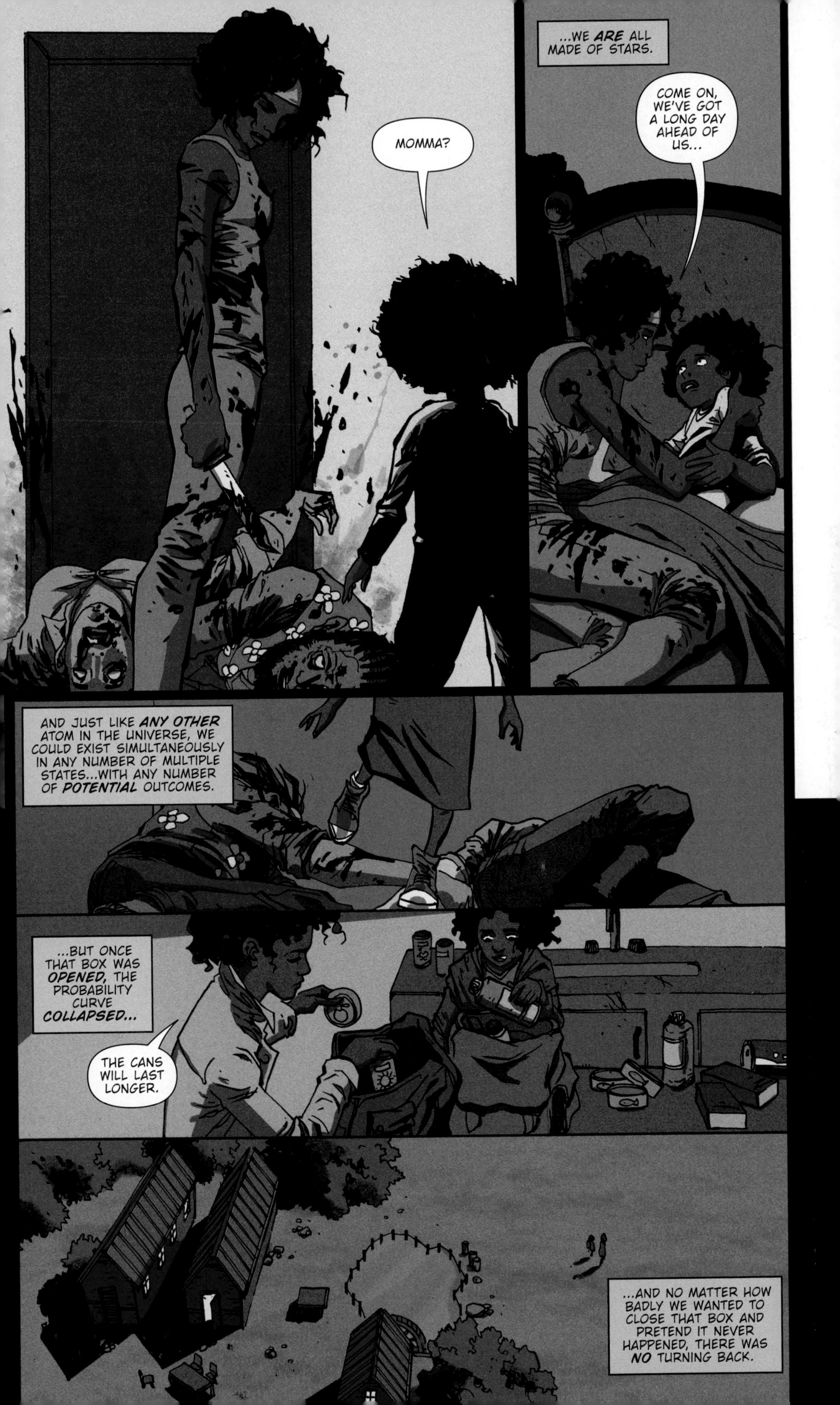

MOMMA?
...WE ARE ALL MADE OF STARS.
COME ON, WE'VE GOT A LONG DAY AHEAD OF US...
AND JUST LIKE ANY OTHER ATOM IN THE UNIVERSE, WE COULD EXIST SIMULTANEOUSLY IN ANY NUMBER OF MULTIPLE STATES...WITH ANY NUMBER OF POTENTIAL OUTCOMES.
...BUT ONCE THAT BOX WAS OPENED, THE PROBABILITY CURVE COLLAPSED...
THE CANS WILL LAST LONGER.
...AND NO MATTER HOW BADLY WE WANTED TO CLOSE THAT BOX AND PRETEND IT NEVER HAPPENED, THERE WAS NO TURNING BACK.

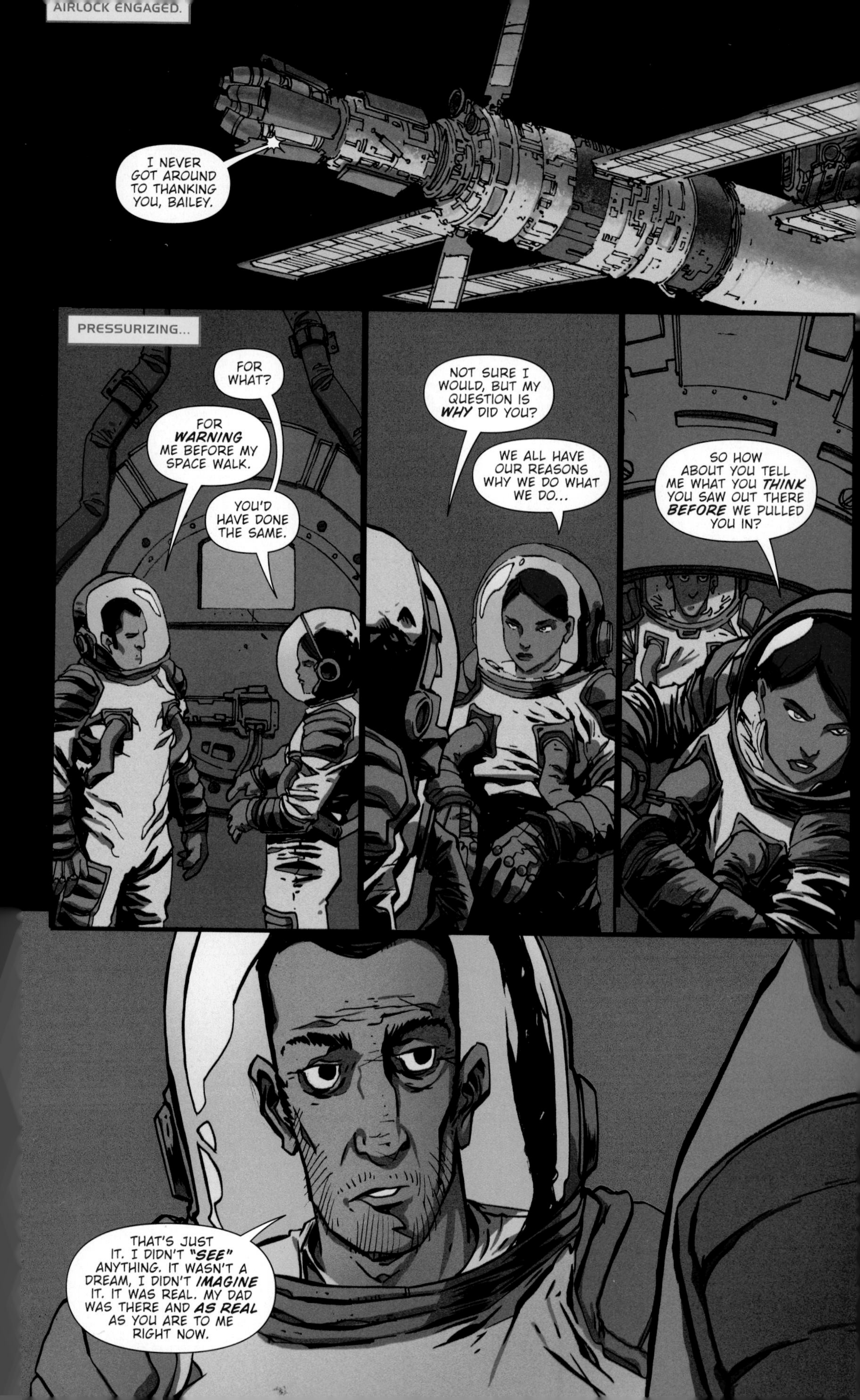

AIRLOCK ENGAGED.
I NEVER GOT AROUND TO THANKING YOU, BAILEY.
PRESSURIZING...
FOR WHAT?
FOR WARNING ME BEFORE MY SPACE WALK.
YOU'D HAVE DONE THE SAME.
NOT SURE I WOULD, BUT MY QUESTION IS WHY DID YOU?
WE ALL HAVE OUR REASONS WHY WE DO WHAT WE DO...
SO HOW ABOUT YOU TELL ME WHAT YOU THINK YOU SAW OUT THERE BEFORE WE PULLED YOU IN?
THAT'S JUST IT. I DIDN'T "SEE" ANYTHING. IT WASN'T A DREAM, I DIDN'T IMAGINE IT. IT WAS REAL. MY DAD WAS THERE AND AS REAL AS YOU ARE TO ME RIGHT NOW.

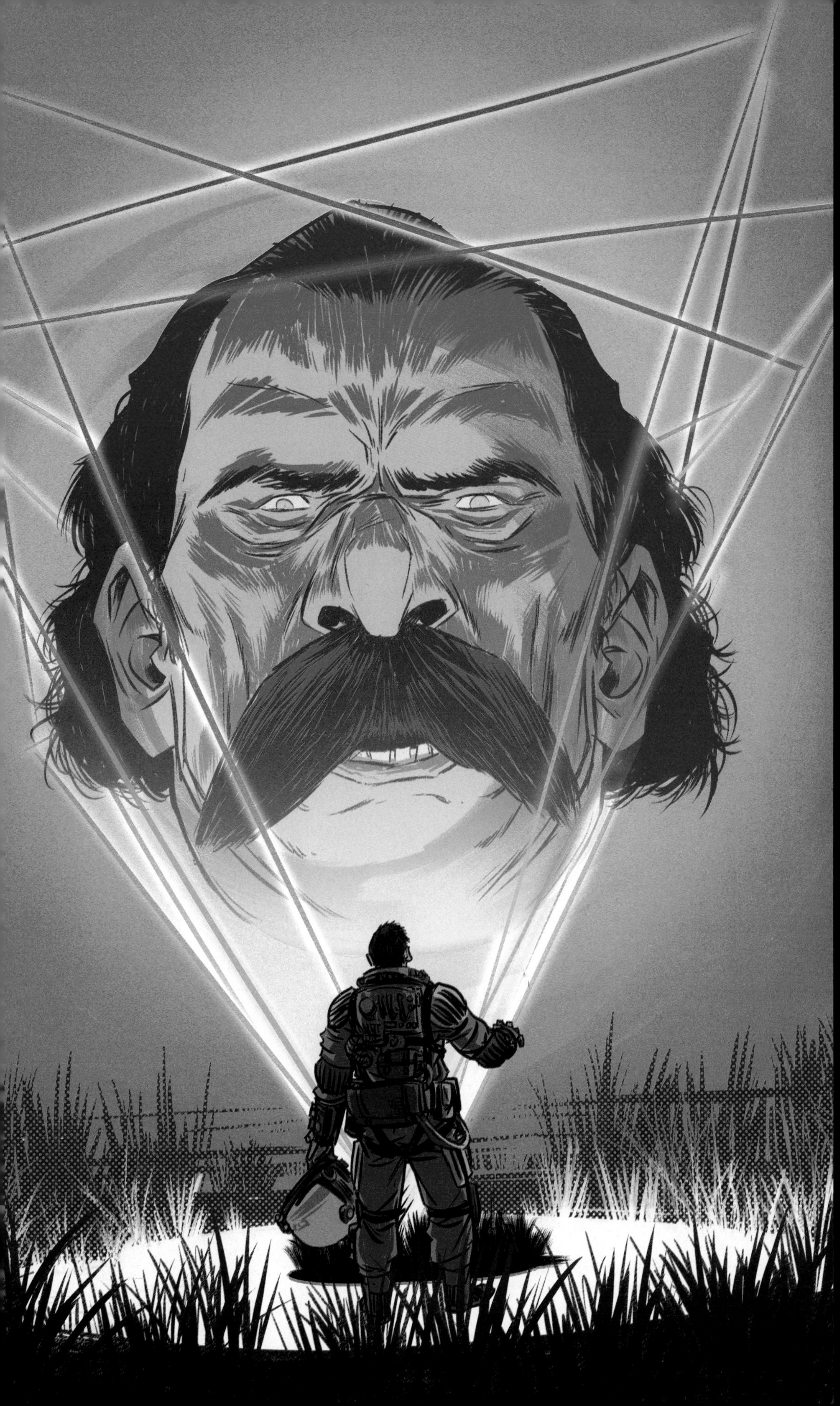

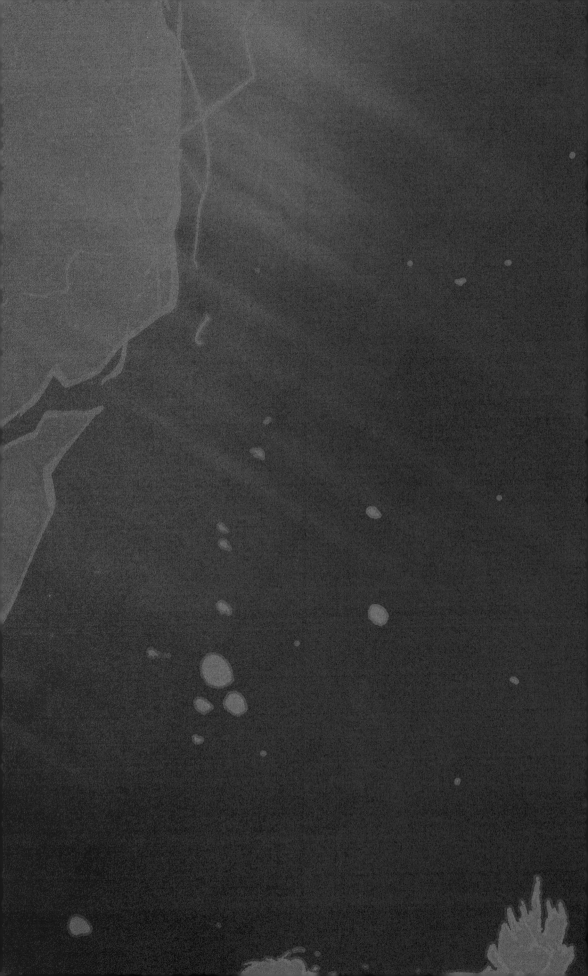

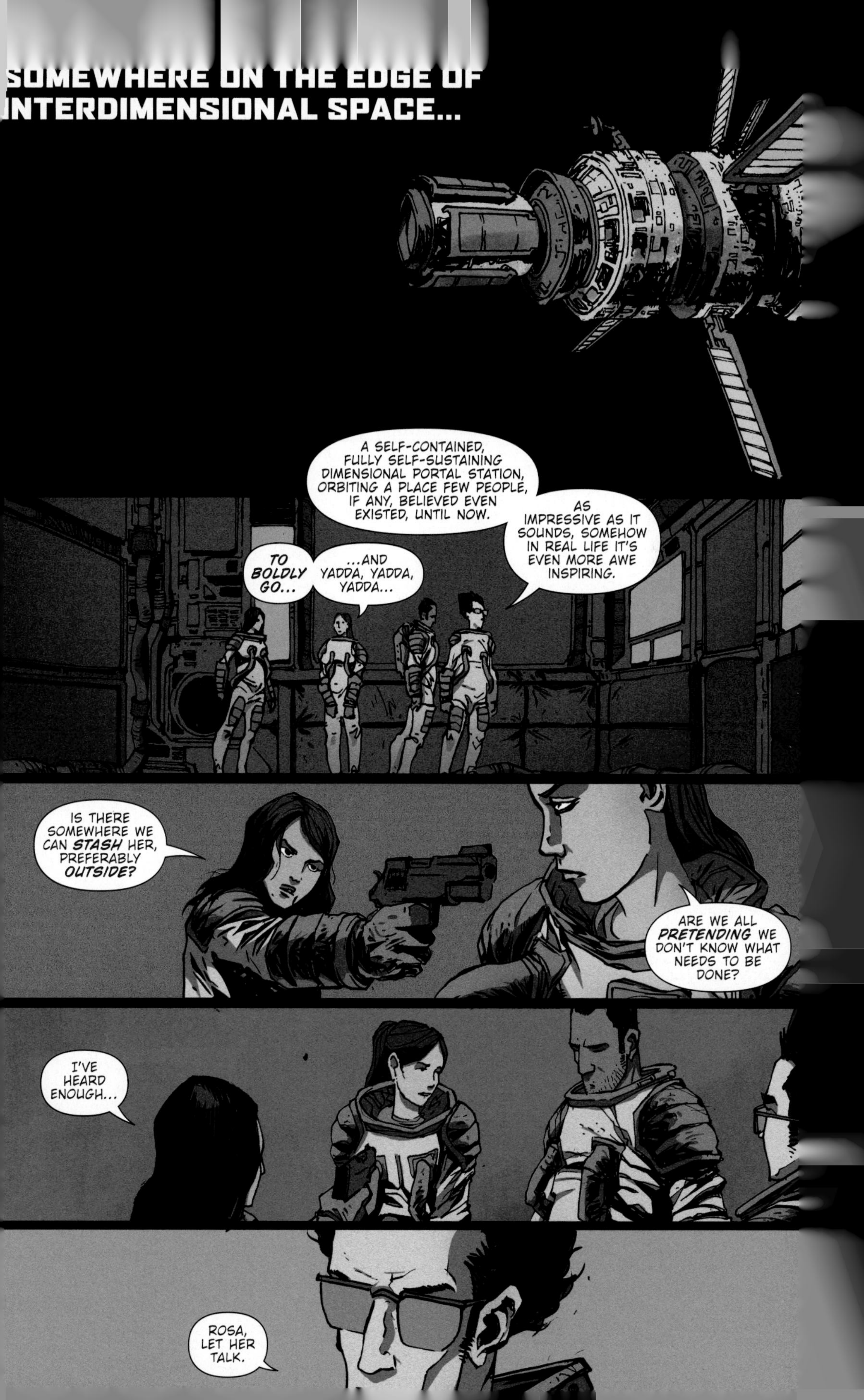
SOMEWHERE ON THE EDGE OF INTERDIMENSIONAL SPACE...
A SELF-CONTAINED, FULLY SELF-SUSTAINING DIMENSIONAL PORTAL STATION, ORBITING A PLACE FEW PEOPLE, IF ANY, BELIEVED EVEN EXISTED, UNTIL NOW.
AS IMPRESSIVE AS IT SOUNDS, SOMEHOW IN REAL LIFE IT'S EVEN MORE AWE INSPIRING.
TO BOLDLY GO...
...AND YADDA, YADDA, YADDA...
IS THERE SOMEWHERE WE CAN STASH HER, PREFERABLY OUTSIDE?
ARE WE ALL PRETENDING WE DON'T KNOW WHAT NEEDS TO BE DONE?
I'VE HEARD ENOUGH...
ROSA, LET HER TALK.

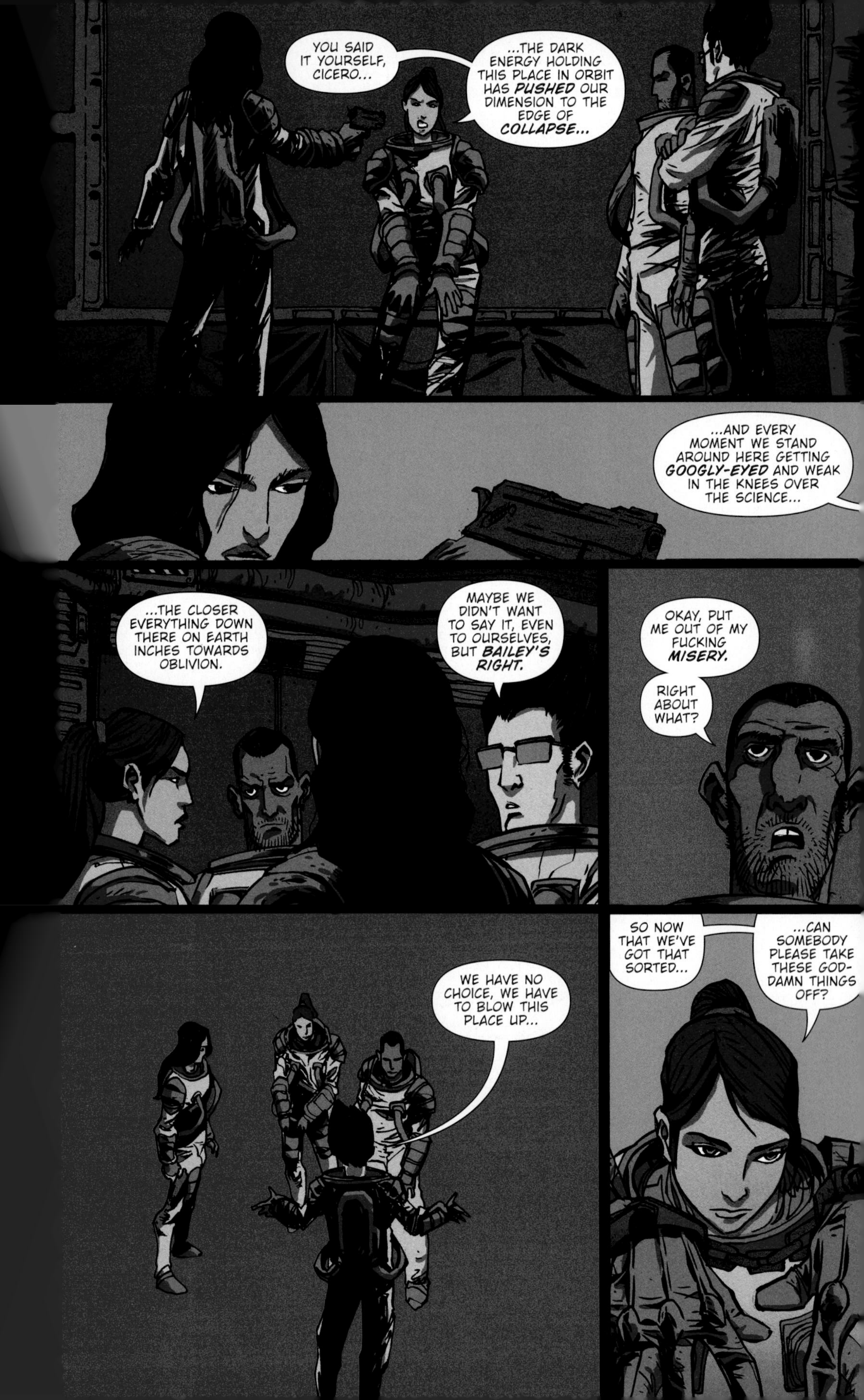
YOU SAID IT YOURSELF, CICERO...
...THE DARK ENERGY HOLDING THIS PLACE IN ORBIT HAS PUSHED OUR DIMENSION TO THE EDGE OF COLLAPSE...
...AND EVERY MOMENT WE STAND AROUND HERE GETTING GOOGLY-EYED AND WEAK IN THE KNEES OVER THE SCIENCE...
...THE CLOSER EVERYTHING DOWN THERE ON EARTH INCHES TOWARDS OBLIVION.
MAYBE WE DIDN'T WANT TO SAY IT, EVEN TO OURSELVES, BUT BAILEY'S RIGHT.
OKAY, PUT ME OUT OF MY FUCKING MISERY.
RIGHT ABOUT WHAT?
WE HAVE NO CHOICE, WE HAVE TO BLOW THIS PLACE UP...
SO NOW THAT WE'VE GOT THAT SORTED...
...CAN SOMEBODY PLEASE TAKE THESE GOD-DAMN THINGS OFF?

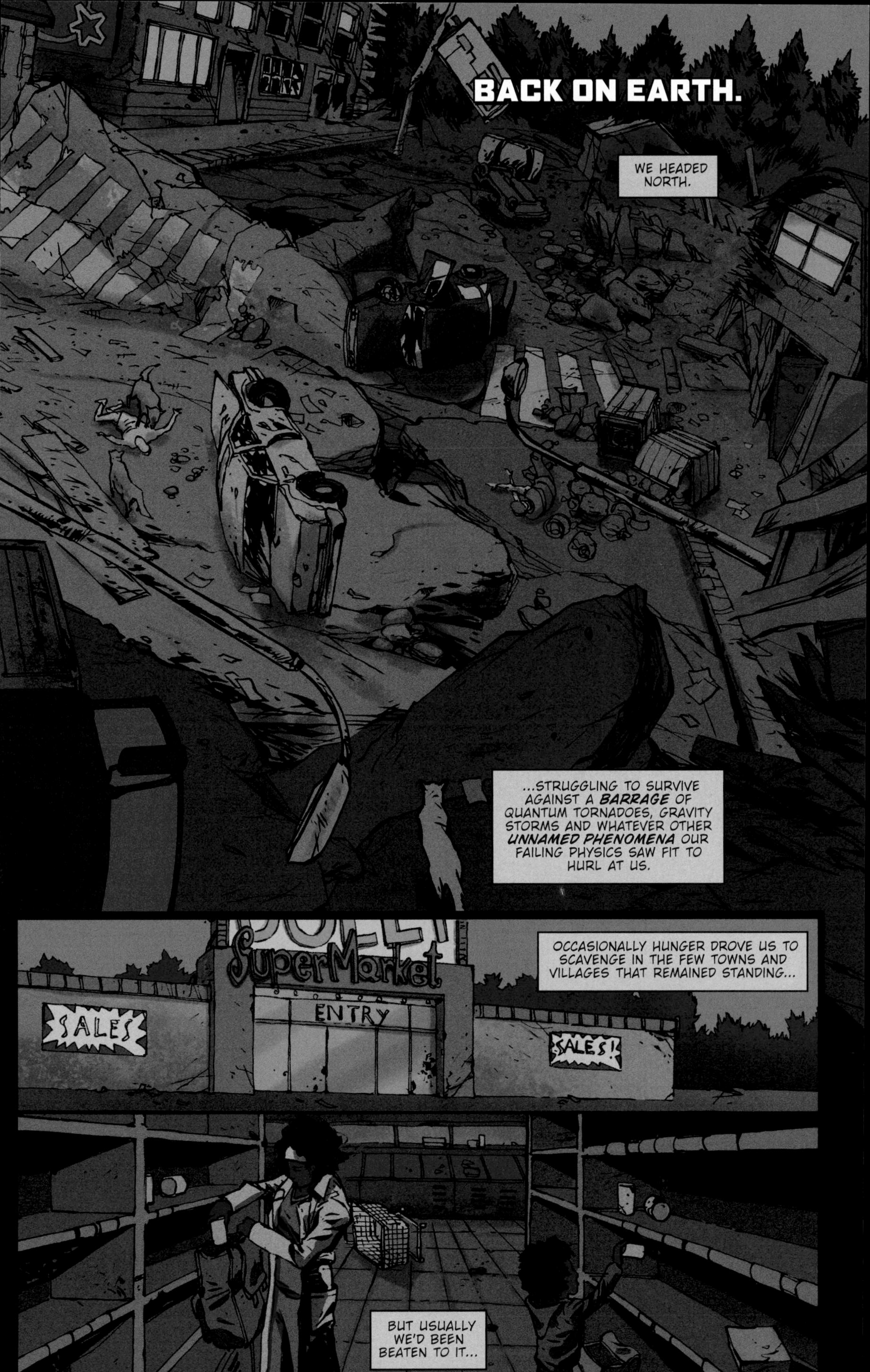
BACK ON EARTH.
WE HEADED NORTH.
...STRUGGLING TO SURVIVE AGAINST A *BARRAGE* OF QUANTUM TORNADOES, GRAVITY STORMS AND WHATEVER OTHER *UNNAMED PHENOMENA* OUR FAILING PHYSICS SAW FIT TO HURL AT US.
SuperMarket
SALES
ENTRY
SALES!
OCCASIONALLY HUNGER DROVE US TO SCAVENGE IN THE FEW TOWNS AND VILLAGES THAT REMAINED STANDING...
BUT USUALLY WE'D BEEN BEATEN TO IT...

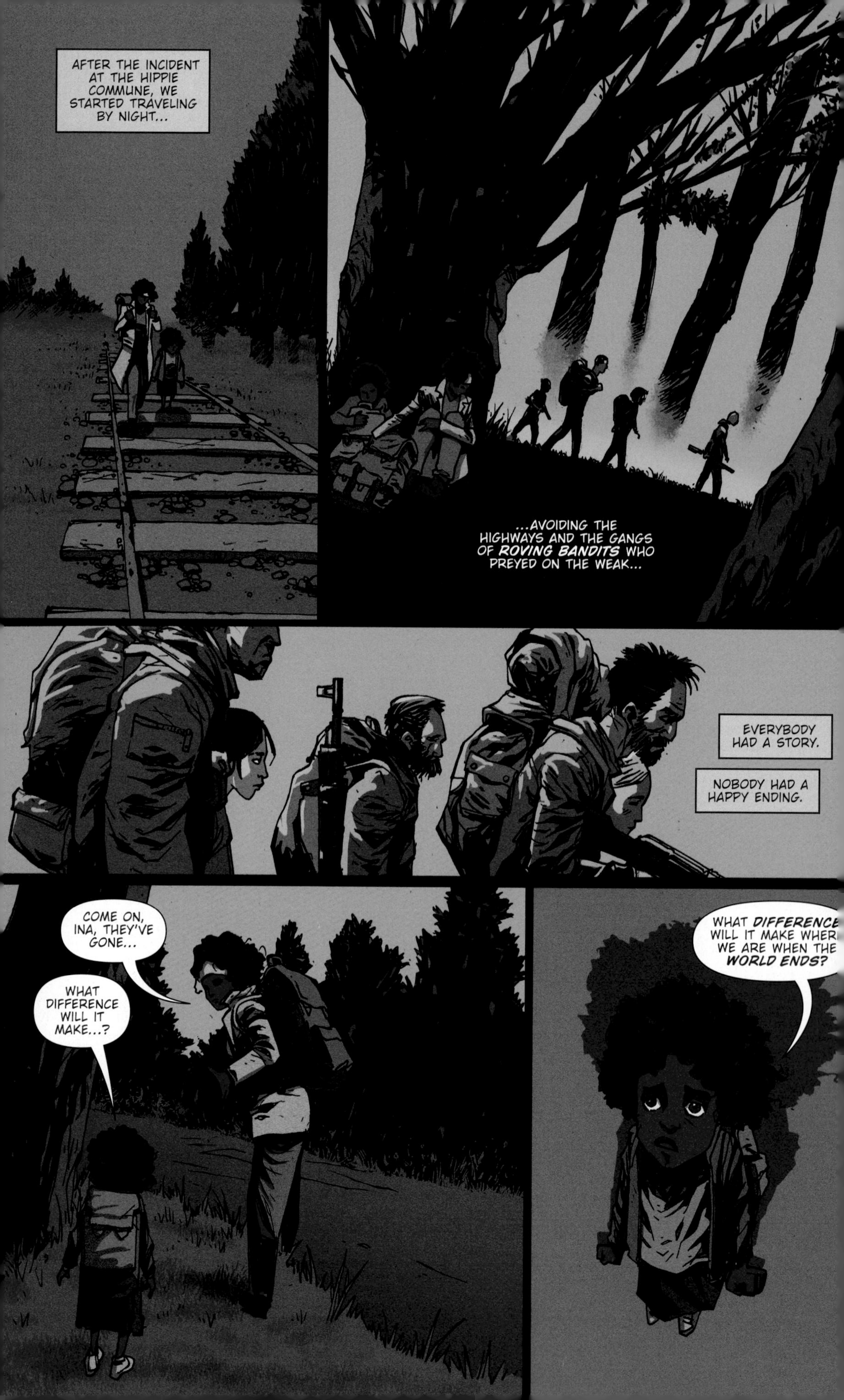
AFTER THE INCIDENT AT THE HIPPIE COMMUNE, WE STARTED TRAVELING BY NIGHT...
...AVOIDING THE HIGHWAYS AND THE GANGS OF ROVING BANDITS WHO PREYED ON THE WEAK...
EVERYBODY HAD A STORY.
NOBODY HAD A HAPPY ENDING.
COME ON, INA, THEY'VE GONE...
WHAT DIFFERENCE WILL IT MAKE...?
WHAT DIFFERENCE WILL IT MAKE WHERE WE ARE WHEN THE WORLD ENDS?

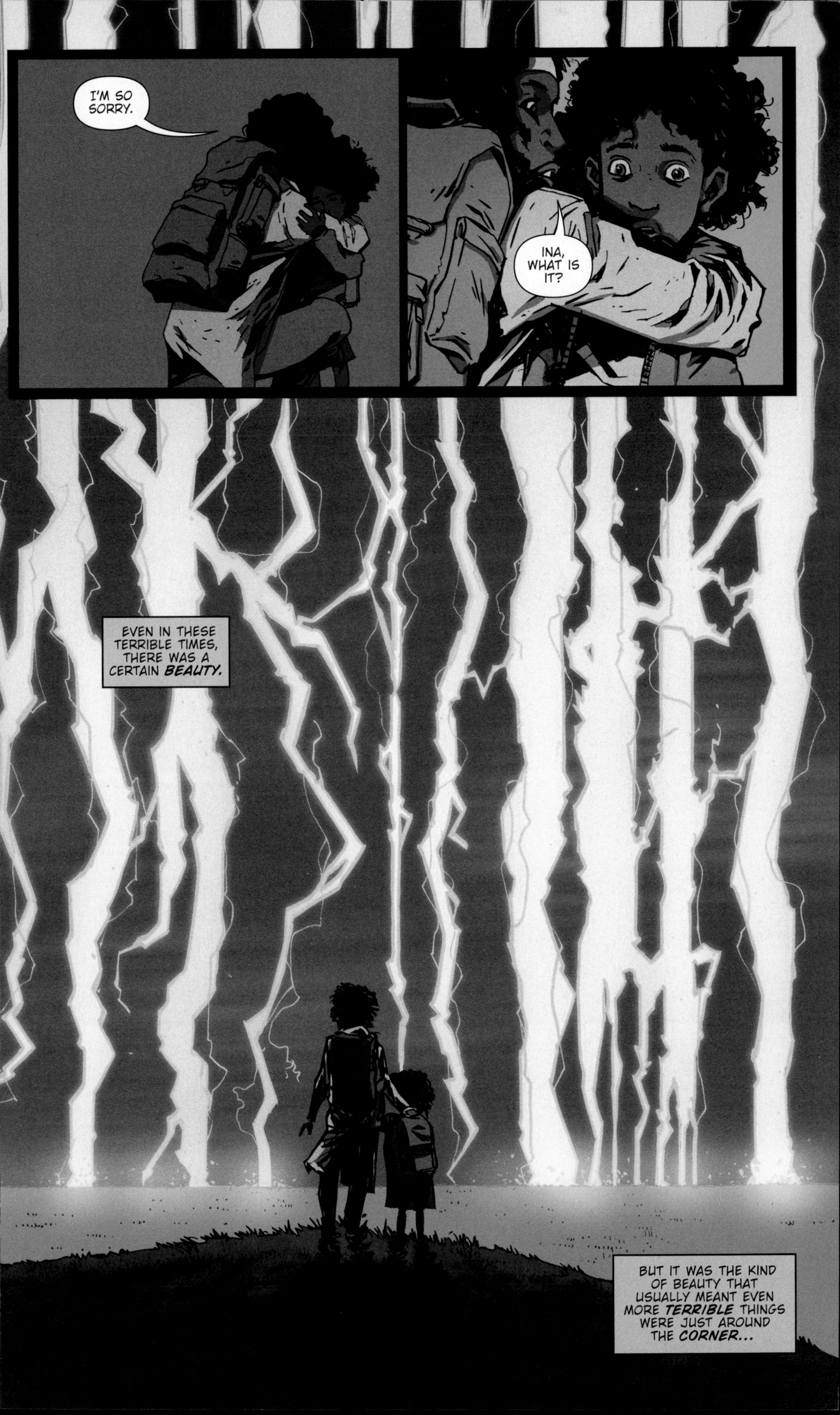
I'M SO SORRY.
INA, WHAT IS IT?
EVEN IN THESE TERRIBLE TIMES, THERE WAS A CERTAIN BEAUTY.
BUT IT WAS THE KIND OF BEAUTY THAT USUALLY MEANT EVEN MORE TERRIBLE THINGS WERE JUST AROUND THE CORNER...

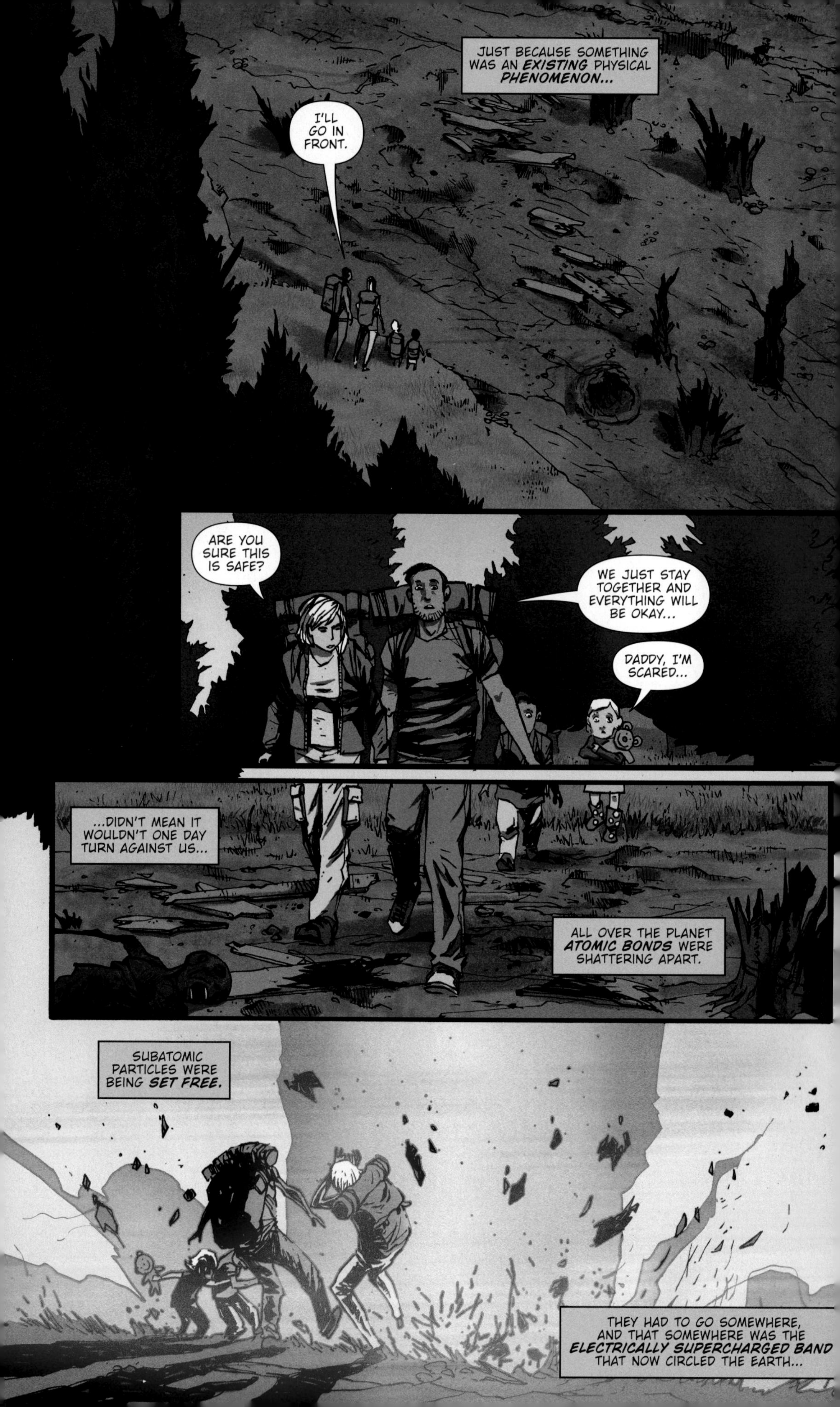
JUST BECAUSE SOMETHING WAS AN ***EXISTING*** PHYSICAL ***PHENOMENON...***
I'LL GO IN FRONT.
ARE YOU SURE THIS IS SAFE?
WE JUST STAY TOGETHER AND EVERYTHING WILL BE OKAY...
DADDY, I'M SCARED...
...DIDN'T MEAN IT WOULDN'T ONE DAY TURN AGAINST US...
ALL OVER THE PLANET ***ATOMIC BONDS*** WERE SHATTERING APART.
SUBATOMIC PARTICLES WERE BEING ***SET FREE.***
THEY HAD TO GO SOMEWHERE, AND THAT SOMEWHERE WAS THE ***ELECTRICALLY SUPERCHARGED BAND*** THAT NOW CIRCLED THE EARTH...

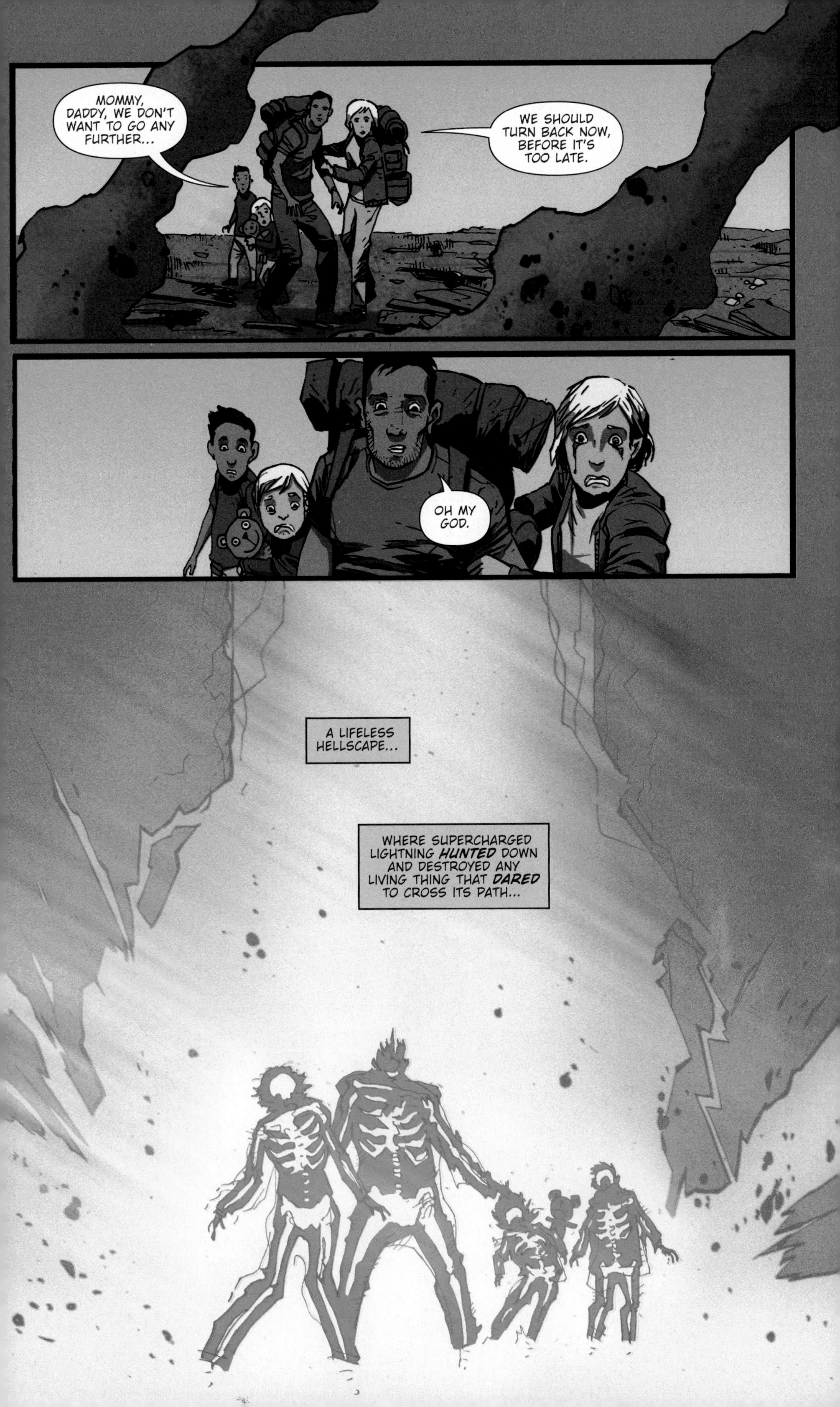

MOMMY, DADDY, WE DON'T WANT TO GO ANY FURTHER...
WE SHOULD TURN BACK NOW, BEFORE IT'S TOO LATE.
OH MY GOD.
A LIFELESS HELLSCAPE...
WHERE SUPERCHARGED LIGHTNING HUNTED DOWN AND DESTROYED ANY LIVING THING THAT DARED TO CROSS ITS PATH...

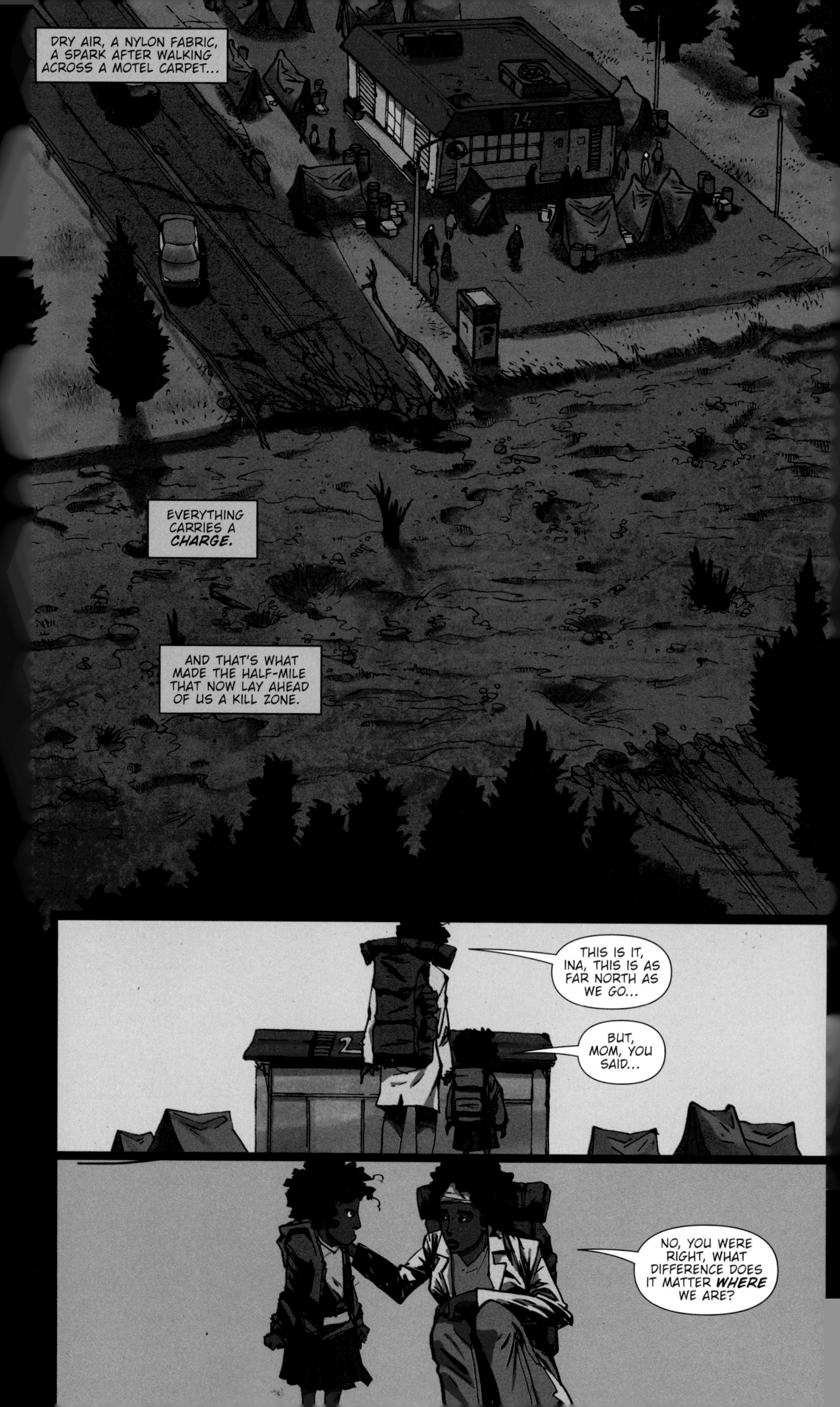
DRY AIR, A NYLON FABRIC, A SPARK AFTER WALKING ACROSS A MOTEL CARPET...
EVERYTHING CARRIES A *CHARGE.*
AND THAT'S WHAT MADE THE HALF-MILE THAT NOW LAY AHEAD OF US A KILL ZONE.
THIS IS IT, INA, THIS IS AS FAR NORTH AS WE GO...
BUT, MOM, YOU SAID...
NO, YOU WERE RIGHT, WHAT DIFFERENCE DOES IT MATTER *WHERE* WE ARE?

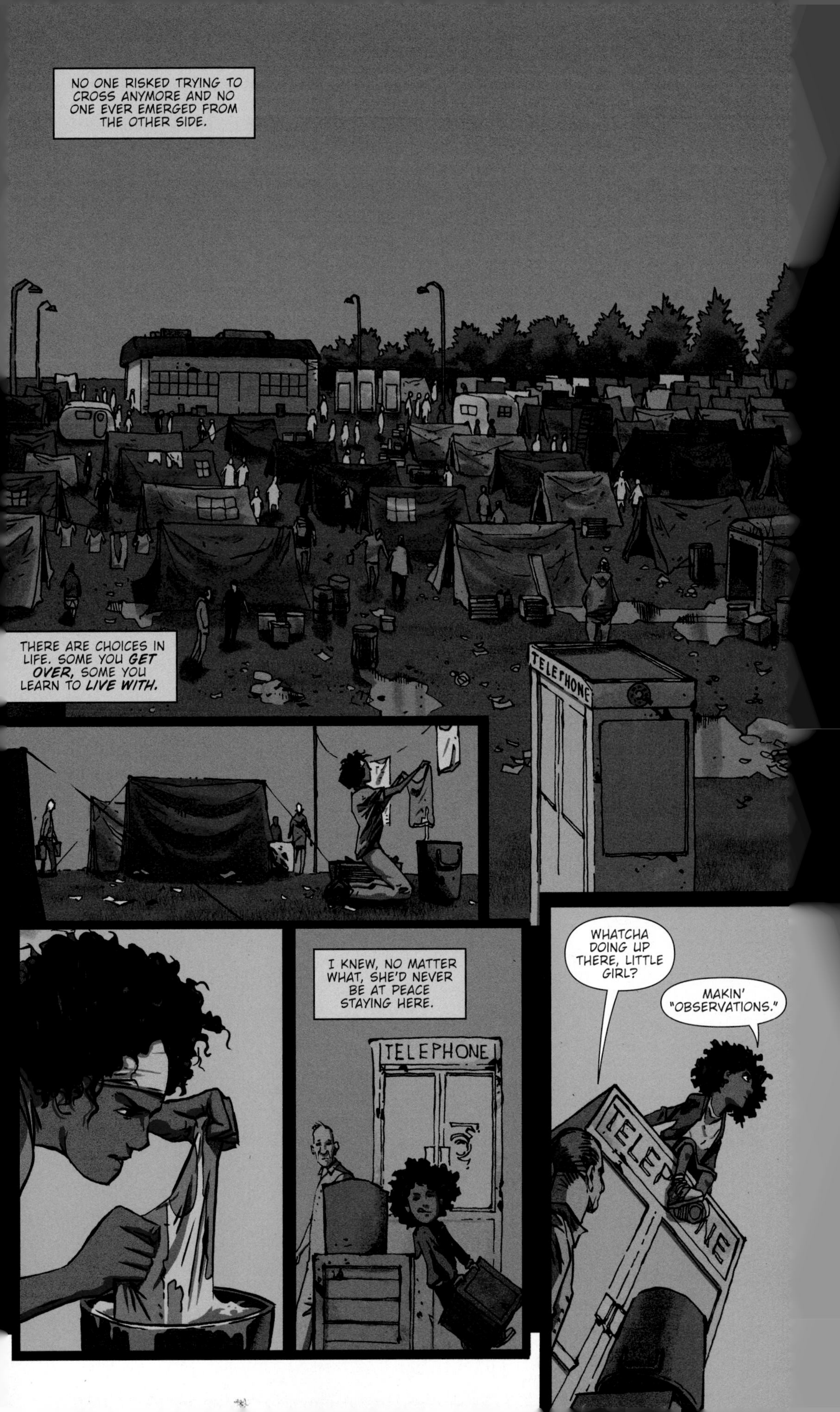

NO ONE RISKED TRYING TO CROSS ANYMORE AND NO ONE EVER EMERGED FROM THE OTHER SIDE.
THERE ARE CHOICES IN LIFE. SOME YOU ***GET OVER,*** SOME YOU LEARN TO ***LIVE WITH.***
TELEPHONE
I KNEW, NO MATTER WHAT, SHE'D NEVER BE AT PEACE STAYING HERE.
TELEPHONE
WHATCHA DOING UP THERE, LITTLE GIRL?
MAKIN' "OBSERVATIONS."
TELEPHONE

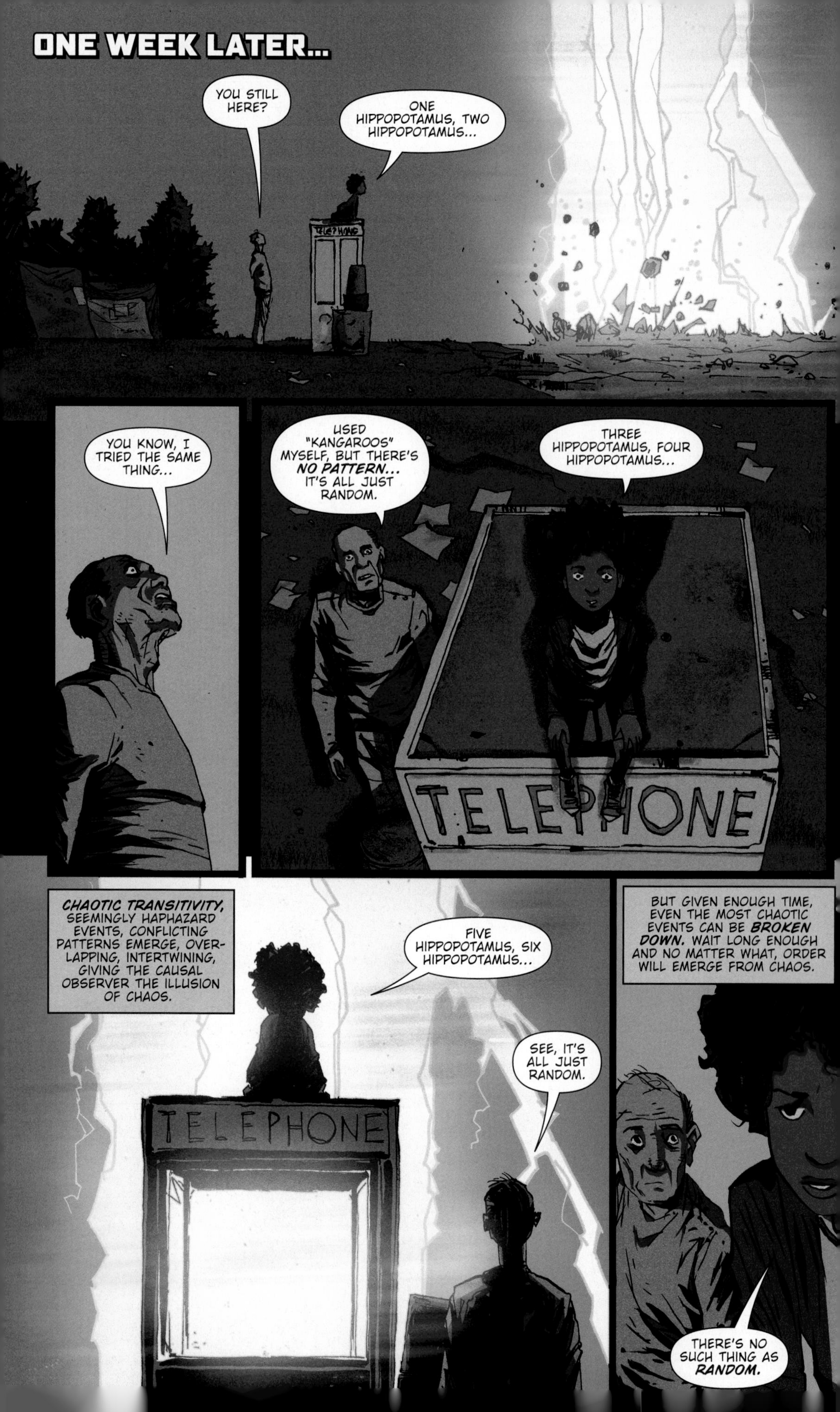
ONE WEEK LATER...
YOU STILL HERE?
ONE HIPPOPOTAMUS, TWO HIPPOPOTAMUS...
YOU KNOW, I TRIED THE SAME THING...
USED "KANGAROOS" MYSELF, BUT THERE'S ***NO PATTERN...*** IT'S ALL JUST RANDOM.
THREE HIPPOPOTAMUS, FOUR HIPPOPOTAMUS...
TELEPHONE
CHAOTIC TRANSITIVITY, SEEMINGLY HAPHAZARD EVENTS, CONFLICTING PATTERNS EMERGE, OVER-LAPPING, INTERTWINING, GIVING THE CAUSAL OBSERVER THE ILLUSION OF CHAOS.
FIVE HIPPOPOTAMUS, SIX HIPPOPOTAMUS...
SEE, IT'S ALL JUST RANDOM.
TELEPHONE
BUT GIVEN ENOUGH TIME, EVEN THE MOST CHAOTIC EVENTS CAN BE ***BROKEN DOWN.*** WAIT LONG ENOUGH AND NO MATTER WHAT, ORDER WILL EMERGE FROM CHAOS.
THERE'S NO SUCH THING AS ***RANDOM.***

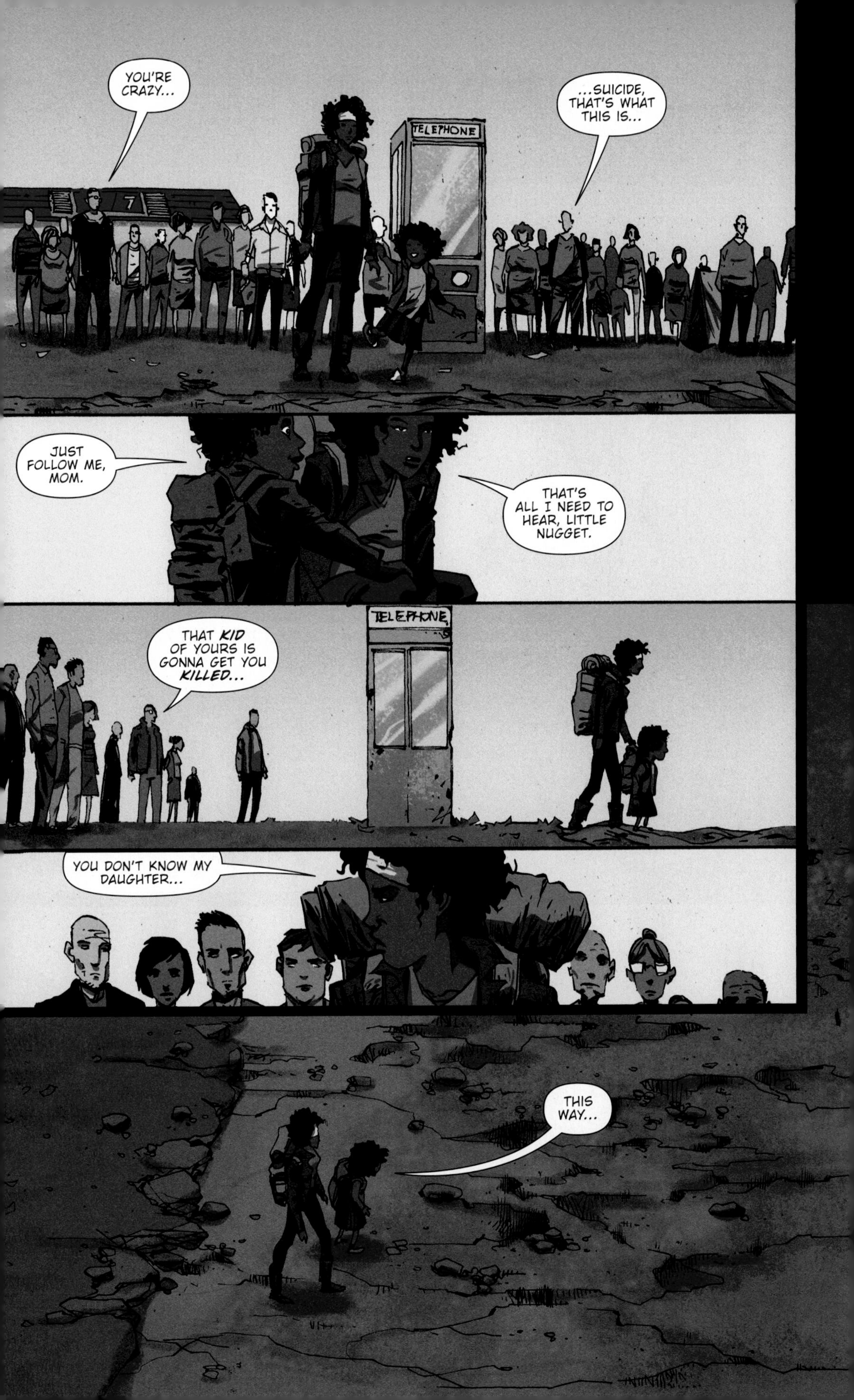
YOU'RE CRAZY...
...SUICIDE, THAT'S WHAT THIS IS...
TELEPHONE
JUST FOLLOW ME, MOM.
THAT'S ALL I NEED TO HEAR, LITTLE NUGGET.
TELEPHONE
THAT KID OF YOURS IS GONNA GET YOU KILLED...
YOU DON'T KNOW MY DAUGHTER...
THIS WAY...

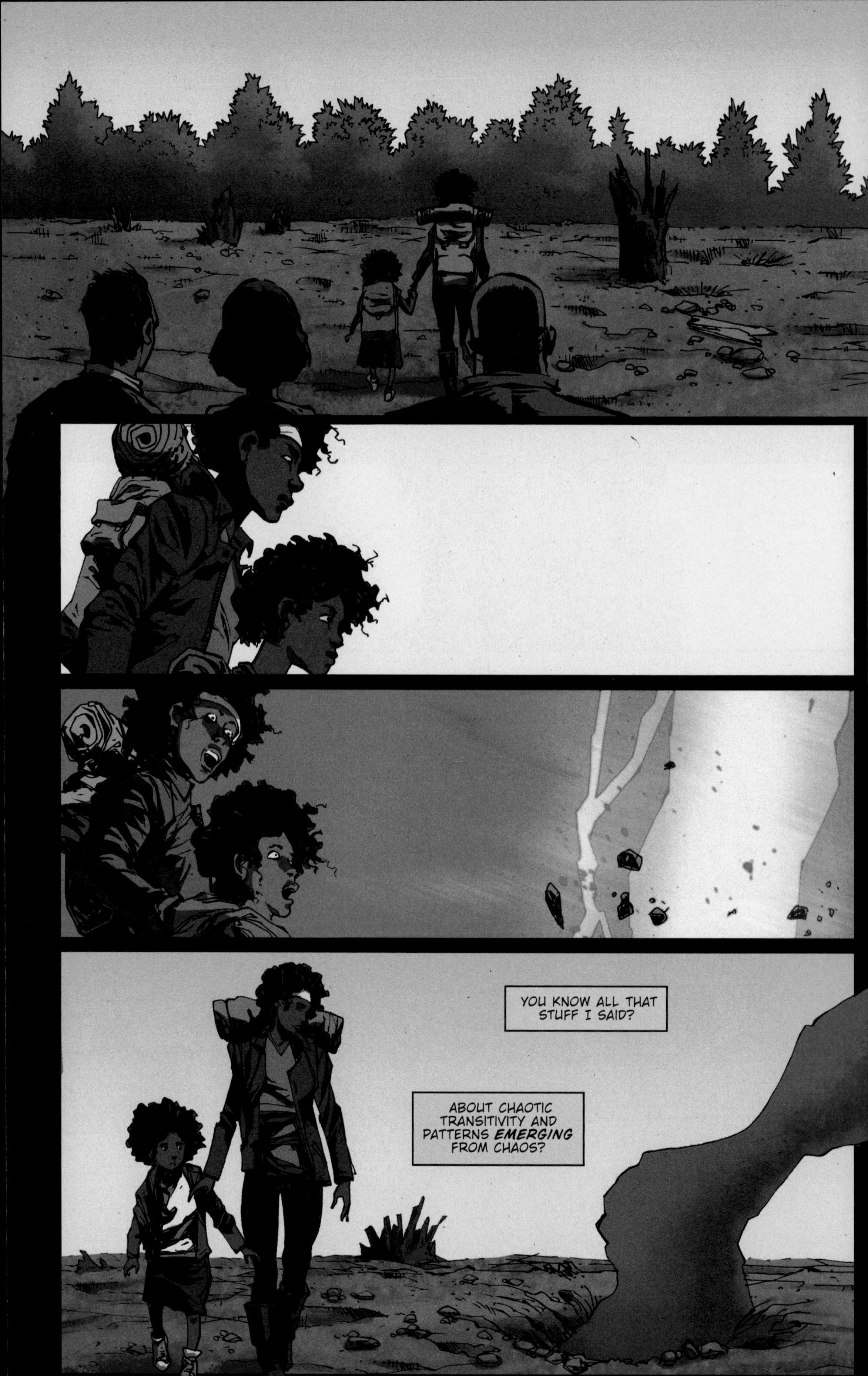
YOU KNOW ALL THAT STUFF I SAID?
ABOUT CHAOTIC TRANSITIVITY AND PATTERNS *EMERGING* FROM CHAOS?

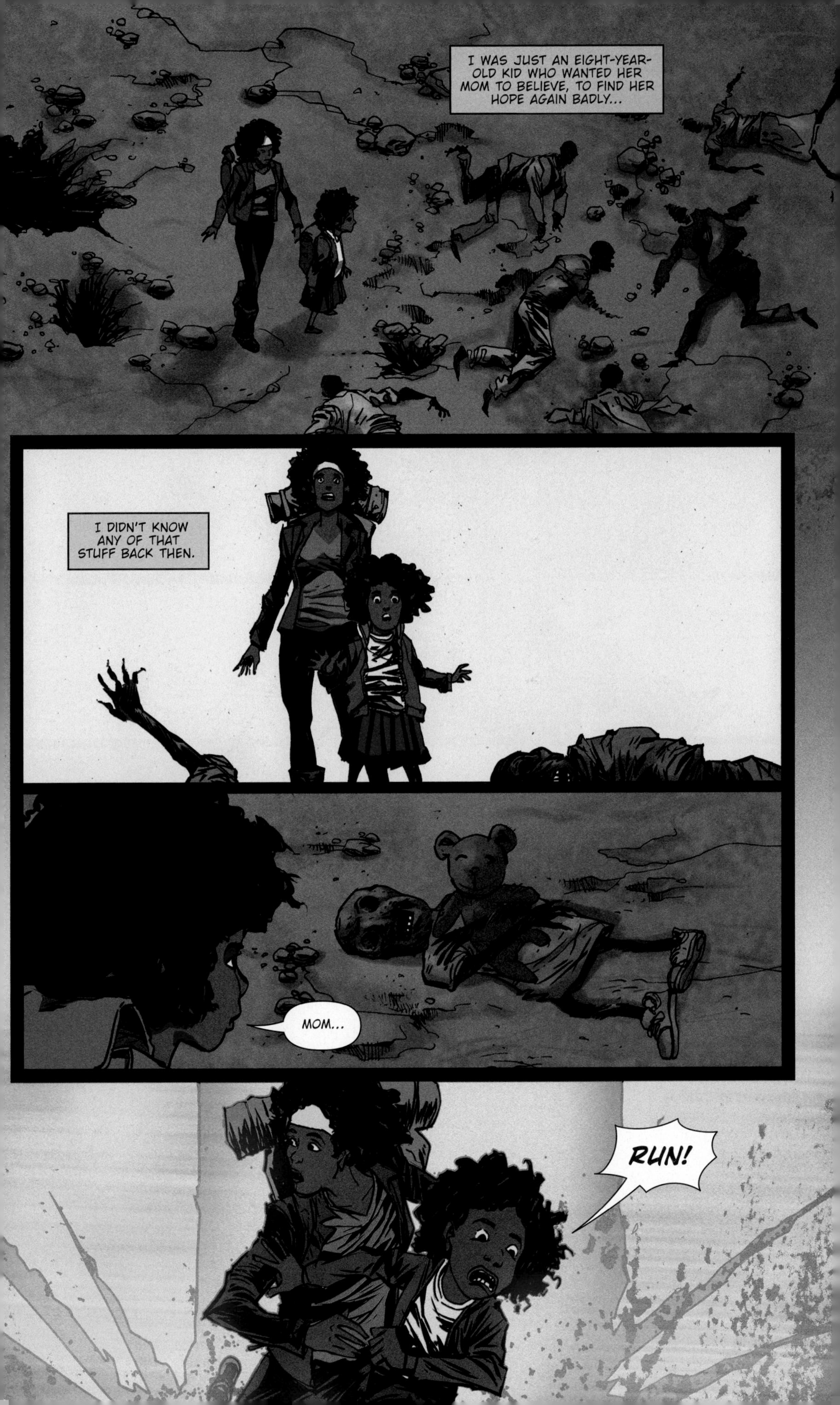
I WAS JUST AN EIGHT-YEAR-OLD KID WHO WANTED HER MOM TO BELIEVE, TO FIND HER HOPE AGAIN BADLY...
I DIDN'T KNOW ANY OF THAT STUFF BACK THEN.
MOM...
RUN!

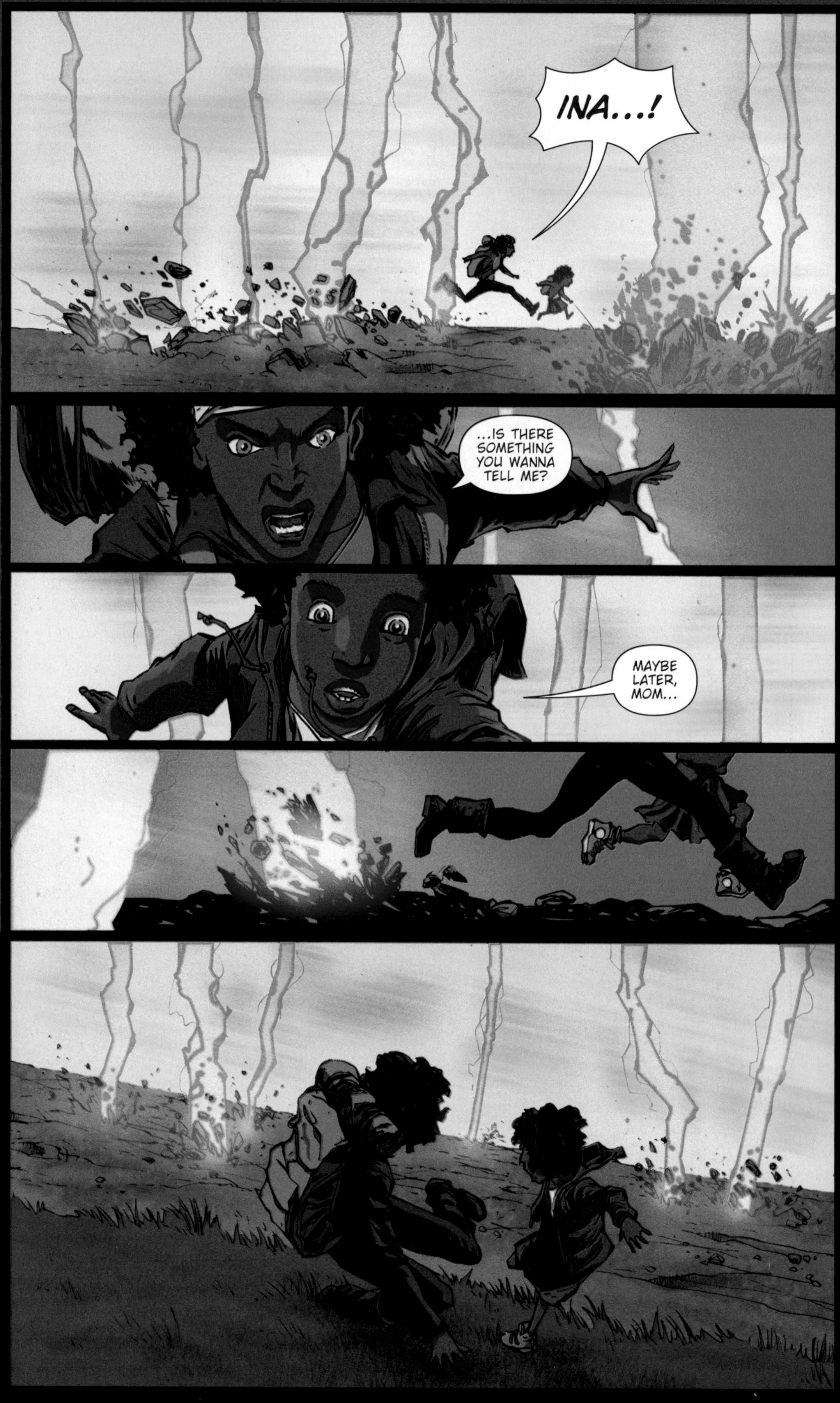
INA...!
...IS THERE SOMETHING YOU WANNA TELL ME?
MAYBE LATER, MOM...

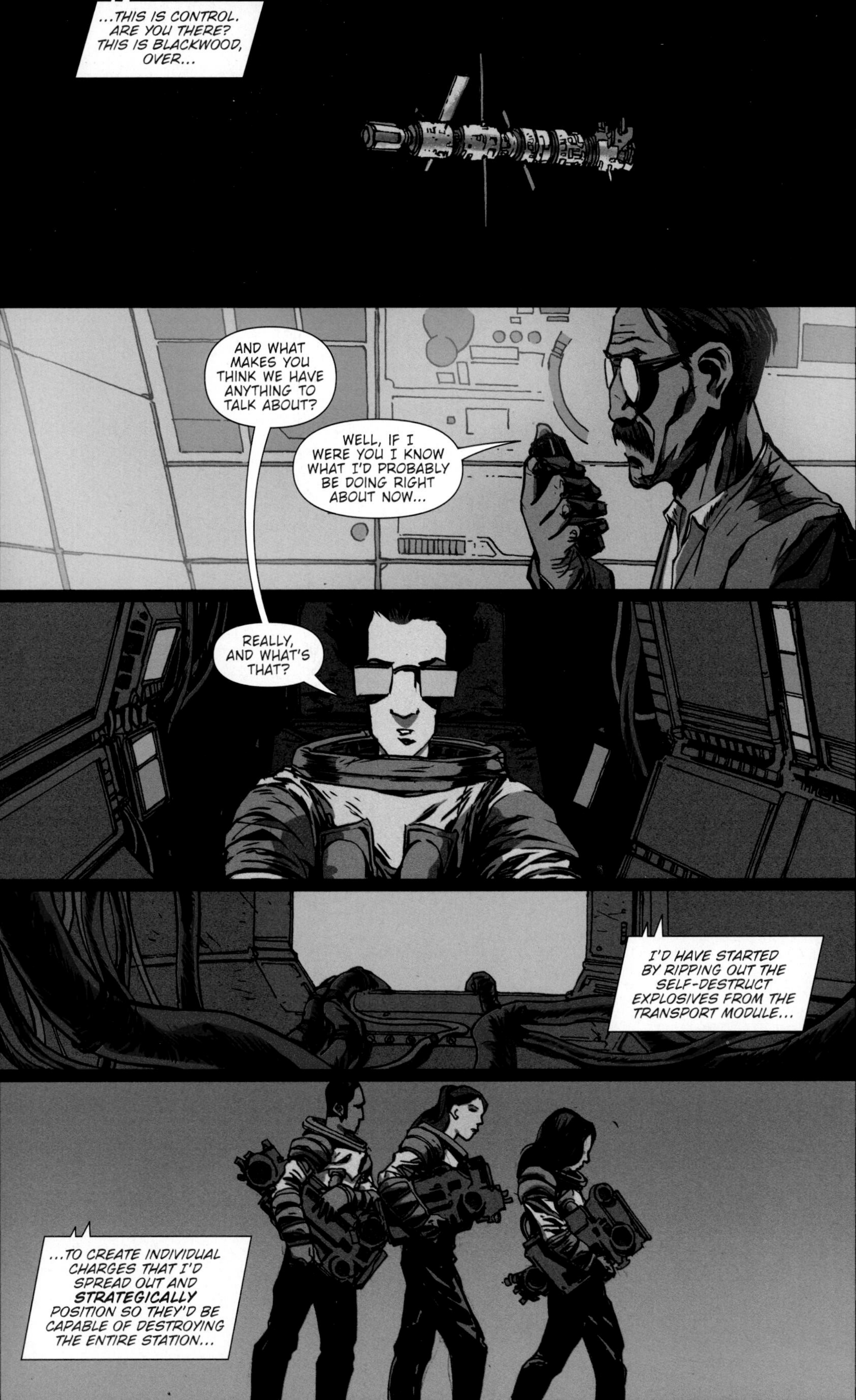
...THIS IS CONTROL. ARE YOU THERE? THIS IS BLACKWOOD, OVER...
AND WHAT MAKES YOU THINK WE HAVE ANYTHING TO TALK ABOUT?
WELL, IF I WERE YOU I KNOW WHAT I'D PROBABLY BE DOING RIGHT ABOUT NOW...
REALLY, AND WHAT'S THAT?
I'D HAVE STARTED BY RIPPING OUT THE SELF-DESTRUCT EXPLOSIVES FROM THE TRANSPORT MODULE...
...TO CREATE INDIVIDUAL CHARGES THAT I'D SPREAD OUT AND **STRATEGICALLY** POSITION SO THEY'D BE CAPABLE OF DESTROYING THE ENTIRE STATION...

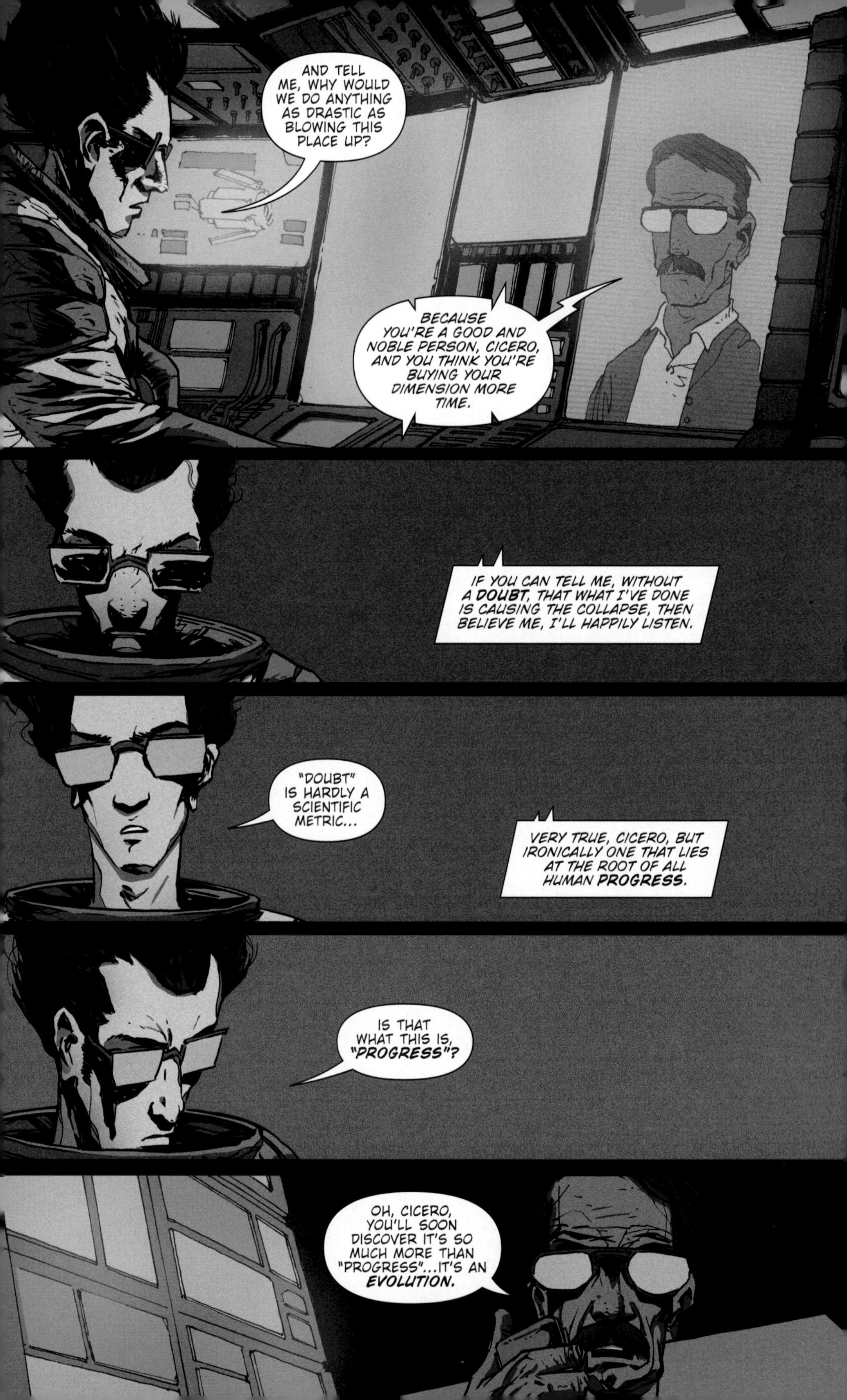
AND TELL ME, WHY WOULD WE DO ANYTHING AS DRASTIC AS BLOWING THIS PLACE UP?
BECAUSE YOU'RE A GOOD AND NOBLE PERSON, CICERO, AND YOU THINK YOU'RE BUYING YOUR DIMENSION MORE TIME.
IF YOU CAN TELL ME, WITHOUT A DOUBT, THAT WHAT I'VE DONE IS CAUSING THE COLLAPSE, THEN BELIEVE ME, I'LL HAPPILY LISTEN.
"DOUBT" IS HARDLY A SCIENTIFIC METRIC...
VERY TRUE, CICERO, BUT IRONICALLY ONE THAT LIES AT THE ROOT OF ALL HUMAN PROGRESS.
IS THAT WHAT THIS IS, "PROGRESS"?
OH, CICERO, YOU'LL SOON DISCOVER IT'S SO MUCH MORE THAN "PROGRESS"...IT'S AN EVOLUTION.

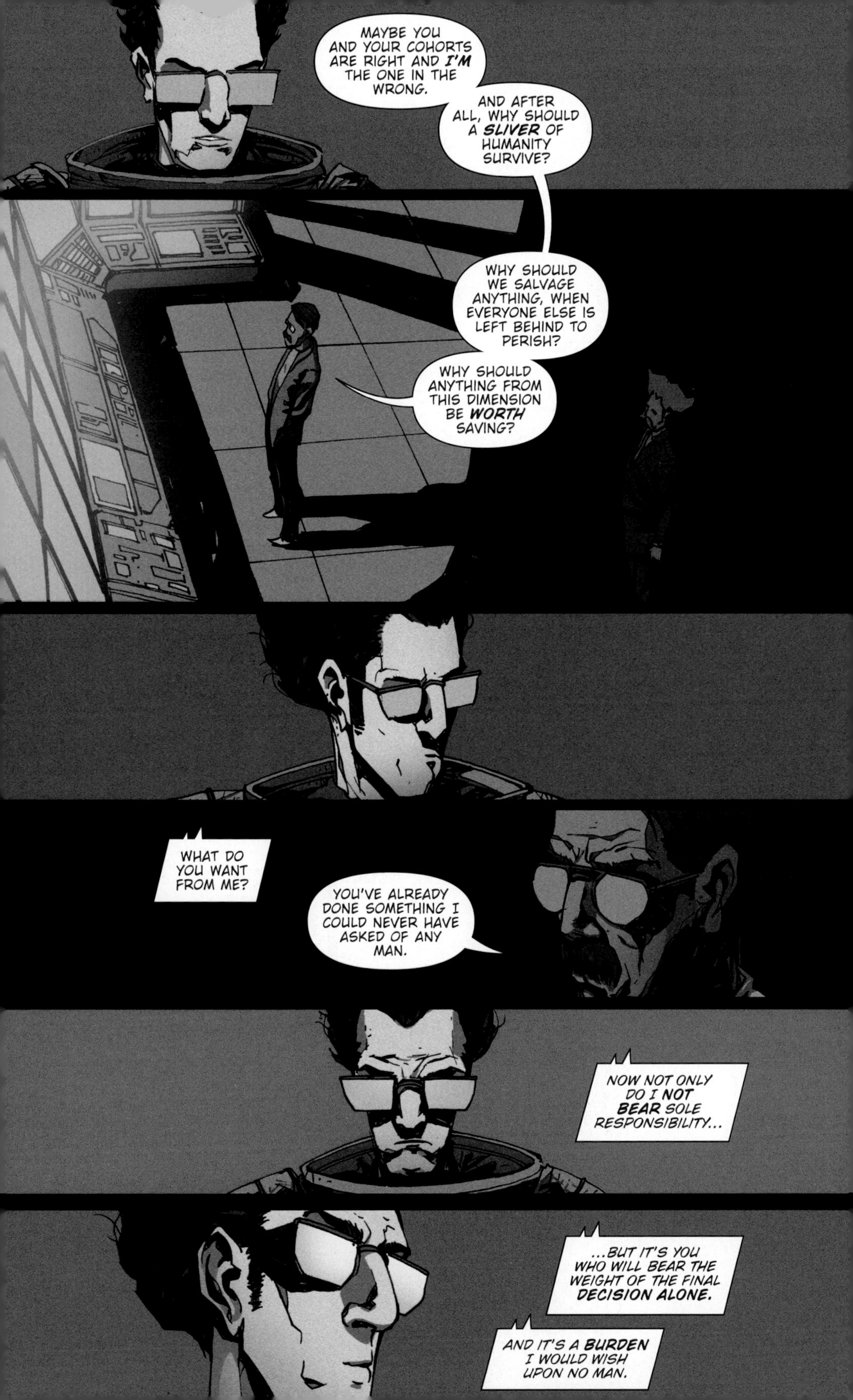
MAYBE YOU AND YOUR COHORTS ARE RIGHT AND *I'M* THE ONE IN THE WRONG.
AND AFTER ALL, WHY SHOULD A **SLIVER** OF HUMANITY SURVIVE?
WHY SHOULD WE SALVAGE ANYTHING, WHEN EVERYONE ELSE IS LEFT BEHIND TO PERISH?
WHY SHOULD ANYTHING FROM THIS DIMENSION BE **WORTH** SAVING?
WHAT DO YOU WANT FROM ME?
YOU'VE ALREADY DONE SOMETHING I COULD NEVER HAVE ASKED OF ANY MAN.
NOW NOT ONLY DO I **NOT BEAR** SOLE RESPONSIBILITY...
...BUT IT'S YOU WHO WILL BEAR THE WEIGHT OF THE FINAL **DECISION ALONE.**
AND IT'S A **BURDEN** I WOULD WISH UPON NO MAN.

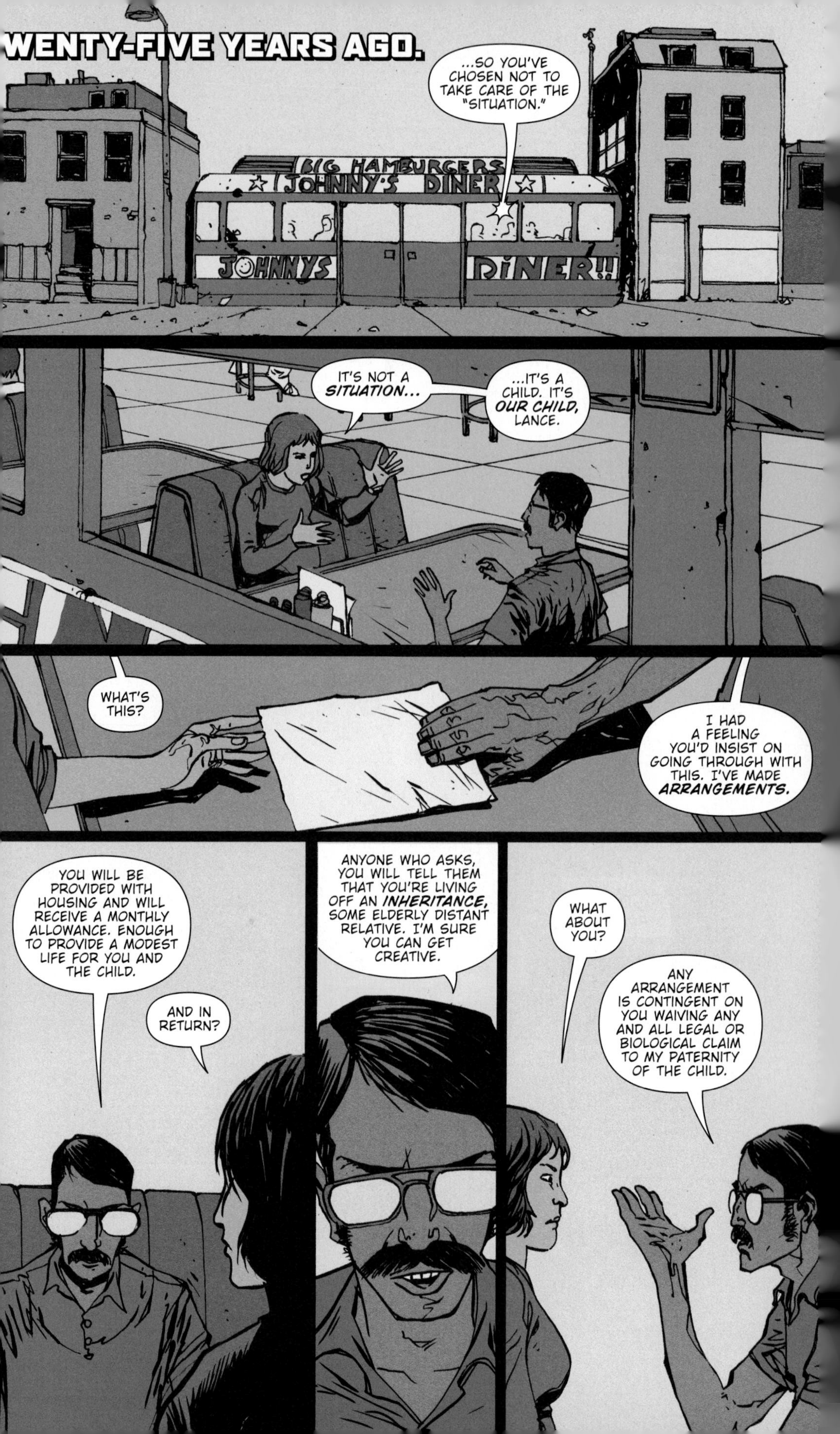
WENTY-FIVE YEARS AGO.
...SO YOU'VE CHOSEN NOT TO TAKE CARE OF THE "SITUATION."
BIG HAMBURGERS
JOHNNY'S DINER
JOHNNYS
DINER!!
IT'S NOT A *SITUATION...*
...IT'S A CHILD. IT'S *OUR CHILD,* LANCE.
WHAT'S THIS?
I HAD A FEELING YOU'D INSIST ON GOING THROUGH WITH THIS. I'VE MADE *ARRANGEMENTS.*
YOU WILL BE PROVIDED WITH HOUSING AND WILL RECEIVE A MONTHLY ALLOWANCE. ENOUGH TO PROVIDE A MODEST LIFE FOR YOU AND THE CHILD.
AND IN RETURN?
ANYONE WHO ASKS, YOU WILL TELL THEM THAT YOU'RE LIVING OFF AN *INHERITANCE,* SOME ELDERLY DISTANT RELATIVE. I'M SURE YOU CAN GET CREATIVE.
WHAT ABOUT YOU?
ANY ARRANGEMENT IS CONTINGENT ON YOU WAIVING ANY AND ALL LEGAL OR BIOLOGICAL CLAIM TO MY PATERNITY OF THE CHILD.

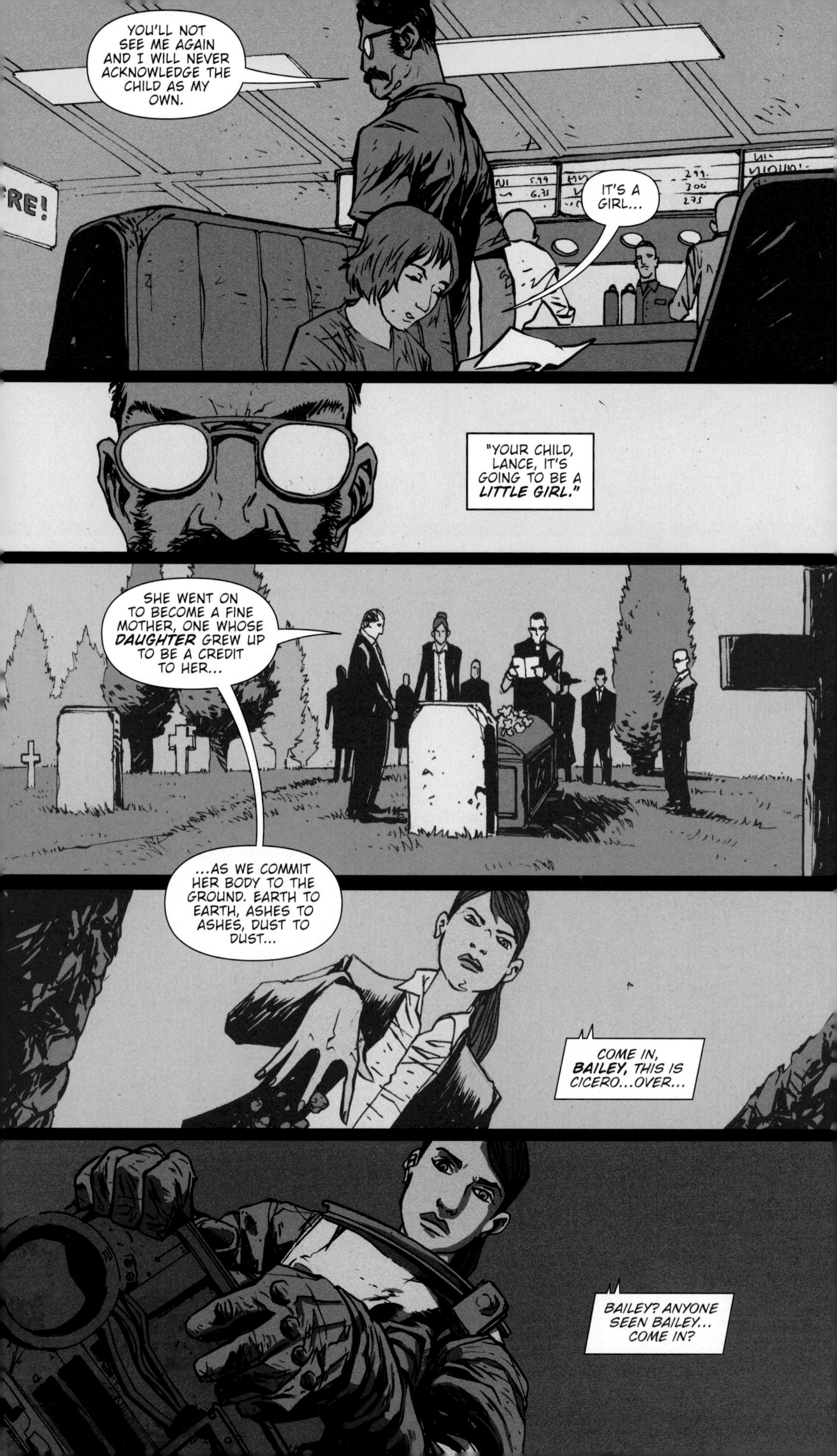
YOU'LL NOT SEE ME AGAIN AND I WILL NEVER ACKNOWLEDGE THE CHILD AS MY OWN.
RE!
IT'S A GIRL...
"YOUR CHILD, LANCE, IT'S GOING TO BE A LITTLE GIRL."
SHE WENT ON TO BECOME A FINE MOTHER, ONE WHOSE DAUGHTER GREW UP TO BE A CREDIT TO HER...
...AS WE COMMIT HER BODY TO THE GROUND. EARTH TO EARTH, ASHES TO ASHES, DUST TO DUST...
COME IN, BAILEY, THIS IS CICERO...OVER...
BAILEY? ANYONE SEEN BAILEY... COME IN?

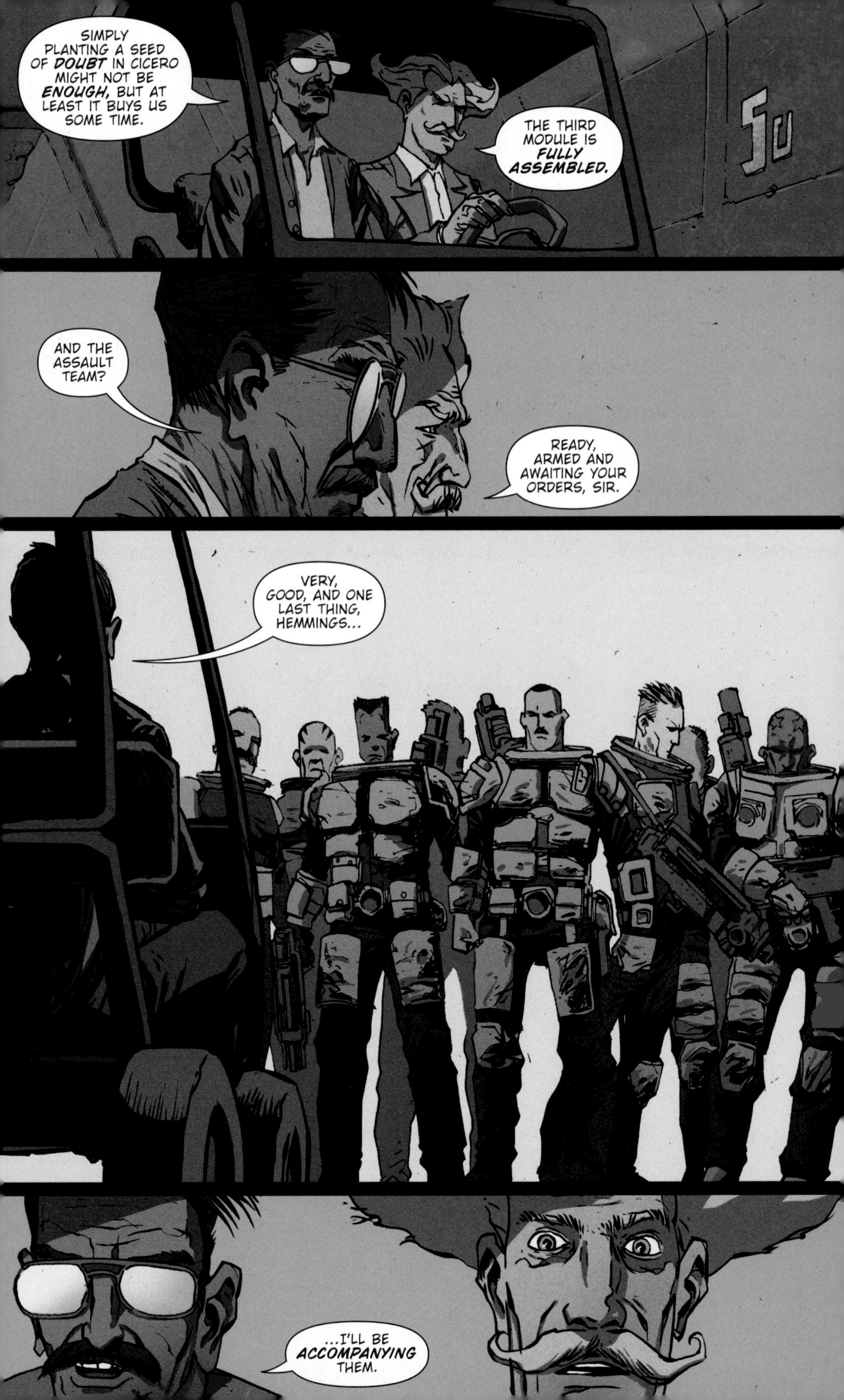
SIMPLY PLANTING A SEED OF DOUBT IN CICERO MIGHT NOT BE ENOUGH, BUT AT LEAST IT BUYS US SOME TIME.
THE THIRD MODULE IS FULLY ASSEMBLED.
AND THE ASSAULT TEAM?
READY, ARMED AND AWAITING YOUR ORDERS, SIR.
VERY, GOOD, AND ONE LAST THING, HEMMINGS...
...I'LL BE ACCOMPANYING THEM.

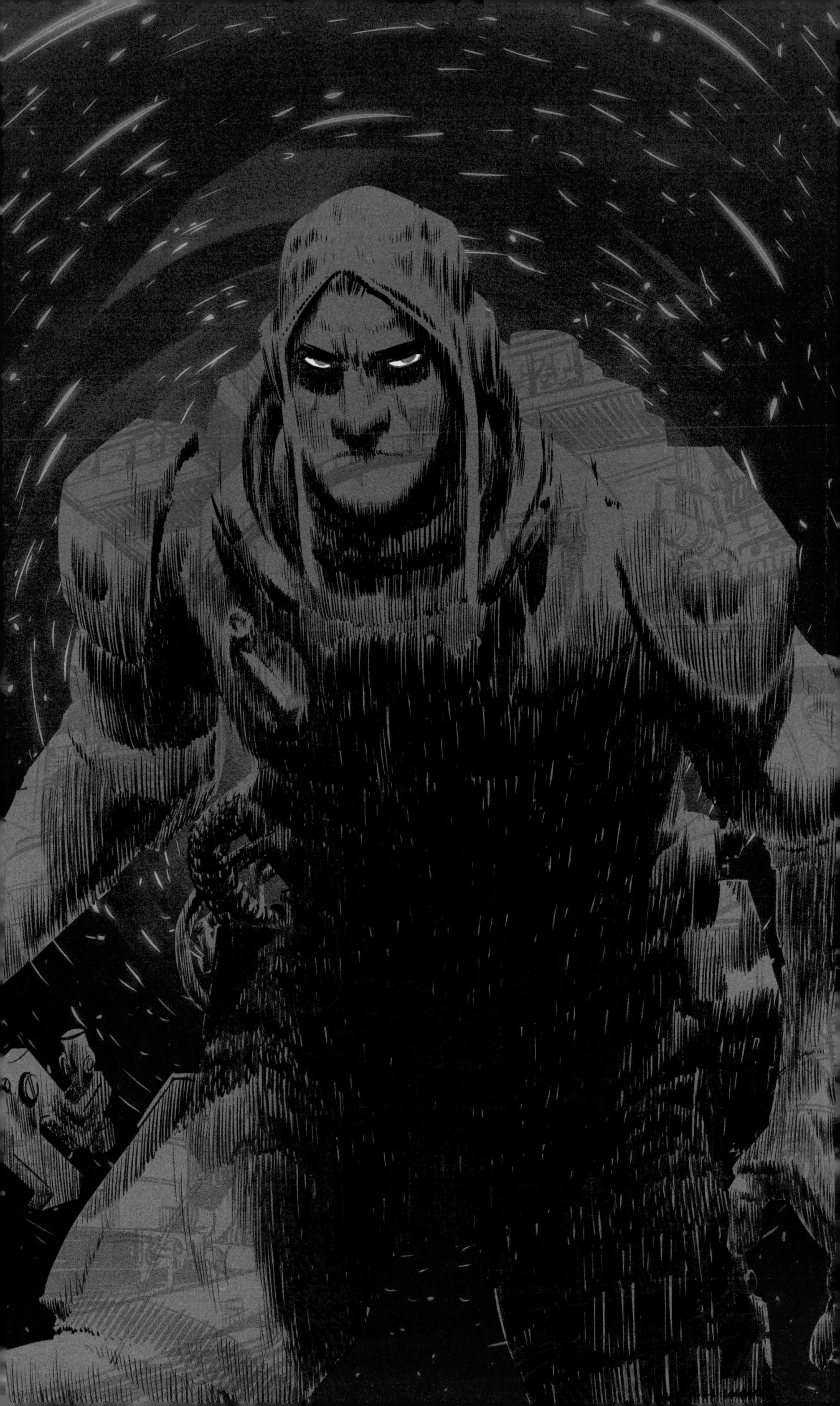

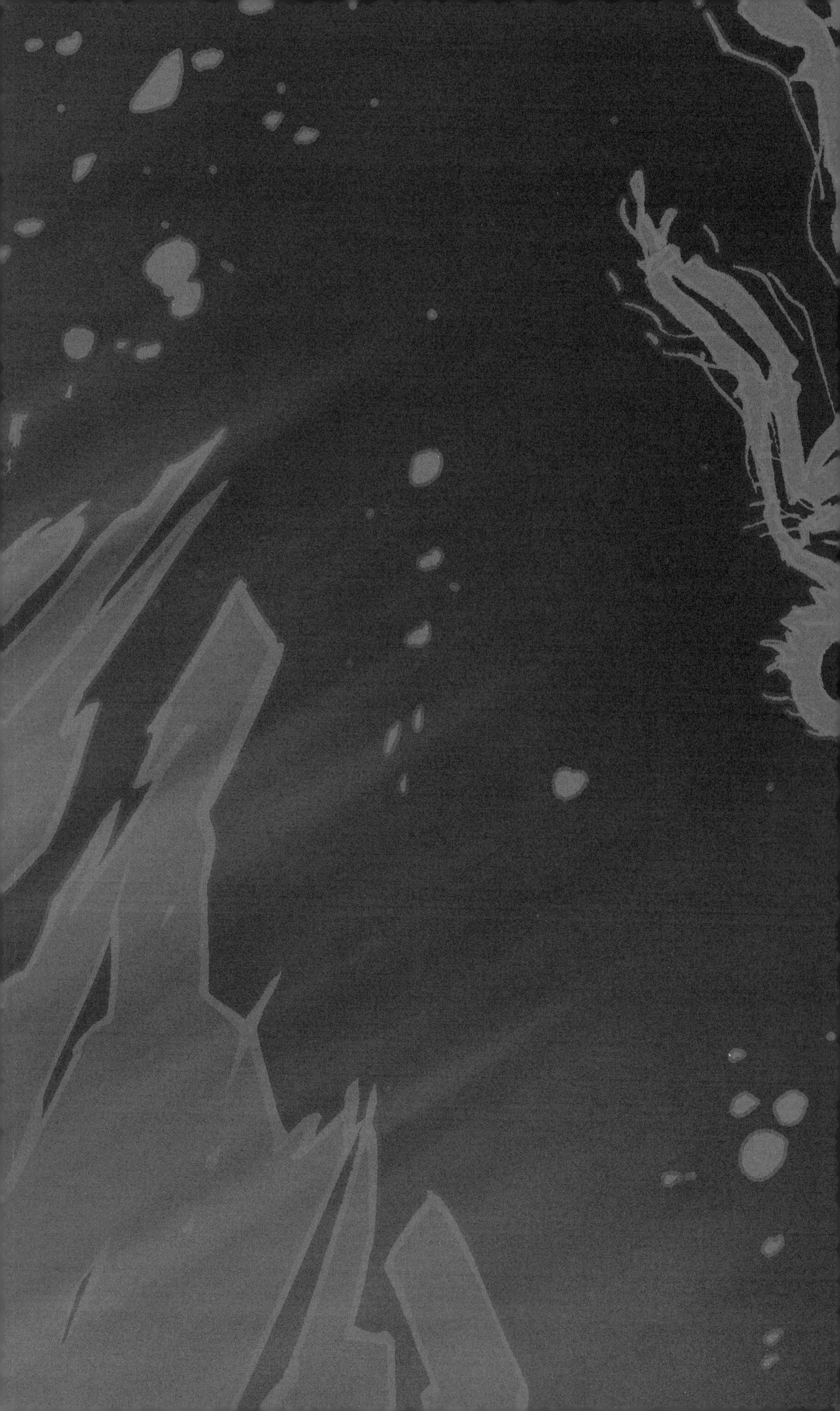

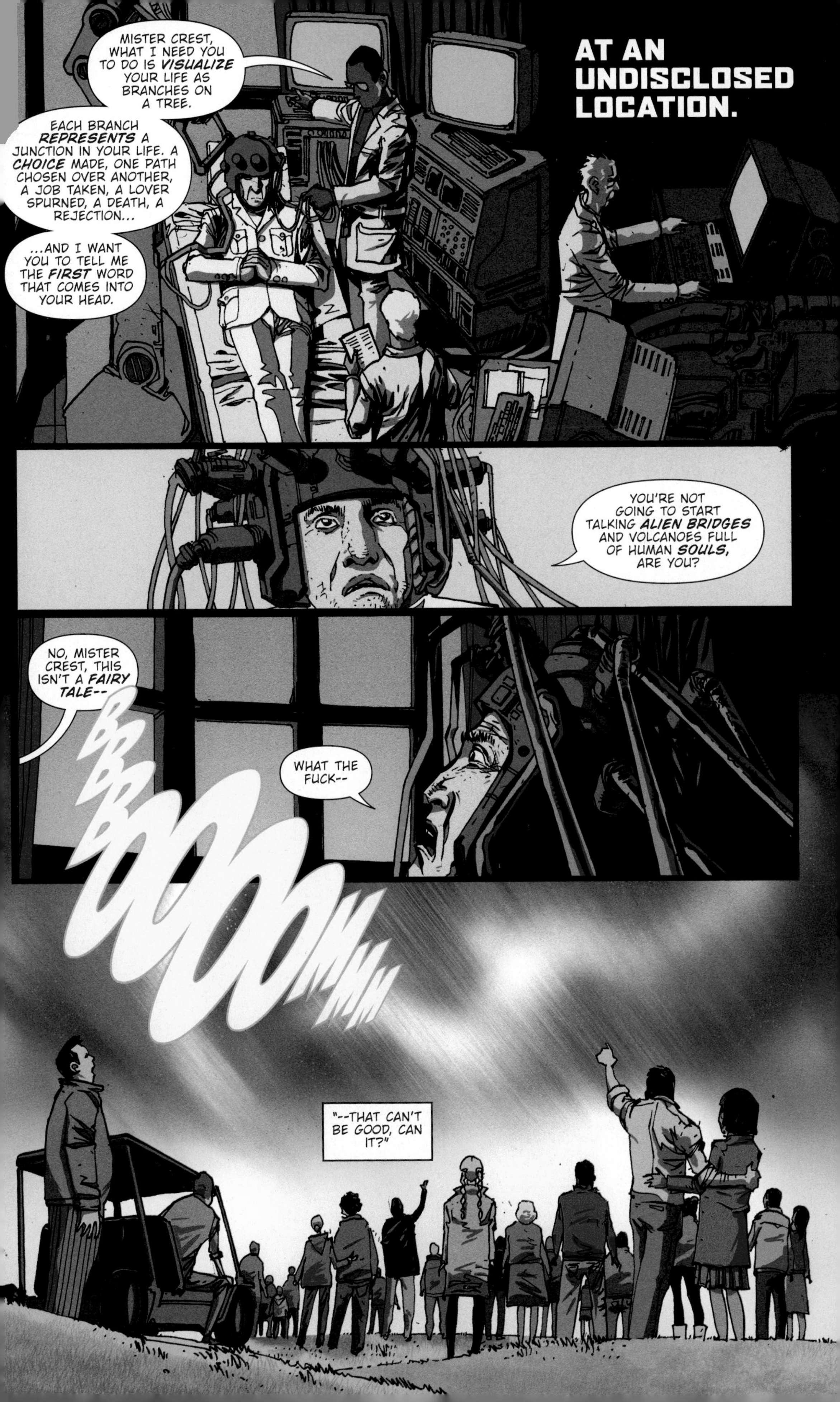
AT AN UNDISCLOSED LOCATION.
MISTER CREST, WHAT I NEED YOU TO DO IS VISUALIZE YOUR LIFE AS BRANCHES ON A TREE.
EACH BRANCH REPRESENTS A JUNCTION IN YOUR LIFE. A CHOICE MADE, ONE PATH CHOSEN OVER ANOTHER, A JOB TAKEN, A LOVER SPURNED, A DEATH, A REJECTION...
...AND I WANT YOU TO TELL ME THE FIRST WORD THAT COMES INTO YOUR HEAD.
YOU'RE NOT GOING TO START TALKING ALIEN BRIDGES AND VOLCANOES FULL OF HUMAN SOULS, ARE YOU?
NO, MISTER CREST, THIS ISN'T A FAIRY TALE--
BBBBBOOOOOMMMM
WHAT THE FUCK--
"--THAT CAN'T BE GOOD, CAN IT?"

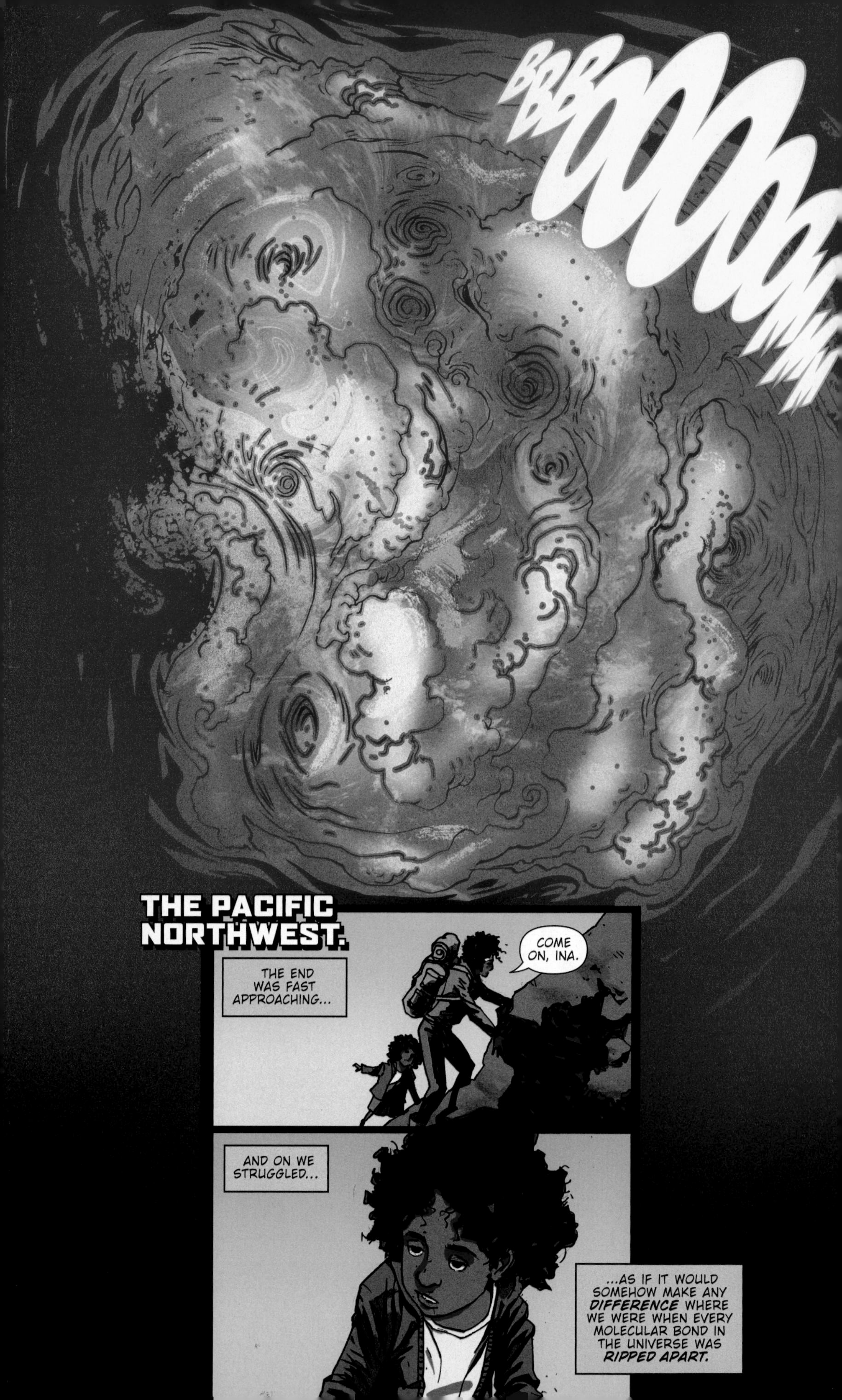
BBBOOOOOOMMM
THE PACIFIC NORTHWEST.
THE END WAS FAST APPROACHING...
COME ON, INA.
AND ON WE STRUGGLED...
...AS IF IT WOULD SOMEHOW MAKE ANY DIFFERENCE WHERE WE WERE WHEN EVERY MOLECULAR BOND IN THE UNIVERSE WAS RIPPED APART.

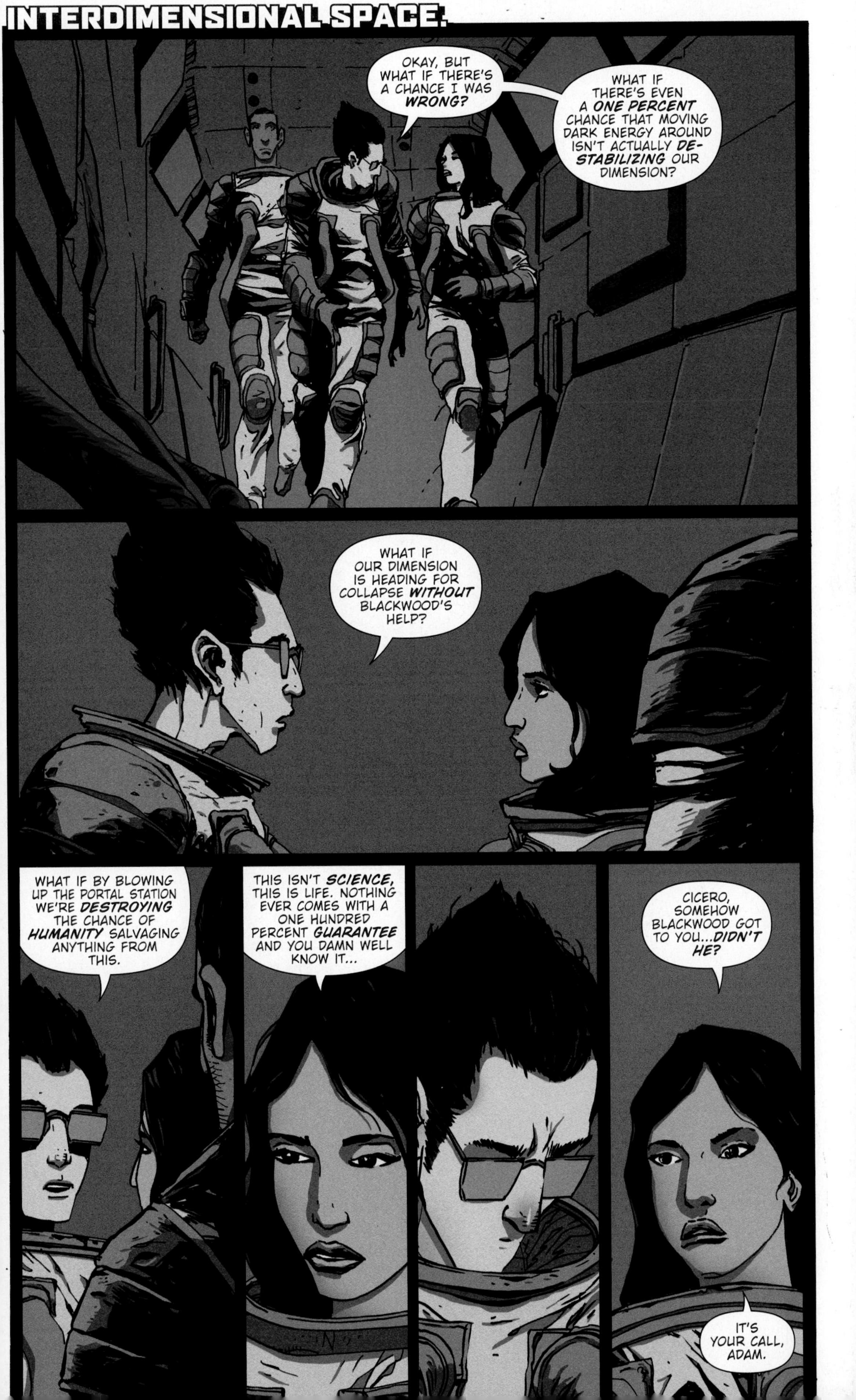
INTERDIMENSIONAL SPACE.
OKAY, BUT WHAT IF THERE'S A CHANCE I WAS WRONG?
WHAT IF THERE'S EVEN A ONE PERCENT CHANCE THAT MOVING DARK ENERGY AROUND ISN'T ACTUALLY DE-STABILIZING OUR DIMENSION?
WHAT IF OUR DIMENSION IS HEADING FOR COLLAPSE WITHOUT BLACKWOOD'S HELP?
WHAT IF BY BLOWING UP THE PORTAL STATION WE'RE DESTROYING THE CHANCE OF HUMANITY SALVAGING ANYTHING FROM THIS.
THIS ISN'T SCIENCE, THIS IS LIFE. NOTHING EVER COMES WITH A ONE HUNDRED PERCENT GUARANTEE AND YOU DAMN WELL KNOW IT...
CICERO, SOMEHOW BLACKWOOD GOT TO YOU...DIDN'T HE?
IT'S YOUR CALL, ADAM.

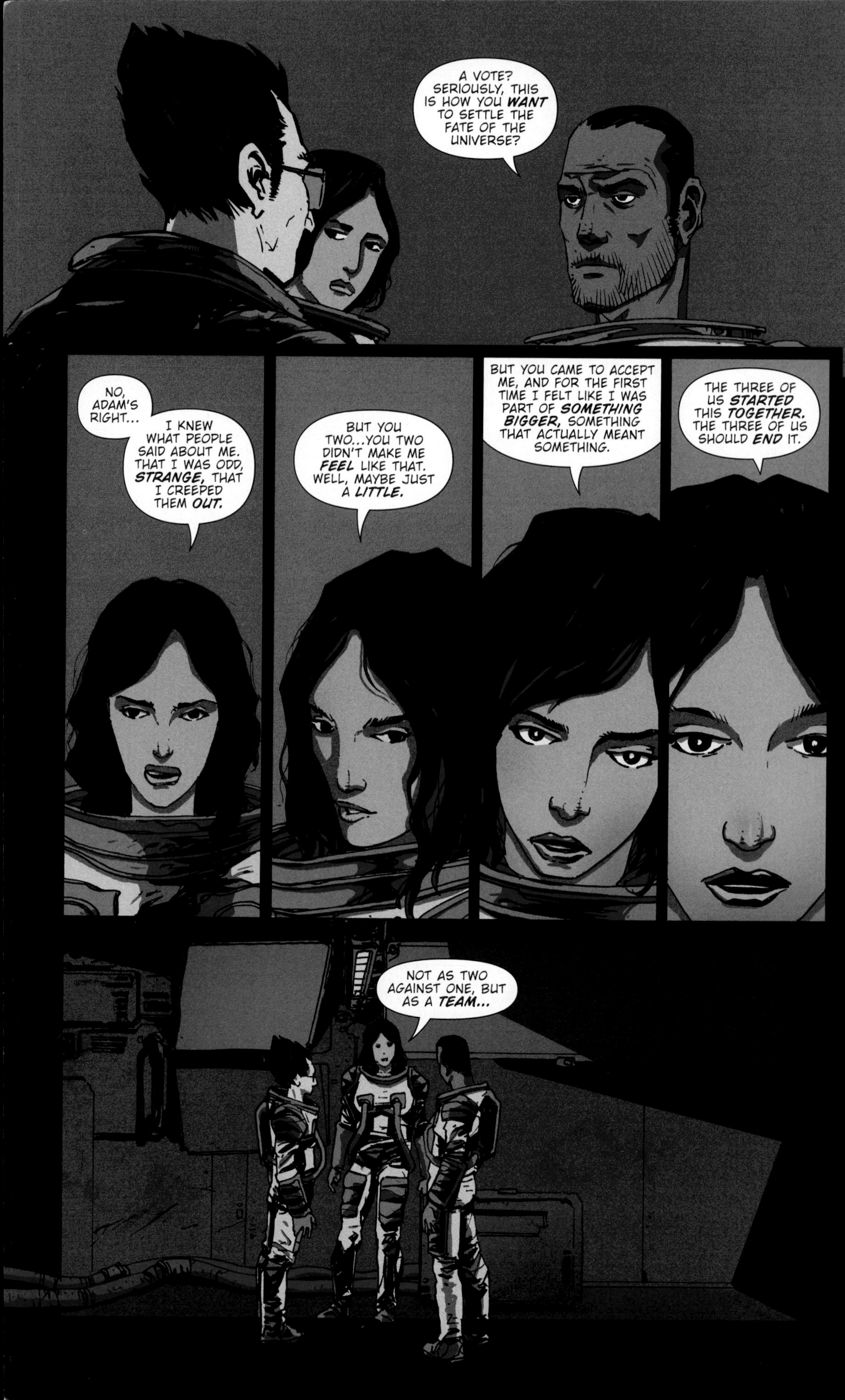
A VOTE? SERIOUSLY, THIS IS HOW YOU WANT TO SETTLE THE FATE OF THE UNIVERSE?
NO, ADAM'S RIGHT...
I KNEW WHAT PEOPLE SAID ABOUT ME. THAT I WAS ODD, STRANGE, THAT I CREEPED THEM OUT.
BUT YOU TWO...YOU TWO DIDN'T MAKE ME FEEL LIKE THAT. WELL, MAYBE JUST A LITTLE.
BUT YOU CAME TO ACCEPT ME, AND FOR THE FIRST TIME I FELT LIKE I WAS PART OF SOMETHING BIGGER, SOMETHING THAT ACTUALLY MEANT SOMETHING.
THE THREE OF US STARTED THIS TOGETHER. THE THREE OF US SHOULD END IT.
NOT AS TWO AGAINST ONE, BUT AS A TEAM...

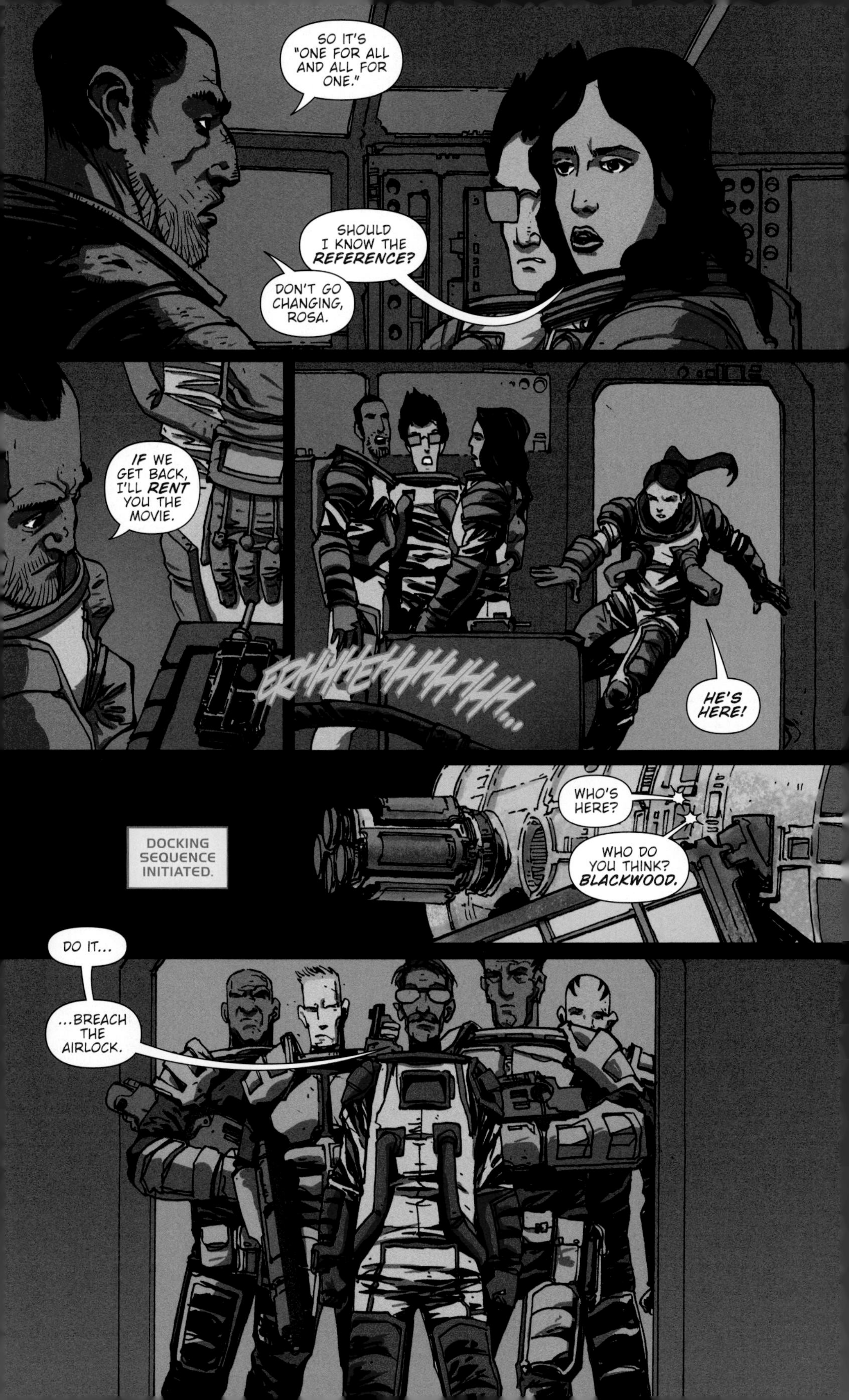
SO IT'S "ONE FOR ALL AND ALL FOR ONE."
SHOULD I KNOW THE REFERENCE?
DON'T GO CHANGING, ROSA.
IF WE GET BACK, I'LL RENT YOU THE MOVIE.
ERHHHEHHHHHHHH...
HE'S HERE!
DOCKING SEQUENCE INITIATED.
WHO'S HERE?
WHO DO YOU THINK? BLACKWOOD.
DO IT...
...BREACH THE AIRLOCK.

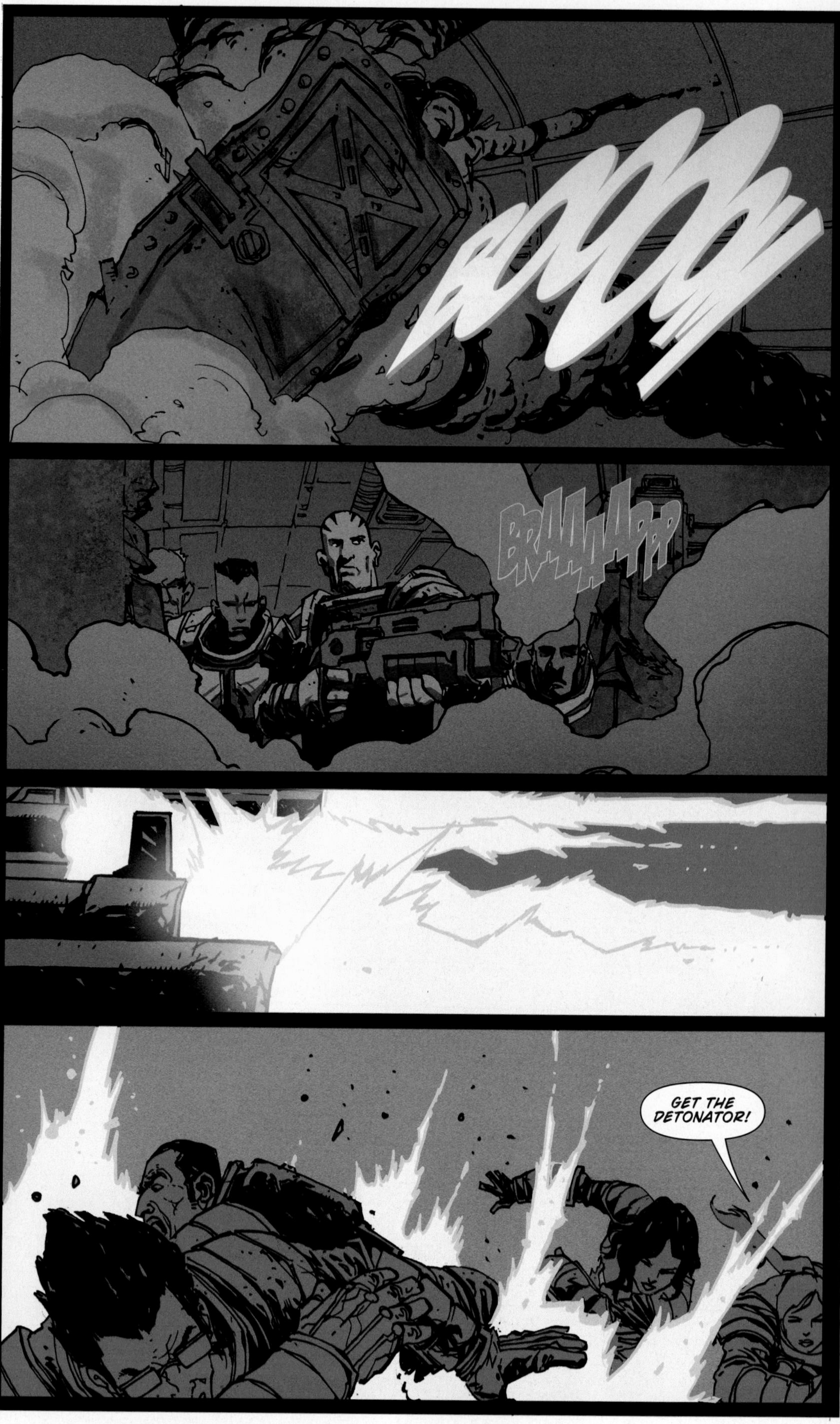
BOOOM
BRAAAAPPP
GET THE DETONATOR!

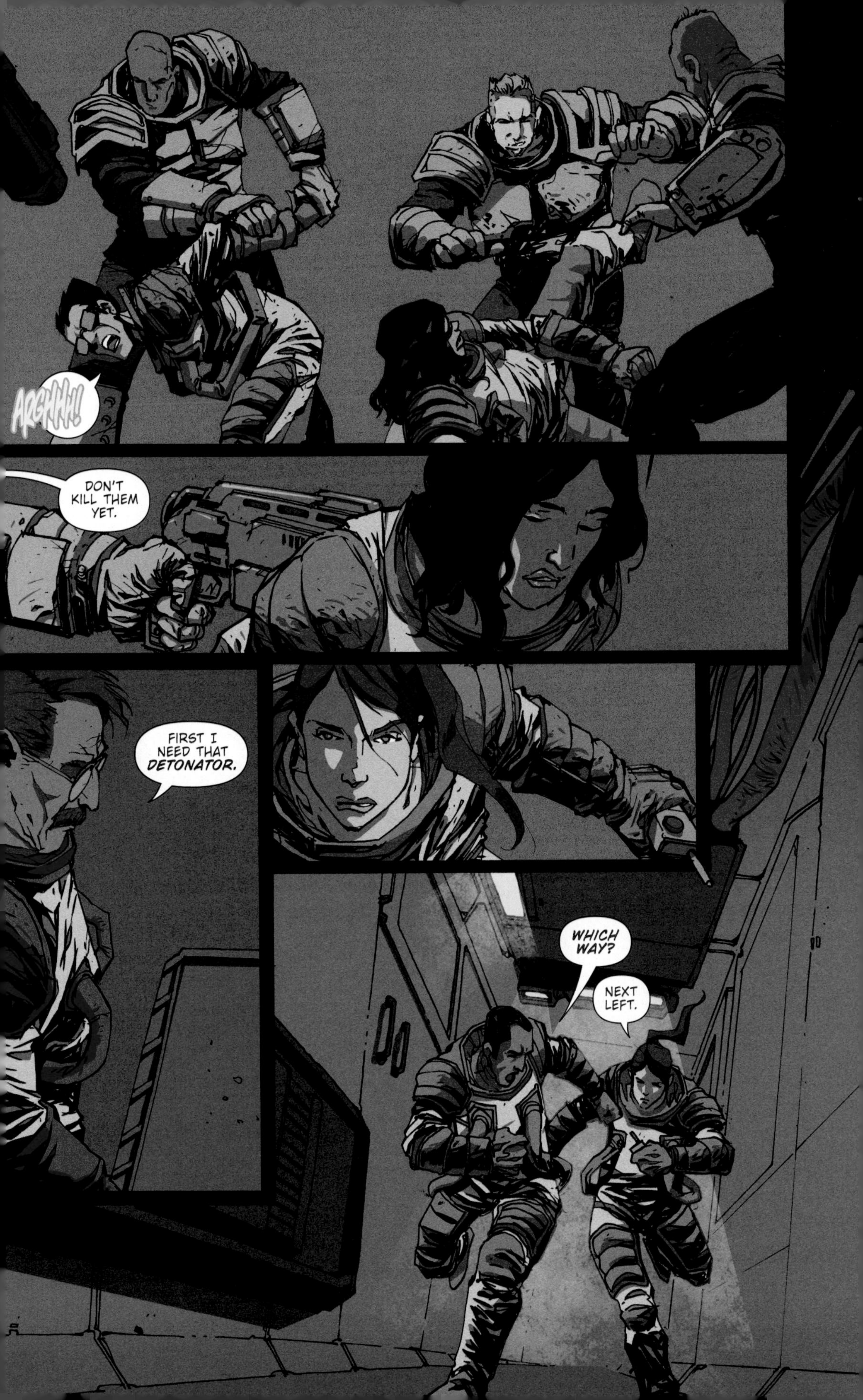
ARGHHH!
DON'T KILL THEM YET.
FIRST I NEED THAT DETONATOR.
WHICH WAY?
NEXT LEFT.

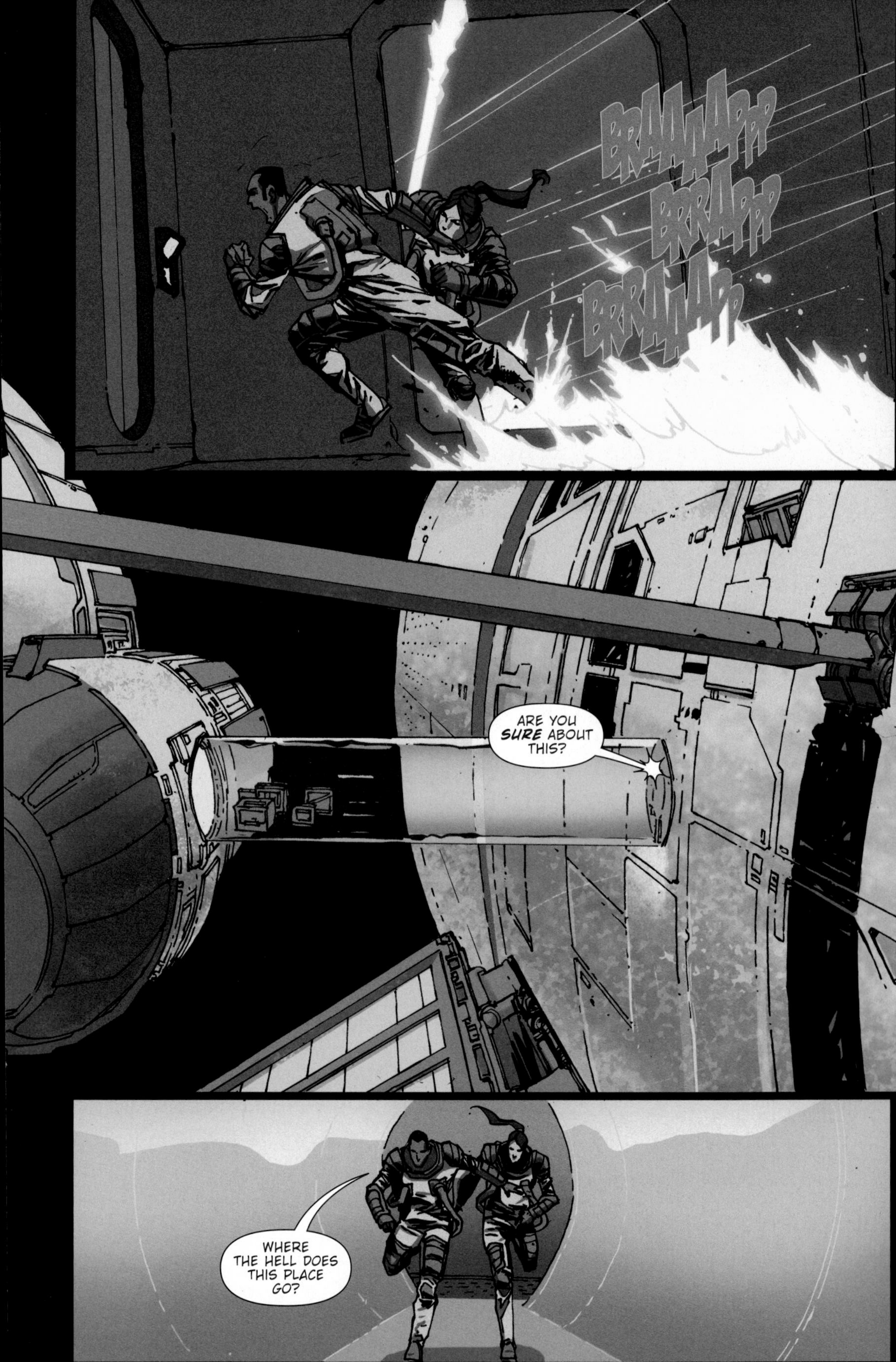
BRAAAAPPP
BRRAPPP
BRRAAAPPP
ARE YOU SURE ABOUT THIS?
WHERE THE HELL DOES THIS PLACE GO?

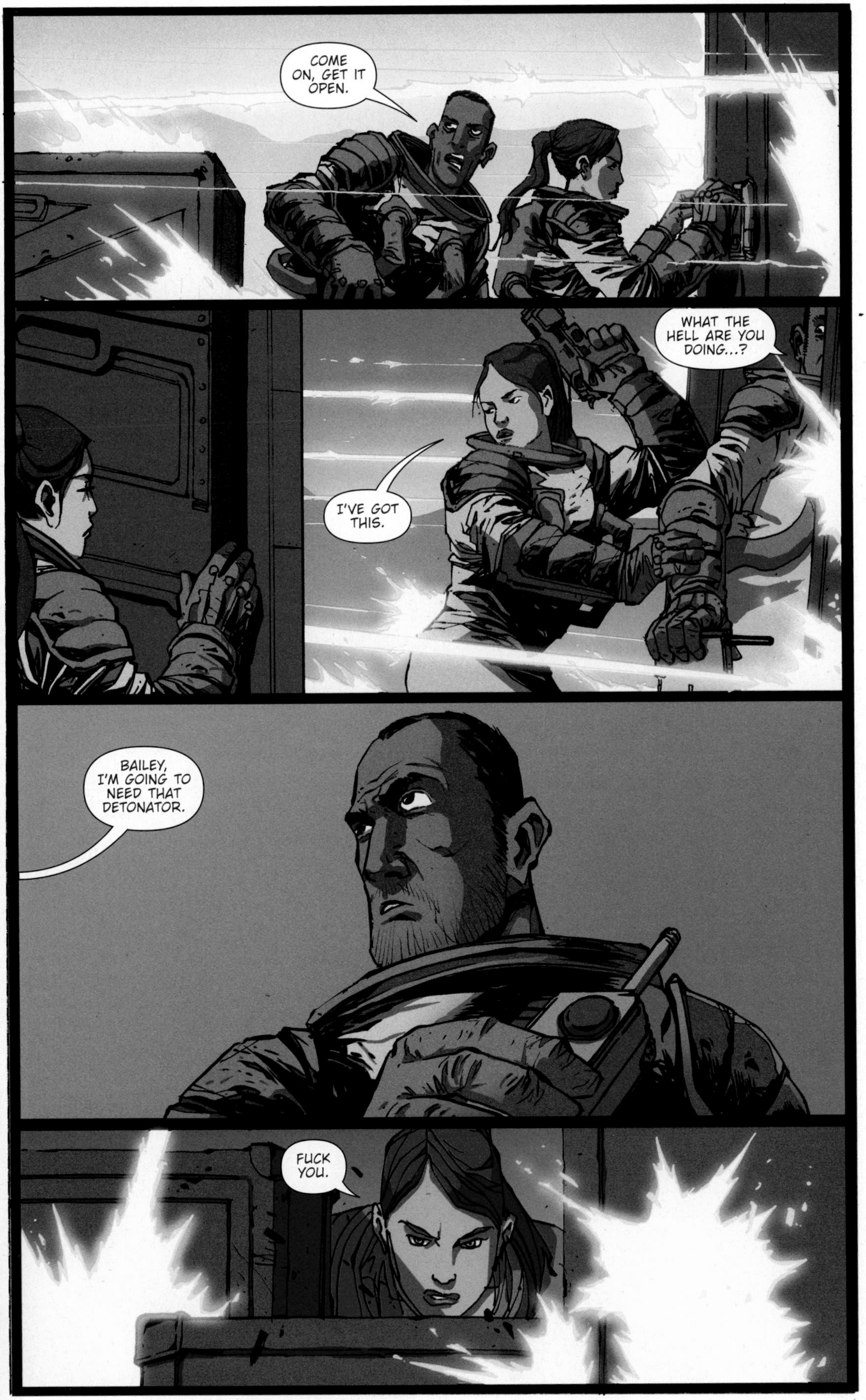
COME ON, GET IT OPEN.
WHAT THE HELL ARE YOU DOING...?
I'VE GOT THIS.
BAILEY, I'M GOING TO NEED THAT DETONATOR.
FUCK YOU.

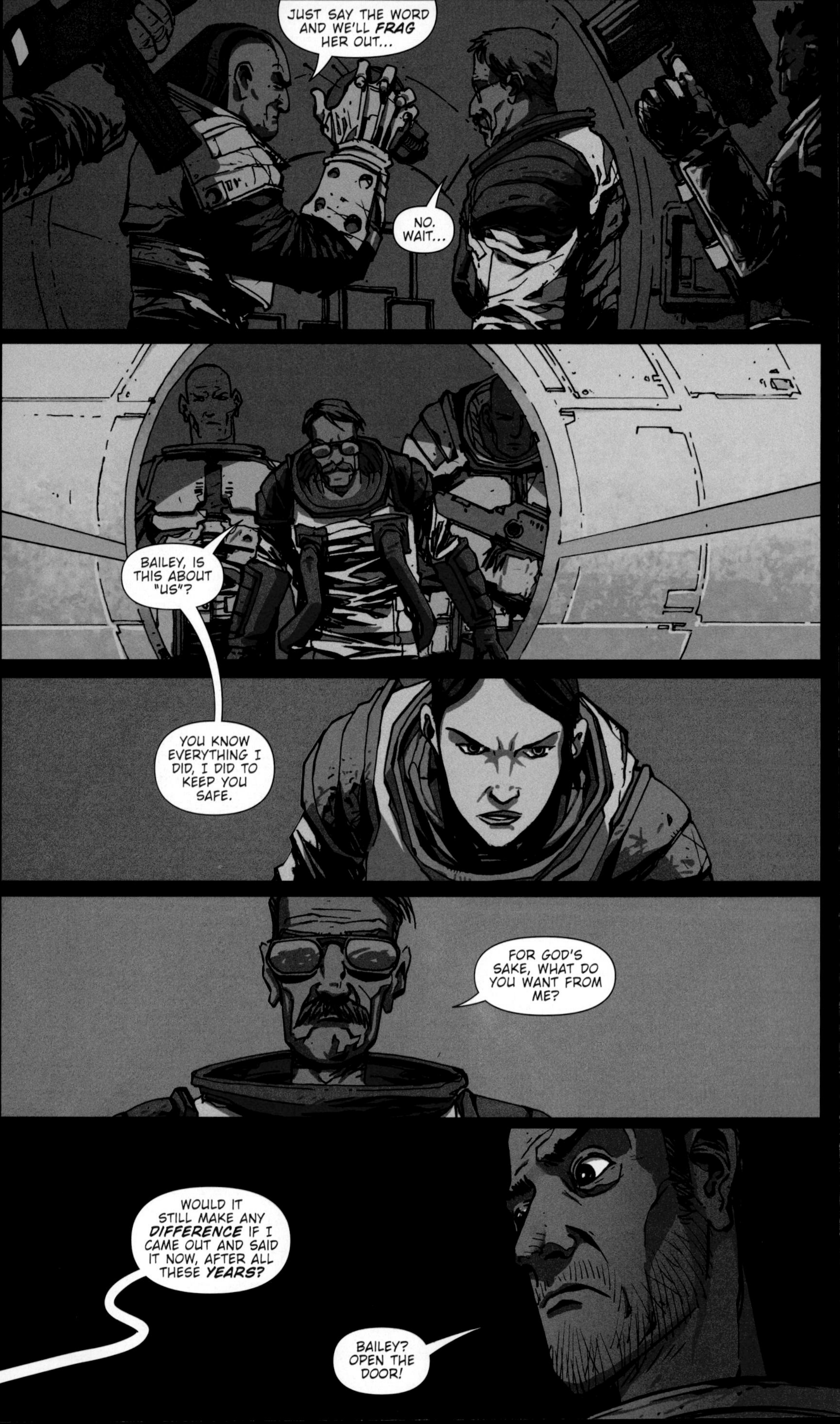
JUST SAY THE WORD AND WE'LL *FRAG* HER OUT...
NO. WAIT...
BAILEY, IS THIS ABOUT "US"?
YOU KNOW EVERYTHING I DID, I DID TO KEEP YOU SAFE.
FOR GOD'S SAKE, WHAT DO YOU WANT FROM ME?
WOULD IT STILL MAKE ANY *DIFFERENCE* IF I CAME OUT AND SAID IT NOW, AFTER ALL THESE *YEARS?*
BAILEY? OPEN THE DOOR!

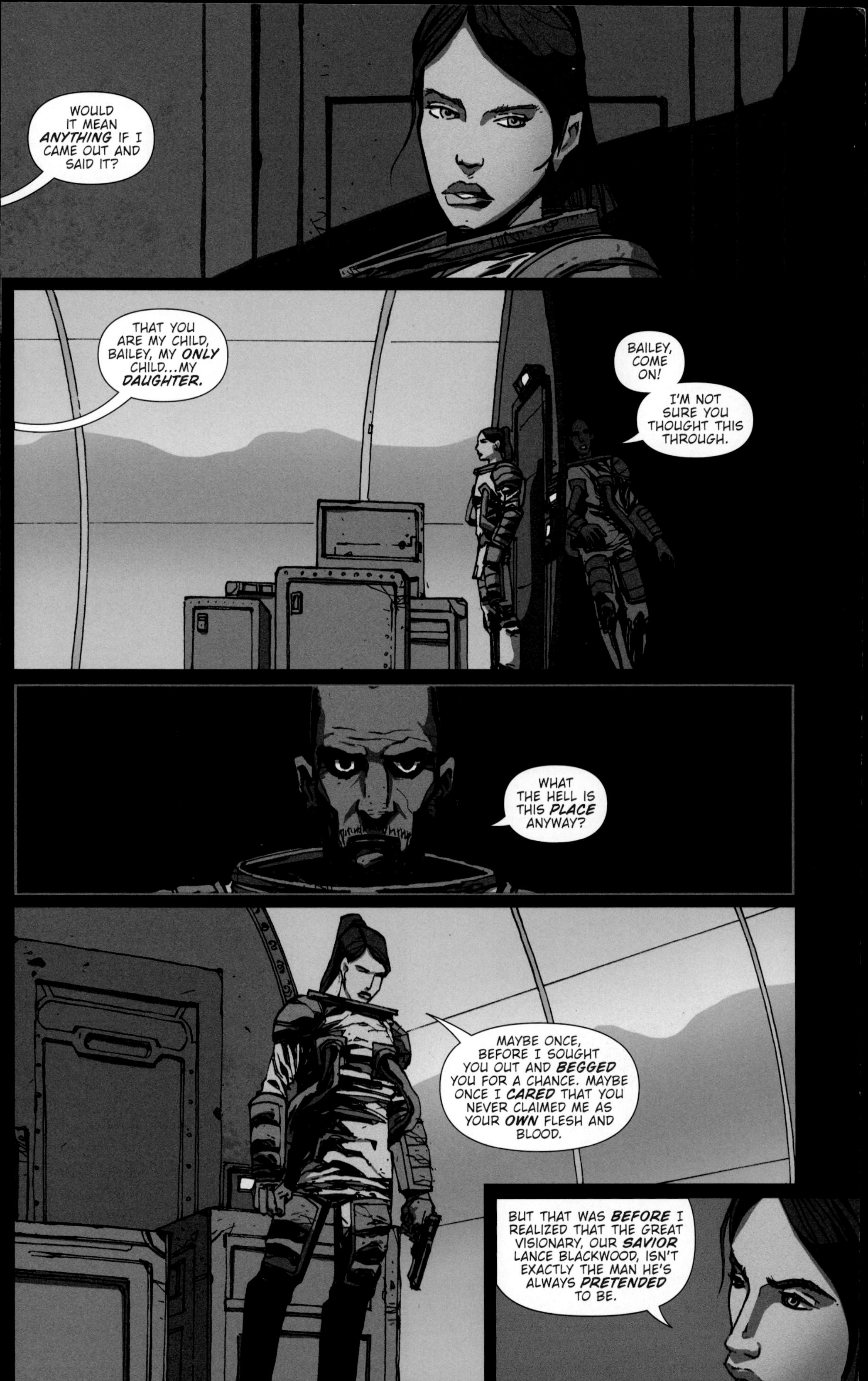
WOULD IT MEAN ANYTHING IF I CAME OUT AND SAID IT?
THAT YOU ARE MY CHILD, BAILEY, MY ONLY CHILD...MY DAUGHTER.
BAILEY, COME ON!
I'M NOT SURE YOU THOUGHT THIS THROUGH.
WHAT THE HELL IS THIS PLACE ANYWAY?
MAYBE ONCE, BEFORE I SOUGHT YOU OUT AND BEGGED YOU FOR A CHANCE. MAYBE ONCE I CARED THAT YOU NEVER CLAIMED ME AS YOUR OWN FLESH AND BLOOD.
BUT THAT WAS BEFORE I REALIZED THAT THE GREAT VISIONARY, OUR SAVIOR LANCE BLACKWOOD, ISN'T EXACTLY THE MAN HE'S ALWAYS PRETENDED TO BE.

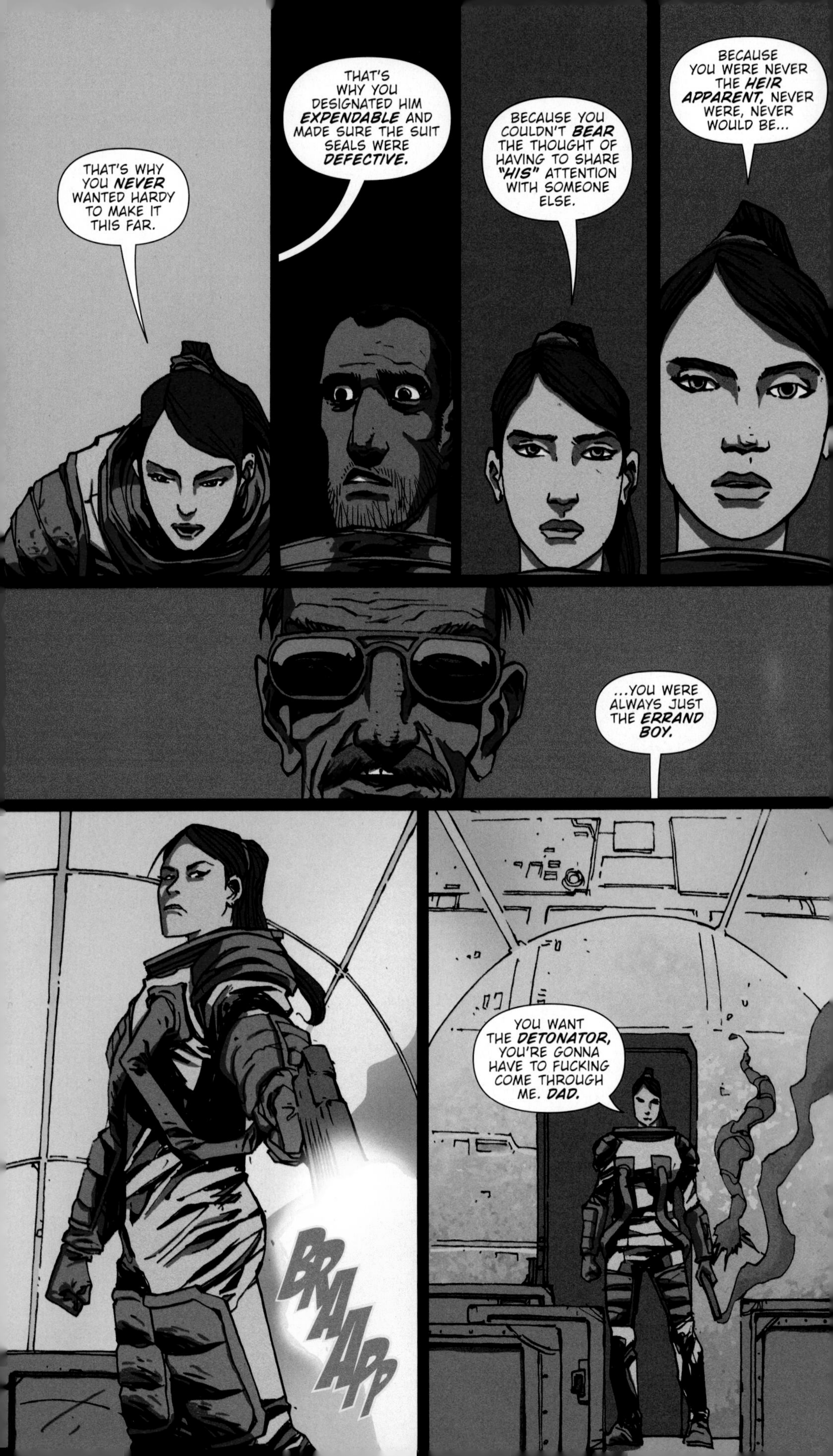
THAT'S WHY YOU NEVER WANTED HARDY TO MAKE IT THIS FAR.
THAT'S WHY YOU DESIGNATED HIM EXPENDABLE AND MADE SURE THE SUIT SEALS WERE DEFECTIVE.
BECAUSE YOU COULDN'T BEAR THE THOUGHT OF HAVING TO SHARE "HIS" ATTENTION WITH SOMEONE ELSE.
BECAUSE YOU WERE NEVER THE HEIR APPARENT, NEVER WERE, NEVER WOULD BE...
...YOU WERE ALWAYS JUST THE ERRAND BOY.
BRAAPP
YOU WANT THE DETONATOR, YOU'RE GONNA HAVE TO FUCKING COME THROUGH ME. DAD.

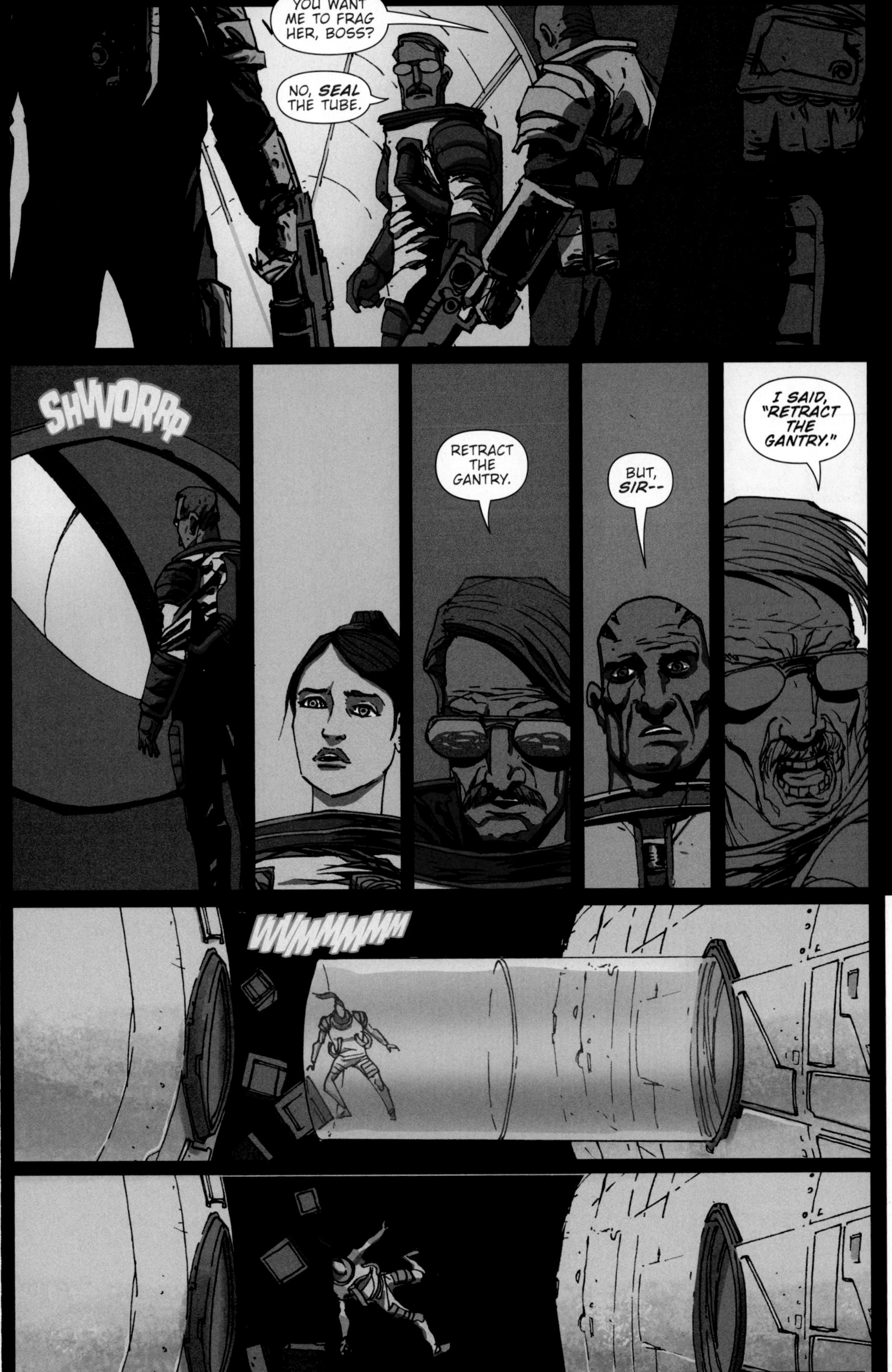
YOU WANT ME TO FRAG HER, BOSS?
NO, SEAL THE TUBE.
SHVVORRP
RETRACT THE GANTRY.
BUT, SIR--
I SAID, "RETRACT THE GANTRY."
VVVMMMMM
"GANTRY RETRACTED."

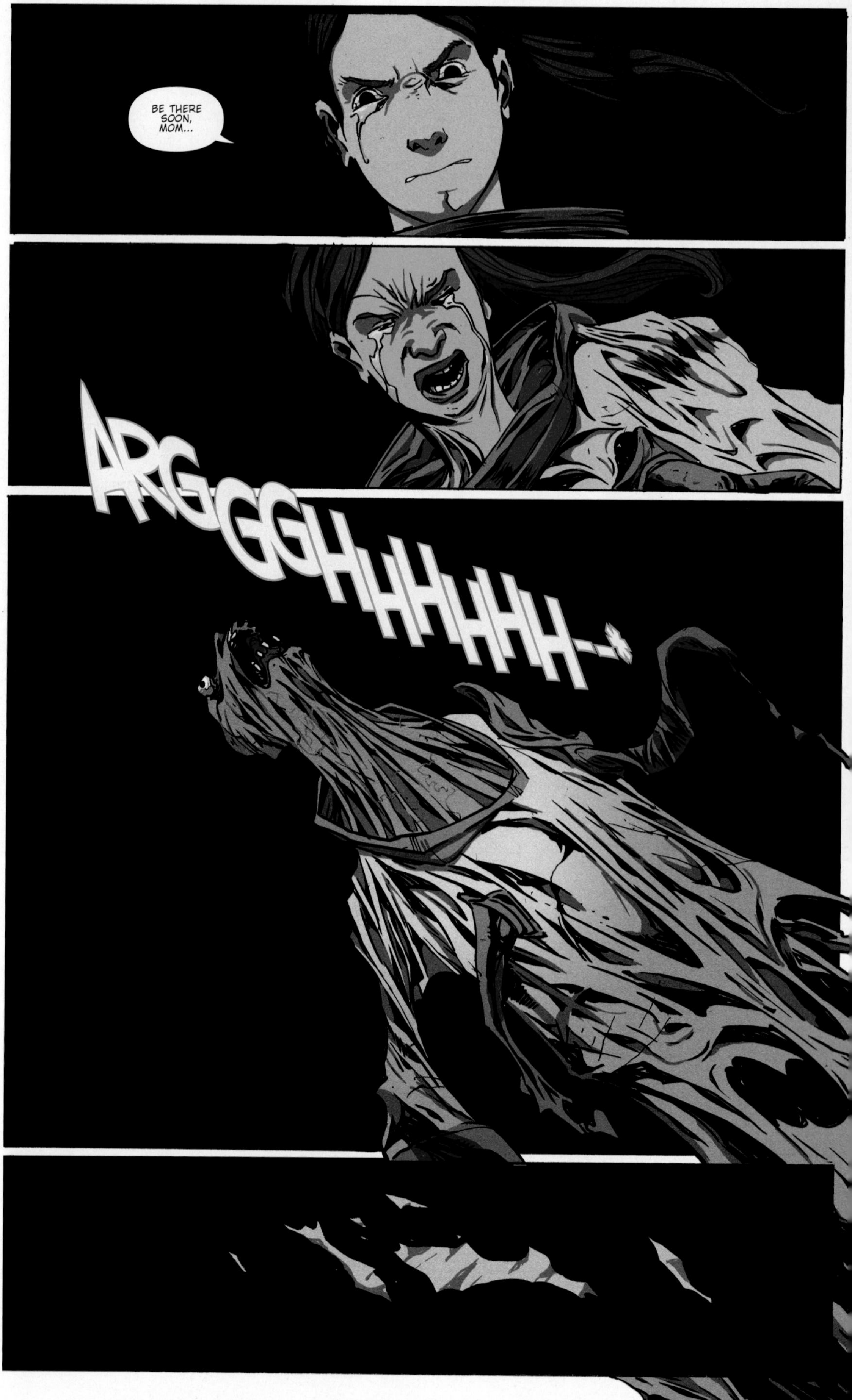
BE THERE SOON, MOM...
ARGGGHHHHHHH--!

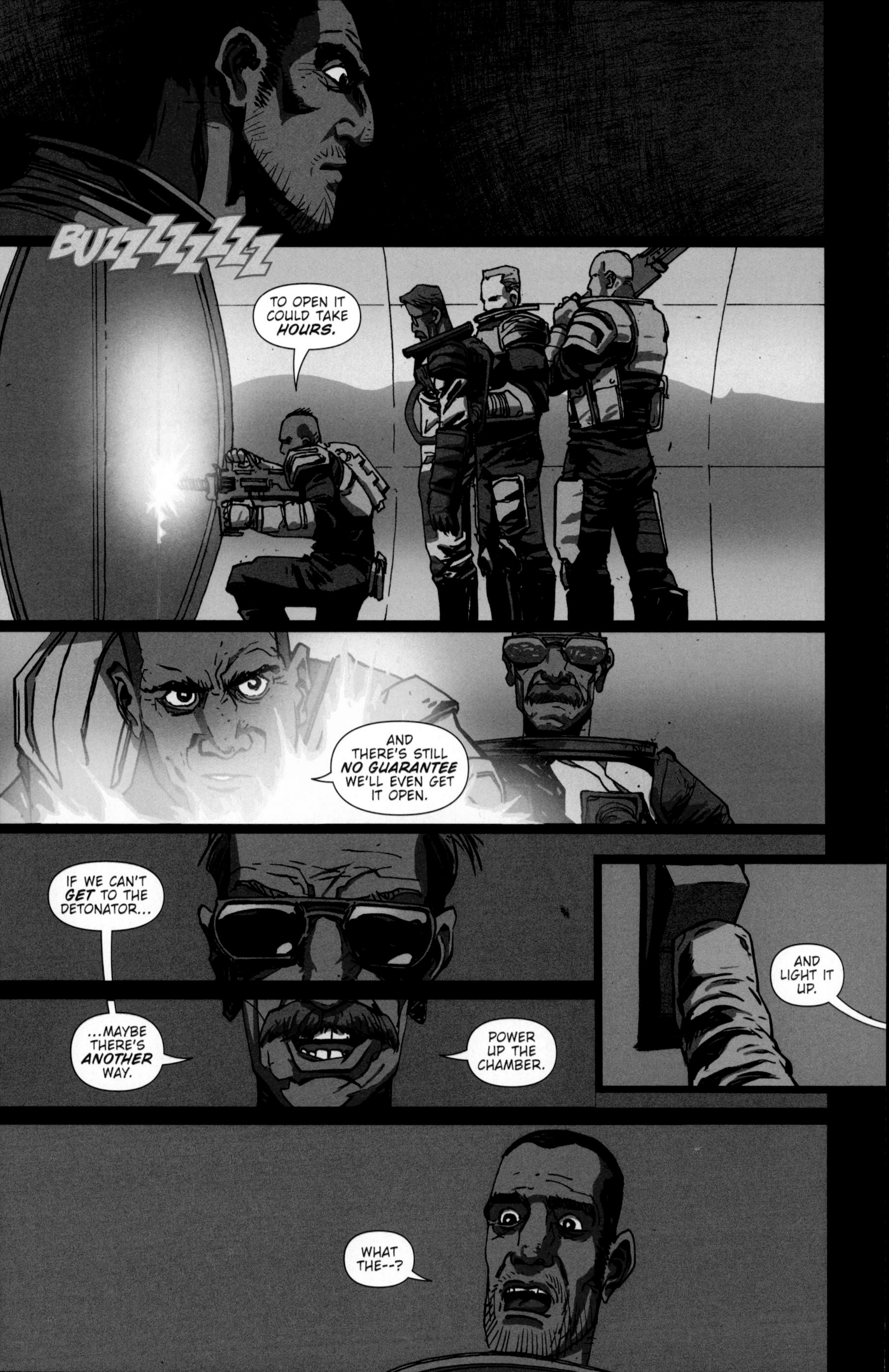

BUZZZZZZZZ
TO OPEN IT COULD TAKE HOURS.
AND THERE'S STILL NO GUARANTEE WE'LL EVEN GET IT OPEN.
IF WE CAN'T GET TO THE DETONATOR...
...MAYBE THERE'S ANOTHER WAY.
POWER UP THE CHAMBER.
AND LIGHT IT UP.
WHAT THE--?

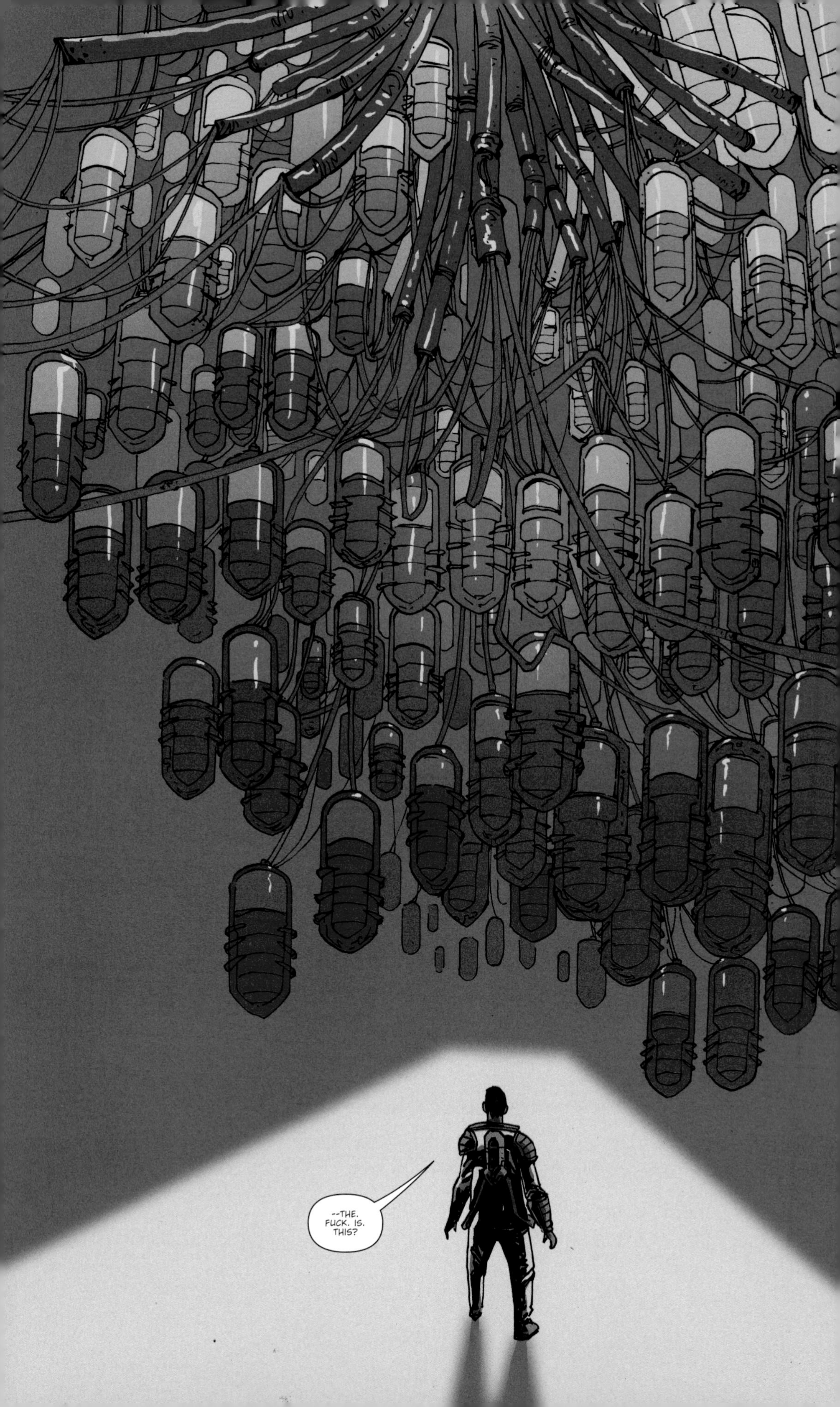
--THE. FUCK. IS. THIS?

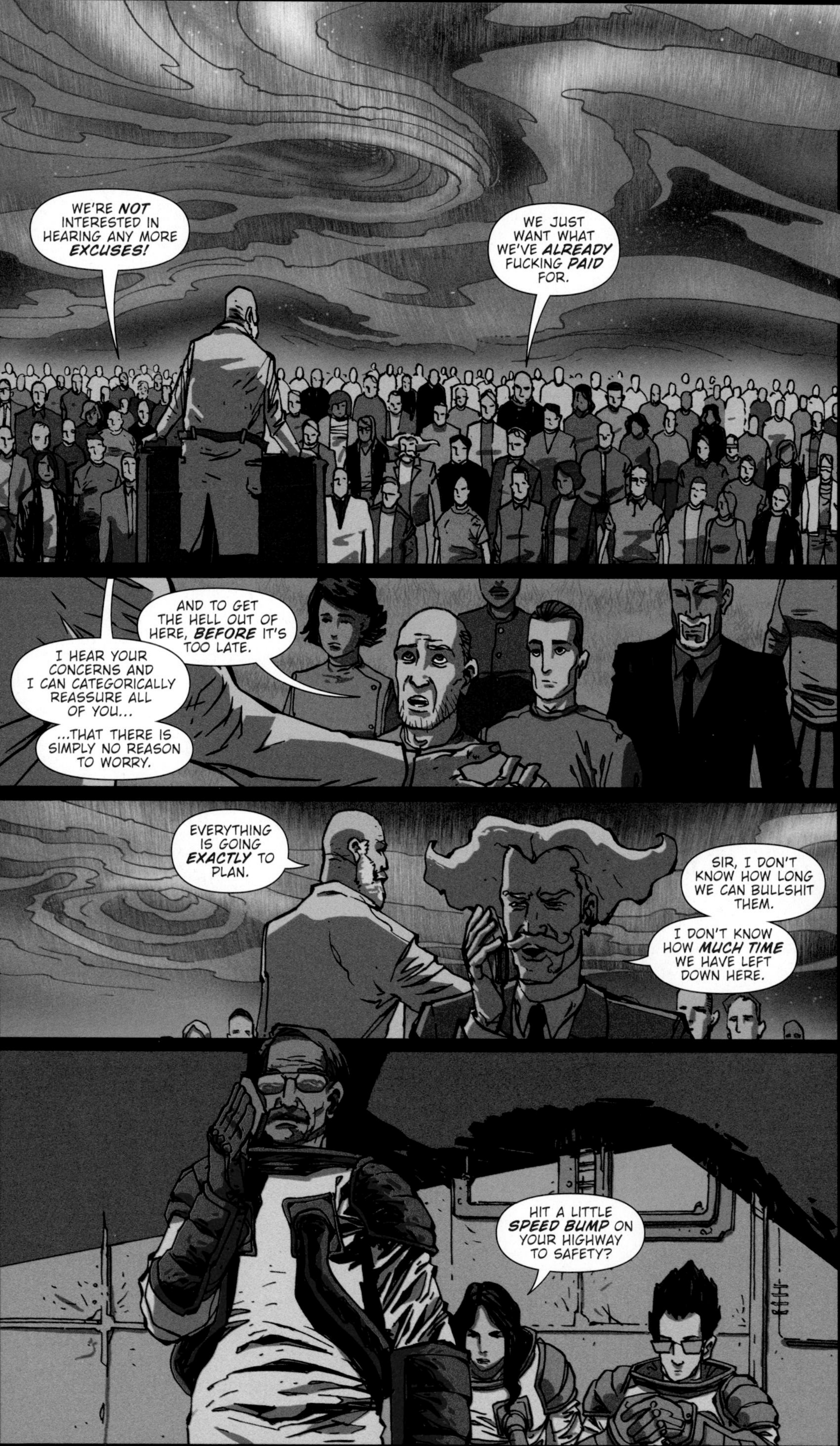
WE'RE **NOT** INTERESTED IN HEARING ANY MORE **EXCUSES!**
WE JUST WANT WHAT WE'VE **ALREADY** FUCKING **PAID** FOR.
AND TO GET THE HELL OUT OF HERE, **BEFORE** IT'S TOO LATE.
I HEAR YOUR CONCERNS AND I CAN CATEGORICALLY REASSURE ALL OF YOU...
...THAT THERE IS SIMPLY NO REASON TO WORRY.
EVERYTHING IS GOING **EXACTLY** TO PLAN.
SIR, I DON'T KNOW HOW LONG WE CAN BULLSHIT THEM.
I DON'T KNOW HOW **MUCH TIME** WE HAVE LEFT DOWN HERE.
HIT A LITTLE **SPEED BUMP** ON YOUR HIGHWAY TO SAFETY?

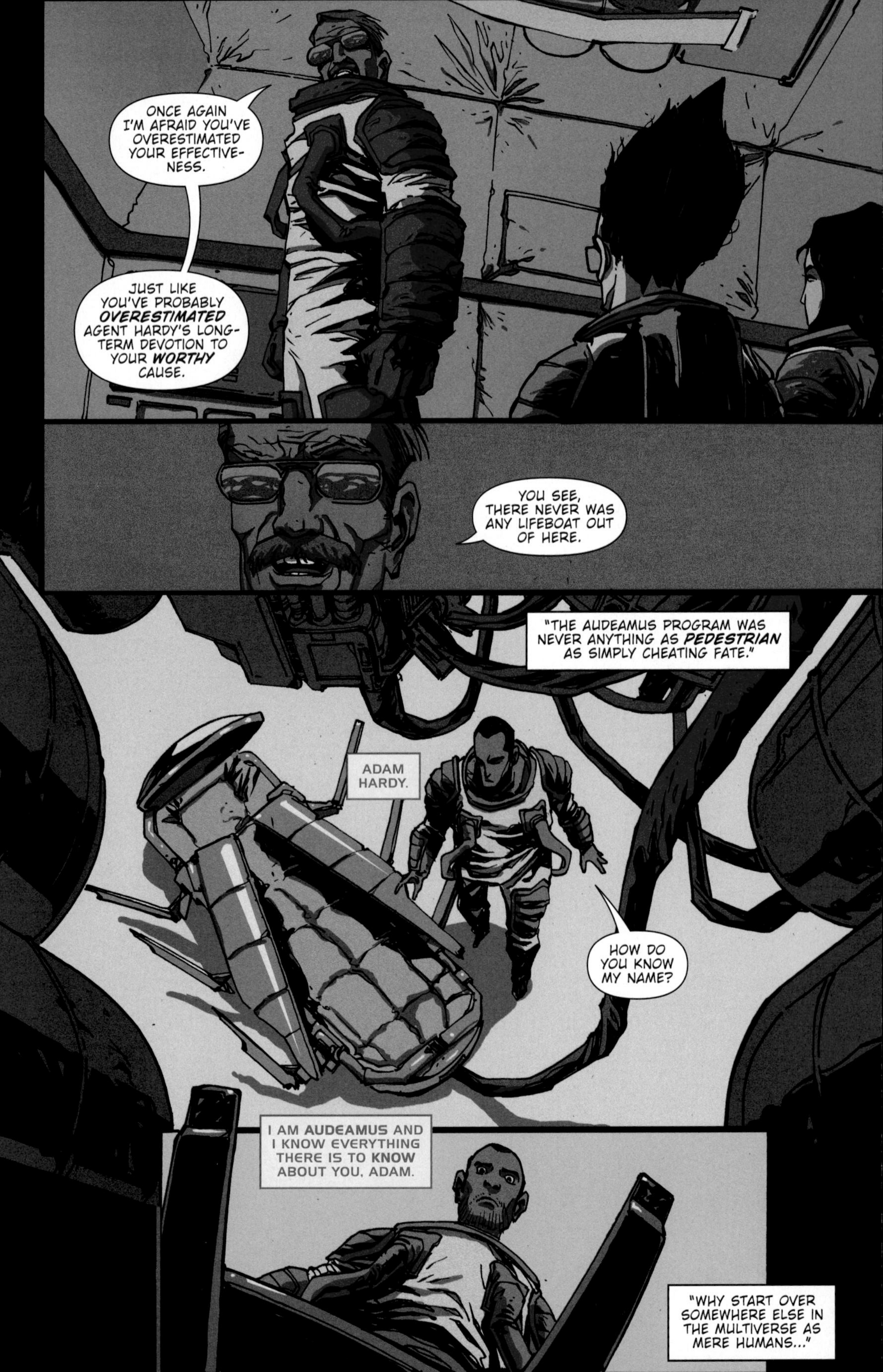
ONCE AGAIN I'M AFRAID YOU'VE OVERESTIMATED YOUR EFFECTIVE-NESS.
JUST LIKE YOU'VE PROBABLY OVERESTIMATED AGENT HARDY'S LONG-TERM DEVOTION TO YOUR WORTHY CAUSE.
YOU SEE, THERE NEVER WAS ANY LIFEBOAT OUT OF HERE.
"THE AUDEAMUS PROGRAM WAS NEVER ANYTHING AS PEDESTRIAN AS SIMPLY CHEATING FATE."
ADAM HARDY.
HOW DO YOU KNOW MY NAME?
I AM AUDEAMUS AND I KNOW EVERYTHING THERE IS TO KNOW ABOUT YOU, ADAM.
"WHY START OVER SOMEWHERE ELSE IN THE MULTIVERSE AS MERE HUMANS..."

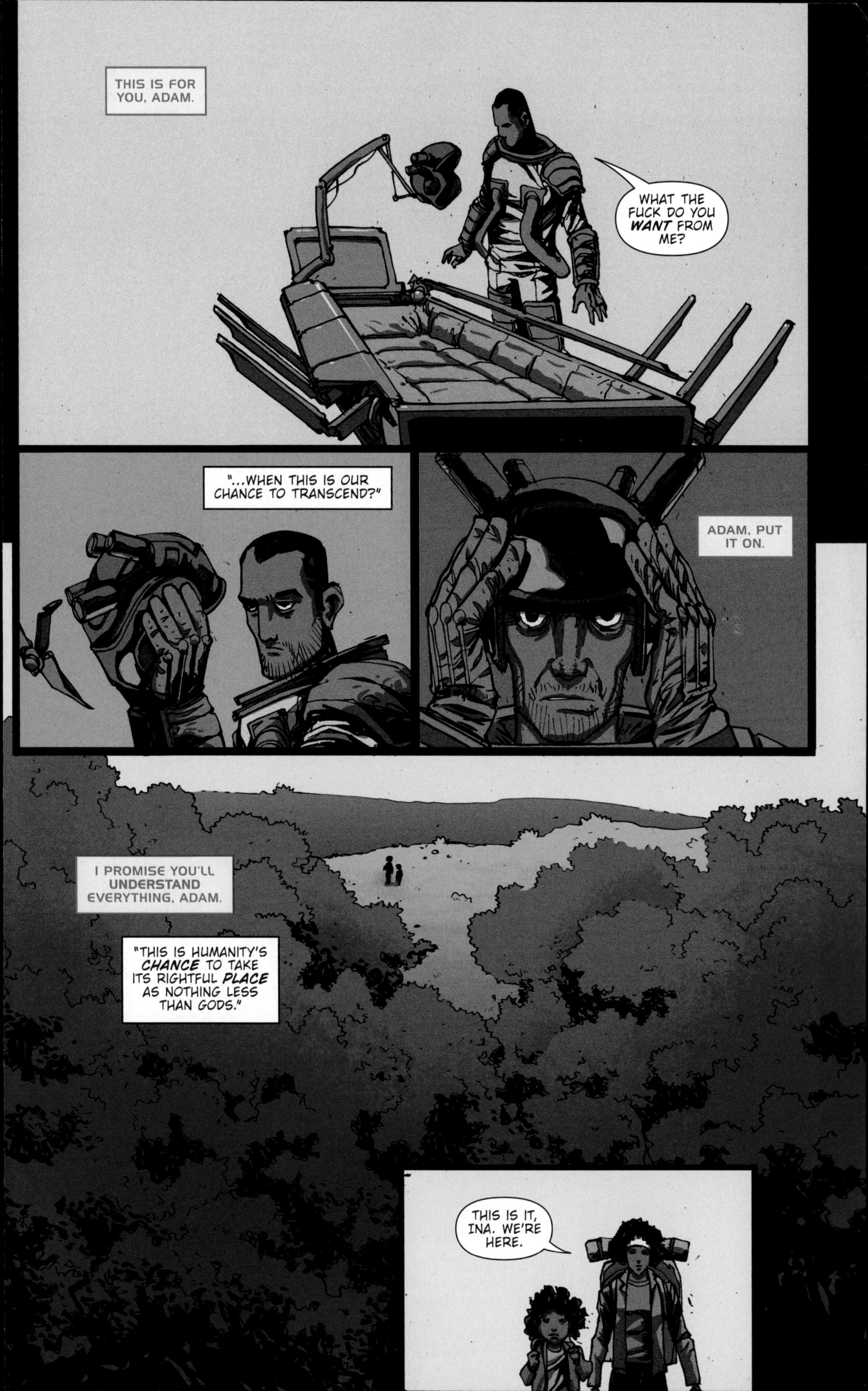
THIS IS FOR YOU, ADAM.
WHAT THE FUCK DO YOU *WANT* FROM ME?
"...WHEN THIS IS OUR CHANCE TO TRANSCEND?"
ADAM, PUT IT ON.
I PROMISE YOU'LL **UNDERSTAND** EVERYTHING, ADAM.
"THIS IS HUMANITY'S *CHANCE* TO TAKE ITS RIGHTFUL *PLACE* AS NOTHING LESS THAN GODS."
THIS IS IT, INA. WE'RE HERE.

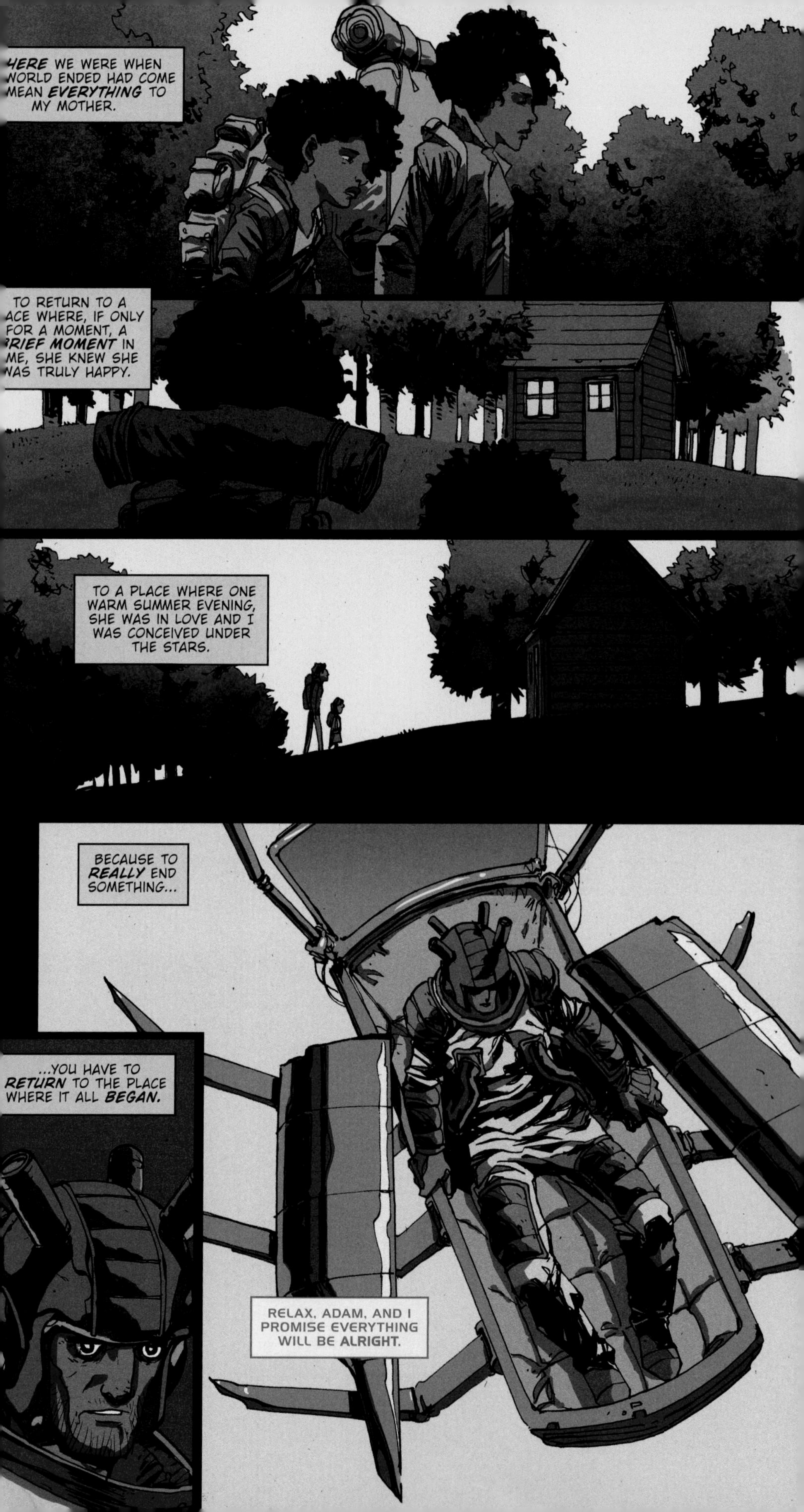
HERE WE WERE WHEN WORLD ENDED HAD COME MEAN EVERYTHING TO MY MOTHER.
TO RETURN TO A ACE WHERE, IF ONLY FOR A MOMENT, A RIEF MOMENT IN ME, SHE KNEW SHE WAS TRULY HAPPY.
TO A PLACE WHERE ONE WARM SUMMER EVENING, SHE WAS IN LOVE AND I WAS CONCEIVED UNDER THE STARS.
BECAUSE TO REALLY END SOMETHING...
...YOU HAVE TO RETURN TO THE PLACE WHERE IT ALL BEGAN.
RELAX, ADAM, AND I PROMISE EVERYTHING WILL BE ALRIGHT.

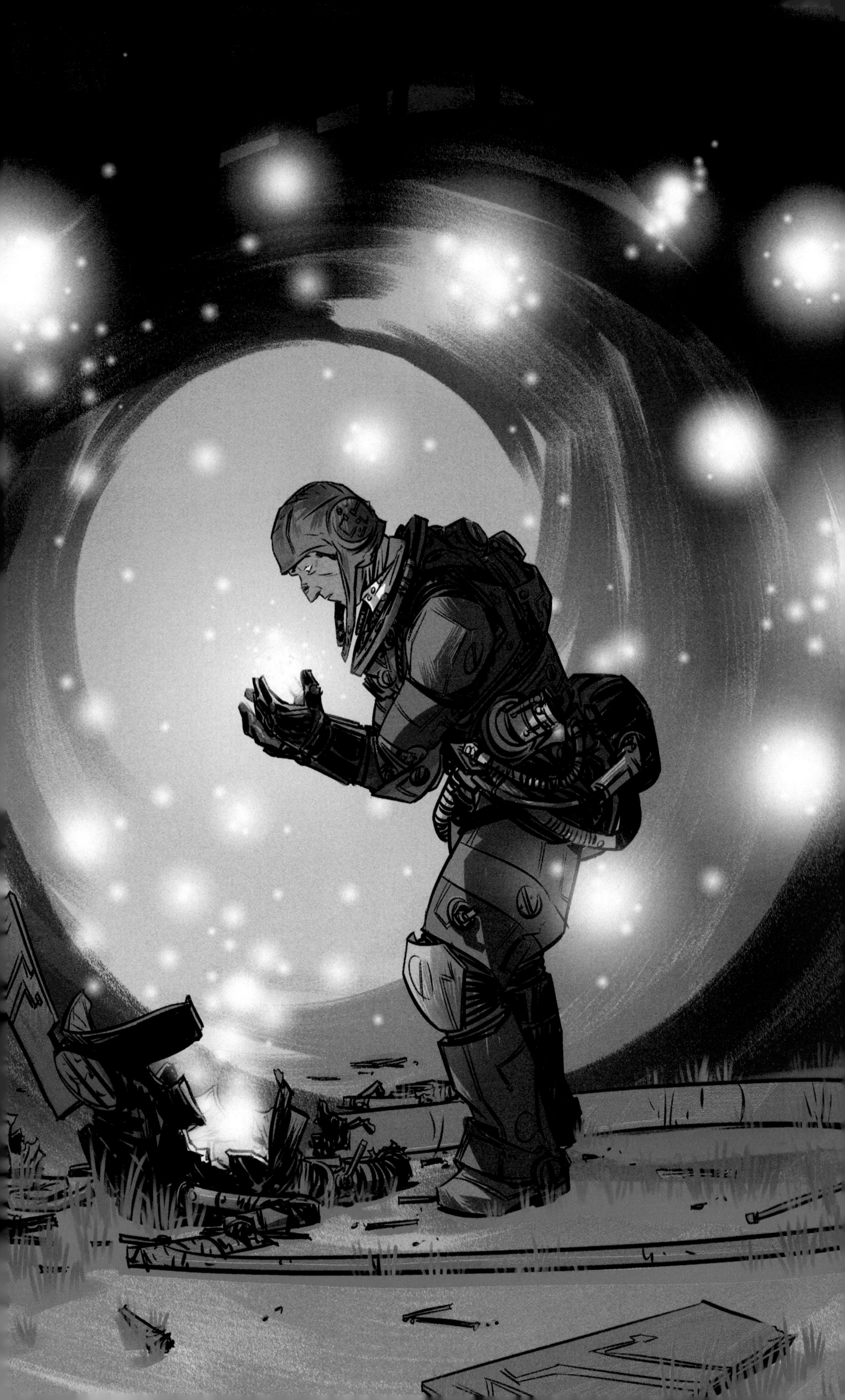

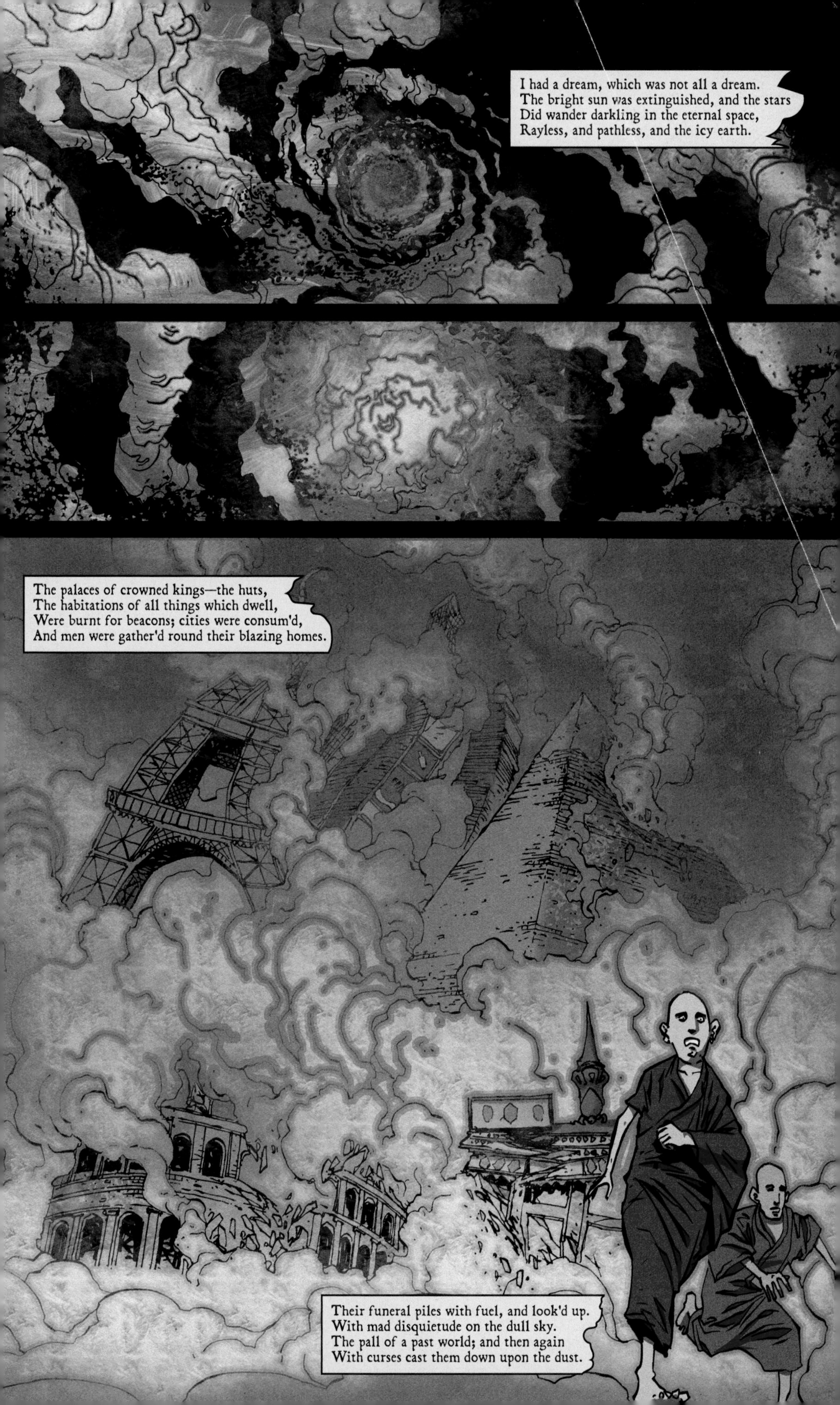
I had a dream, which was not all a dream.
The bright sun was extinguished, and the stars
Did wander darkling in the eternal space,
Rayless, and pathless, and the icy earth.
The palaces of crowned kings—the huts,
The habitations of all things which dwell,
Were burnt for beacons; cities were consum'd,
And men were gather'd round their blazing homes.
Their funeral piles with fuel, and look'd up.
With mad disquietude on the dull sky.
The pall of a past world; and then again
With curses cast them down upon the dust.

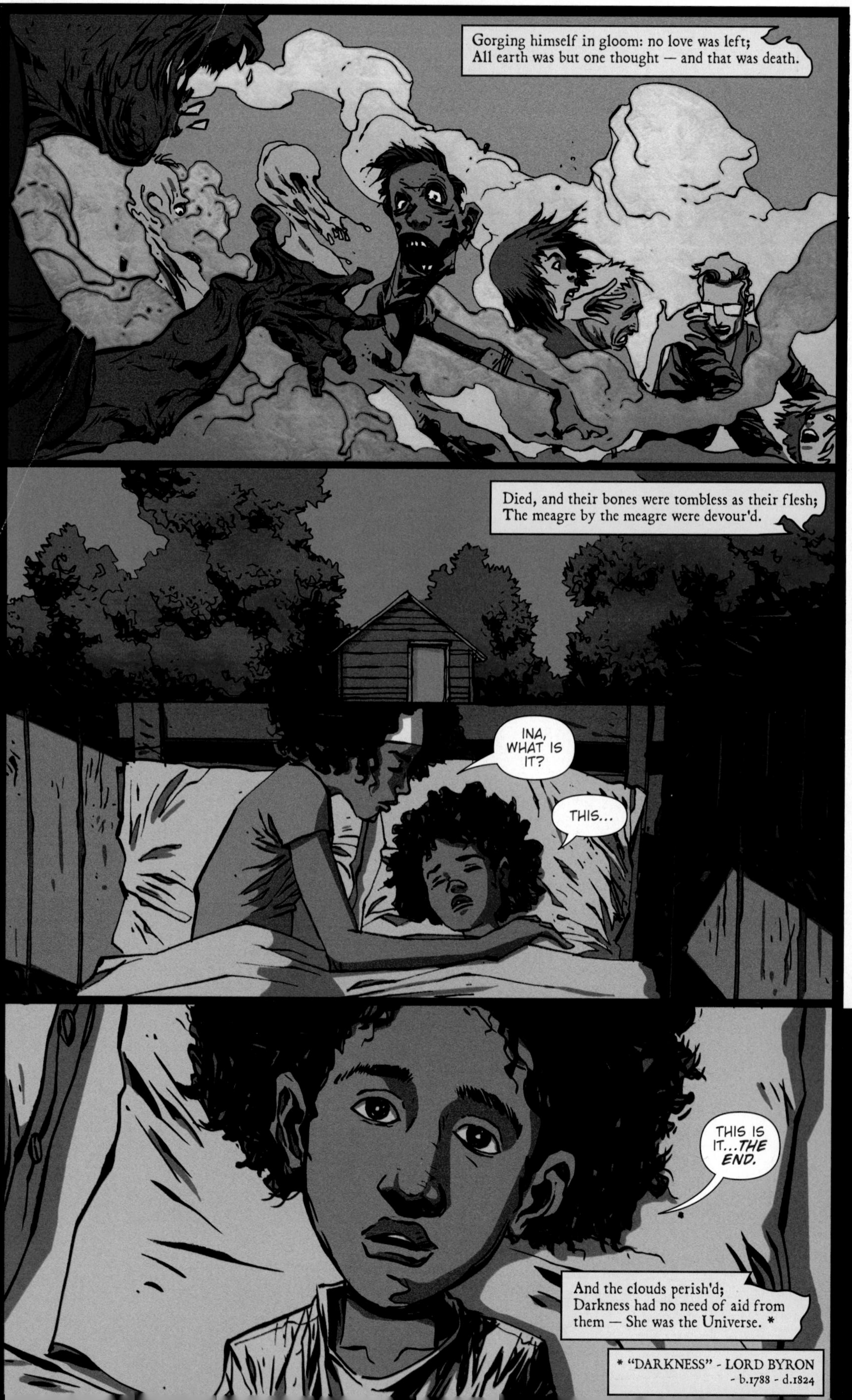
Gorging himself in gloom: no love was left;
All earth was but one thought — and that was death.
Died, and their bones were tombless as their flesh;
The meagre by the meagre were devour'd.
INA, WHAT IS IT?
THIS...
THIS IS IT...THE END.
And the clouds perish'd;
Darkness had no need of aid from them — She was the Universe. *
* "DARKNESS" - LORD BYRON
- b.1788 - d.1824

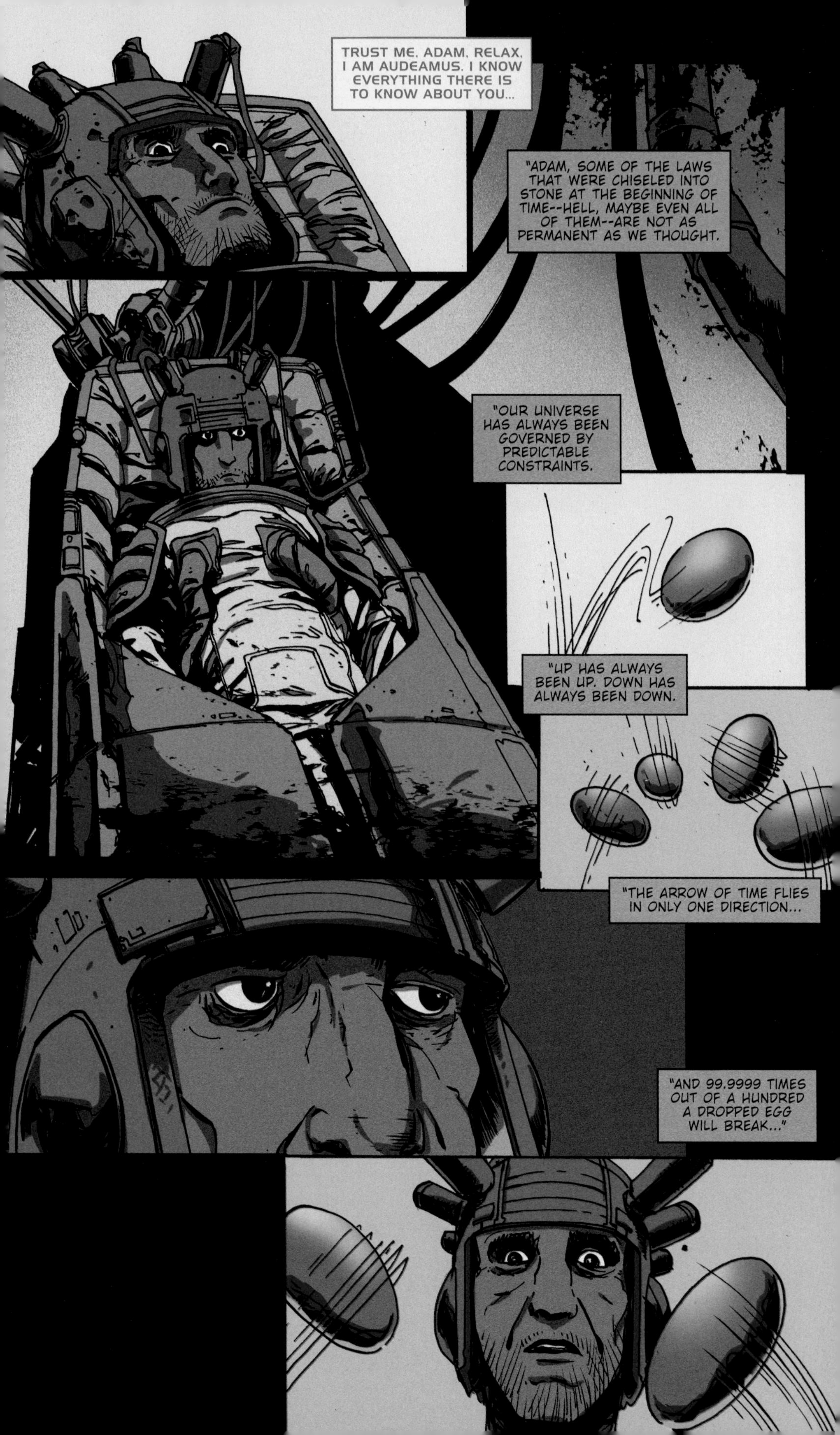
TRUST ME, ADAM. RELAX. I AM AUDEAMUS. I KNOW EVERYTHING THERE IS TO KNOW ABOUT YOU...
"ADAM, SOME OF THE LAWS THAT WERE CHISELED INTO STONE AT THE BEGINNING OF TIME--HELL, MAYBE EVEN ALL OF THEM--ARE NOT AS PERMANENT AS WE THOUGHT.
"OUR UNIVERSE HAS ALWAYS BEEN GOVERNED BY PREDICTABLE CONSTRAINTS.
"UP HAS ALWAYS BEEN UP. DOWN HAS ALWAYS BEEN DOWN.
"THE ARROW OF TIME FLIES IN ONLY ONE DIRECTION...
"AND 99.9999 TIMES OUT OF A HUNDRED A DROPPED EGG WILL BREAK..."

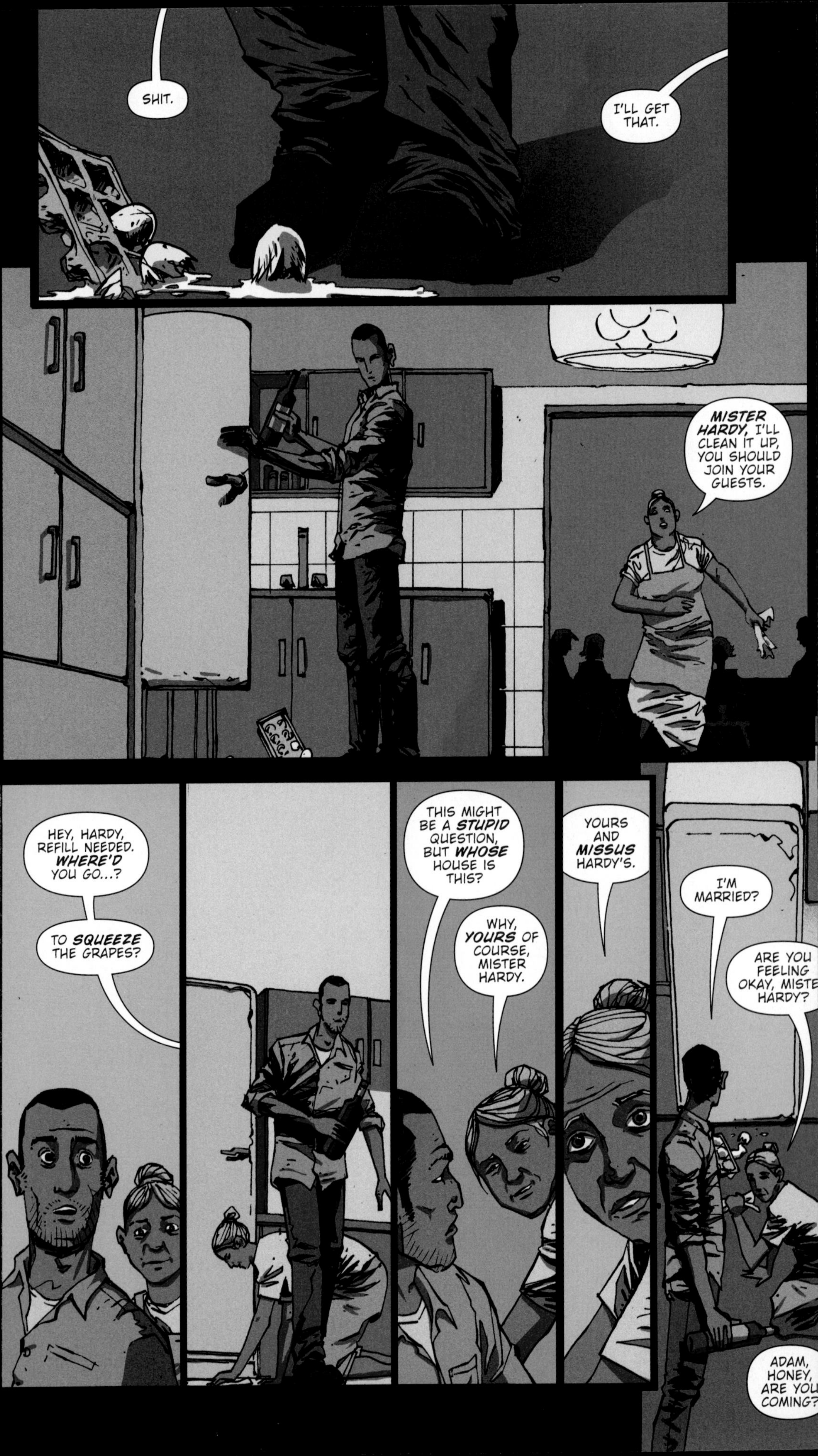
SHIT.
I'LL GET THAT.
MISTER HARDY, I'LL CLEAN IT UP, YOU SHOULD JOIN YOUR GUESTS.
HEY, HARDY, REFILL NEEDED. WHERE'D YOU GO...?
TO SQUEEZE THE GRAPES?
THIS MIGHT BE A STUPID QUESTION, BUT WHOSE HOUSE IS THIS?
WHY, YOURS OF COURSE, MISTER HARDY.
YOURS AND MISSUS HARDY'S.
I'M MARRIED?
ARE YOU FEELING OKAY, MISTE HARDY?
ADAM, HONEY, ARE YOU COMING?

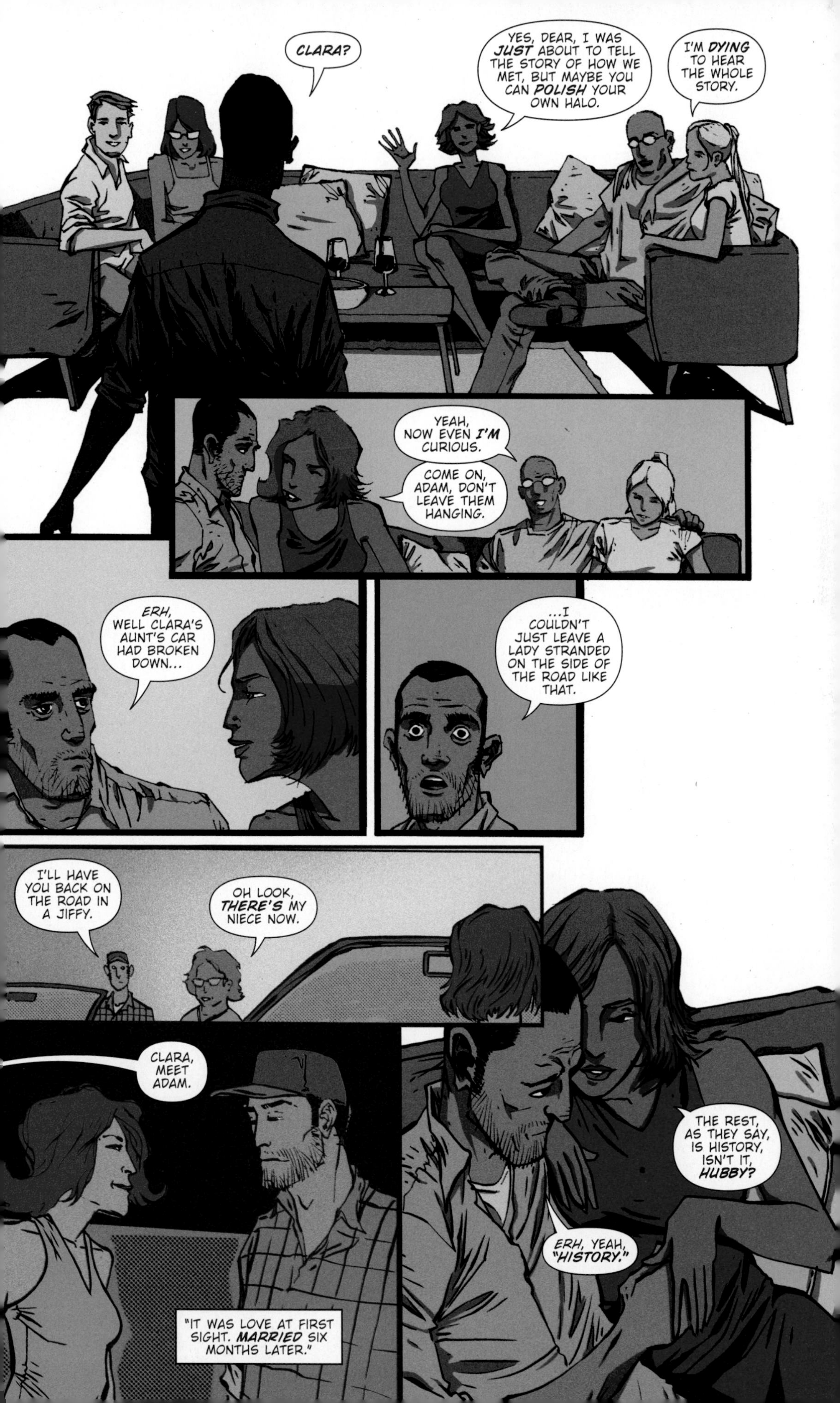

CLARA?
YES, DEAR, I WAS JUST ABOUT TO TELL THE STORY OF HOW WE MET, BUT MAYBE YOU CAN POLISH YOUR OWN HALO.
I'M DYING TO HEAR THE WHOLE STORY.
YEAH, NOW EVEN I'M CURIOUS.
COME ON, ADAM, DON'T LEAVE THEM HANGING.
ERH, WELL CLARA'S AUNT'S CAR HAD BROKEN DOWN...
...I COULDN'T JUST LEAVE A LADY STRANDED ON THE SIDE OF THE ROAD LIKE THAT.
I'LL HAVE YOU BACK ON THE ROAD IN A JIFFY.
OH LOOK, THERE'S MY NIECE NOW.
CLARA, MEET ADAM.
"IT WAS LOVE AT FIRST SIGHT. MARRIED SIX MONTHS LATER."
THE REST, AS THEY SAY, IS HISTORY, ISN'T IT, HUBBY?
ERH, YEAH, "HISTORY."

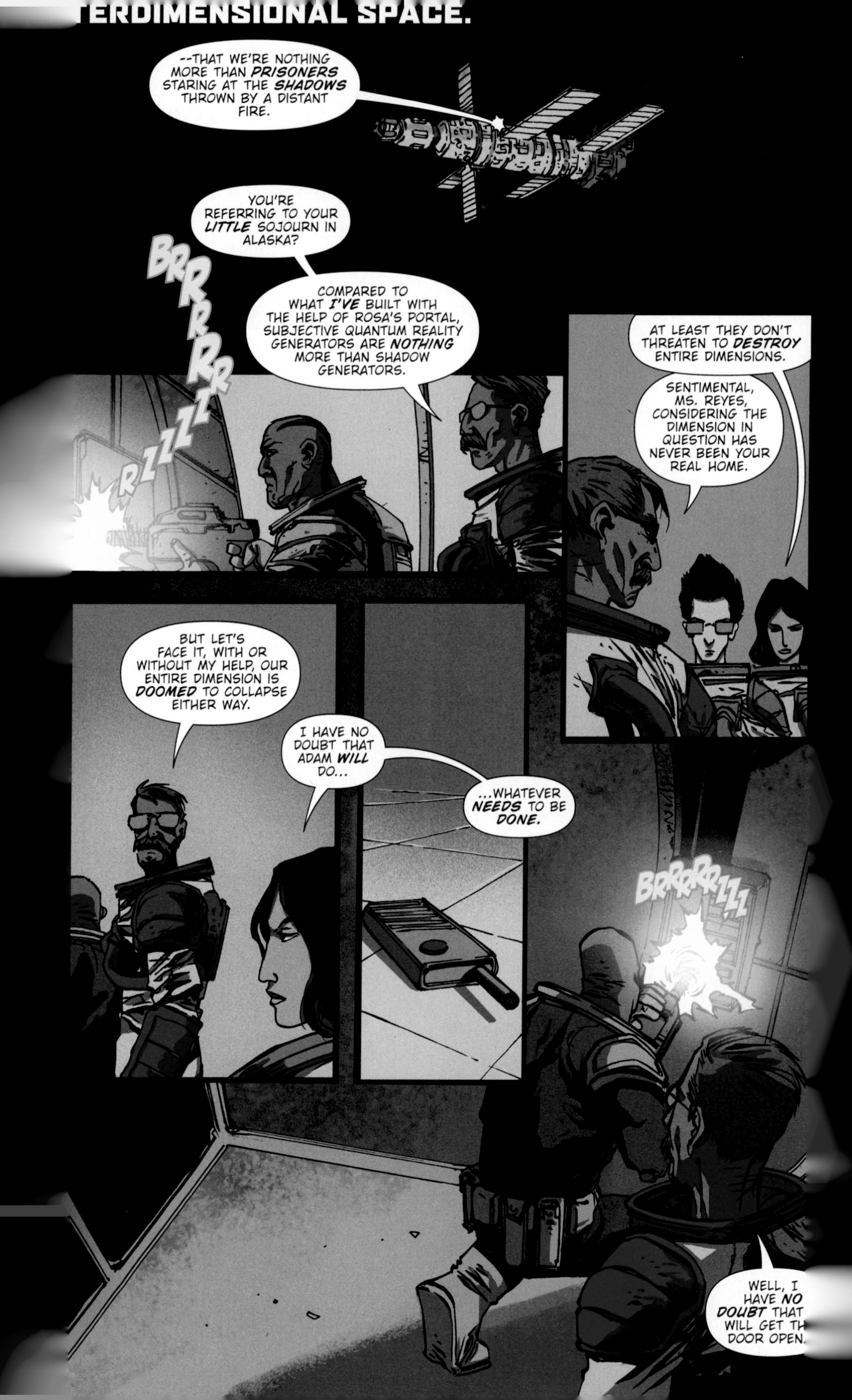

TERDIMENSIONAL SPACE.
--THAT WE'RE NOTHING MORE THAN PRISONERS STARING AT THE SHADOWS THROWN BY A DISTANT FIRE.
YOU'RE REFERRING TO YOUR LITTLE SOJOURN IN ALASKA?
BRRRRRRRZZZZZ
COMPARED TO WHAT I'VE BUILT WITH THE HELP OF ROSA'S PORTAL, SUBJECTIVE QUANTUM REALITY GENERATORS ARE NOTHING MORE THAN SHADOW GENERATORS.
AT LEAST THEY DON'T THREATEN TO DESTROY ENTIRE DIMENSIONS.
SENTIMENTAL, MS. REYES, CONSIDERING THE DIMENSION IN QUESTION HAS NEVER BEEN YOUR REAL HOME.
BUT LET'S FACE IT, WITH OR WITHOUT MY HELP, OUR ENTIRE DIMENSION IS DOOMED TO COLLAPSE EITHER WAY.
I HAVE NO DOUBT THAT ADAM WILL DO...
...WHATEVER NEEDS TO BE DONE.
BRRRRRZZZ
WELL, I HAVE NO DOUBT THAT WILL GET TH DOOR OPEN.

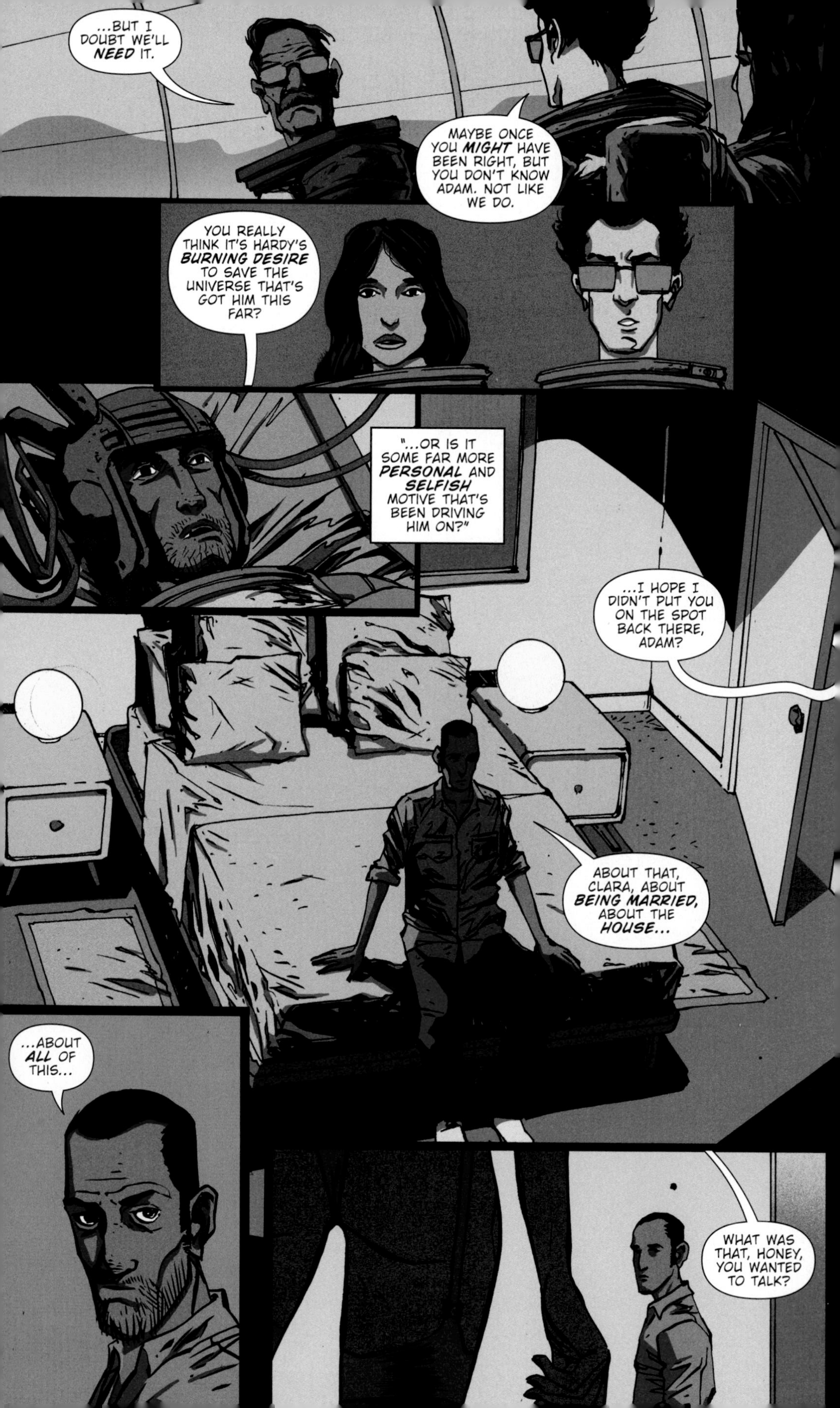
...BUT I DOUBT WE'LL NEED IT.
MAYBE ONCE YOU MIGHT HAVE BEEN RIGHT, BUT YOU DON'T KNOW ADAM. NOT LIKE WE DO.
YOU REALLY THINK IT'S HARDY'S BURNING DESIRE TO SAVE THE UNIVERSE THAT'S GOT HIM THIS FAR?
"...OR IS IT SOME FAR MORE PERSONAL AND SELFISH MOTIVE THAT'S BEEN DRIVING HIM ON?"
...I HOPE I DIDN'T PUT YOU ON THE SPOT BACK THERE, ADAM?
ABOUT THAT, CLARA, ABOUT BEING MARRIED, ABOUT THE HOUSE...
...ABOUT ALL OF THIS...
WHAT WAS THAT, HONEY, YOU WANTED TO TALK?

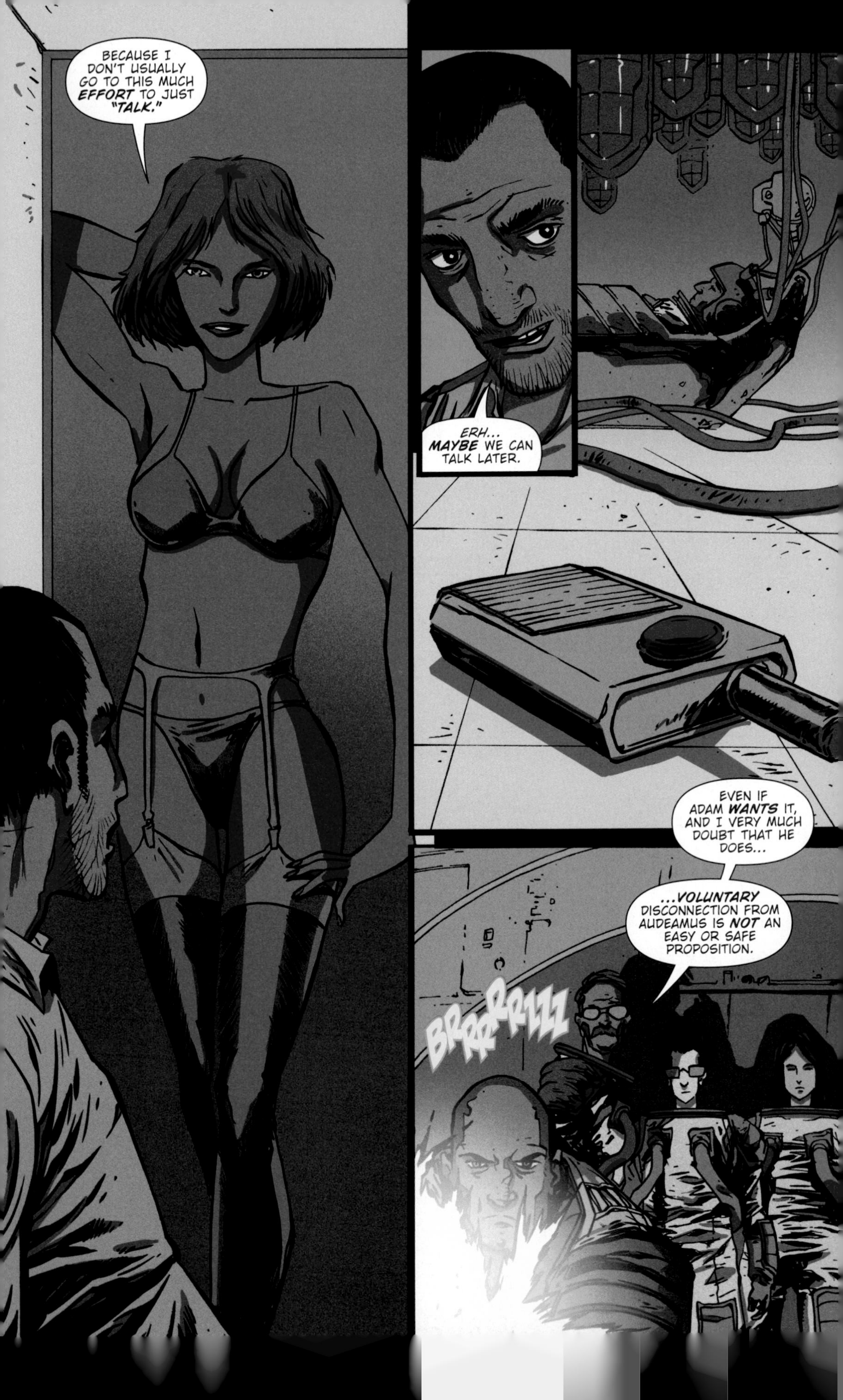
BECAUSE I DON'T USUALLY GO TO THIS MUCH EFFORT TO JUST "TALK."
ERH... MAYBE WE CAN TALK LATER.
EVEN IF ADAM WANTS IT, AND I VERY MUCH DOUBT THAT HE DOES...
...VOLUNTARY DISCONNECTION FROM AUDEAMUS IS NOT AN EASY OR SAFE PROPOSITION.
BRRRRRZZZZ

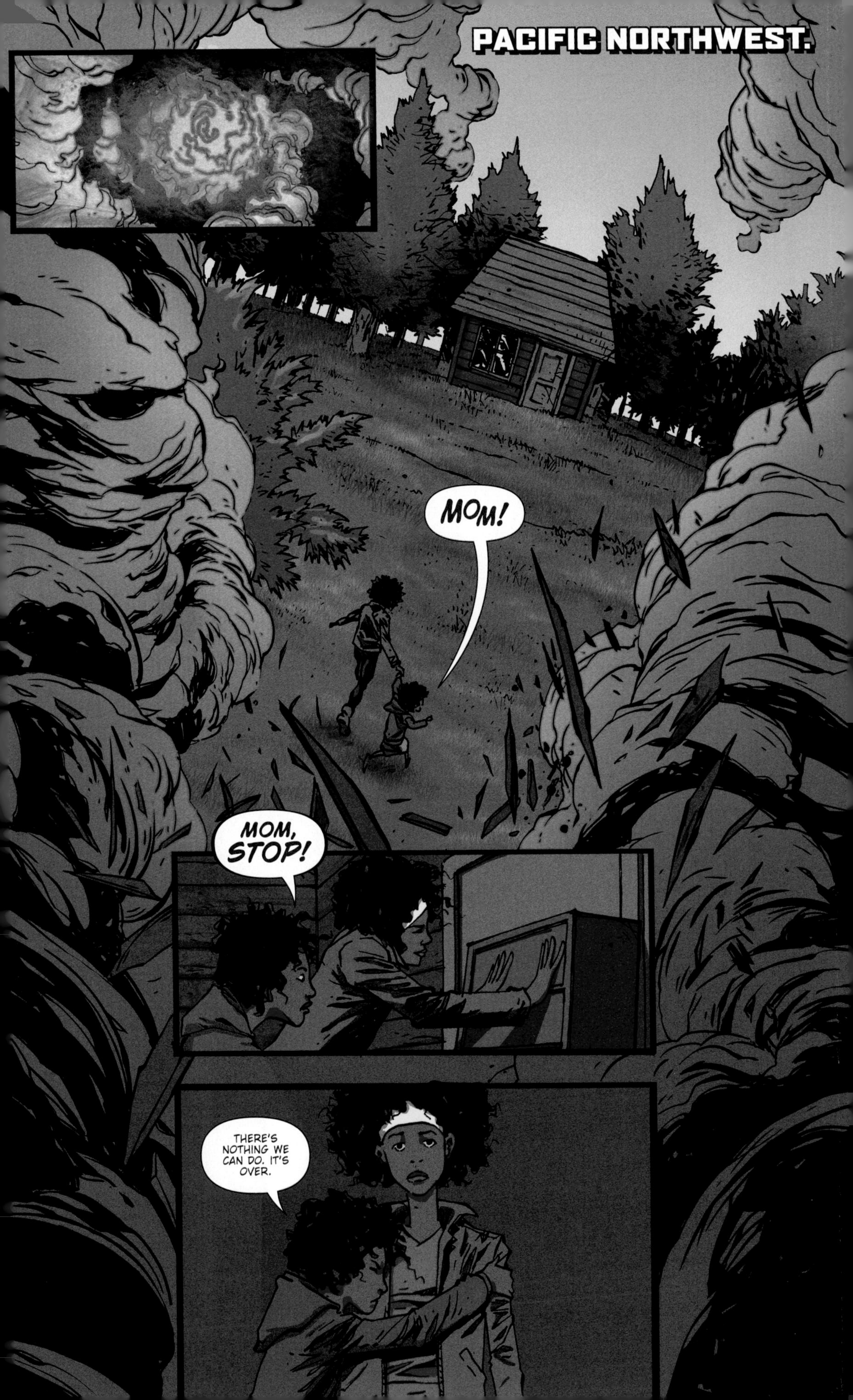
PACIFIC NORTHWEST.
MOM!
MOM, STOP!
THERE'S NOTHING WE CAN DO. IT'S OVER.

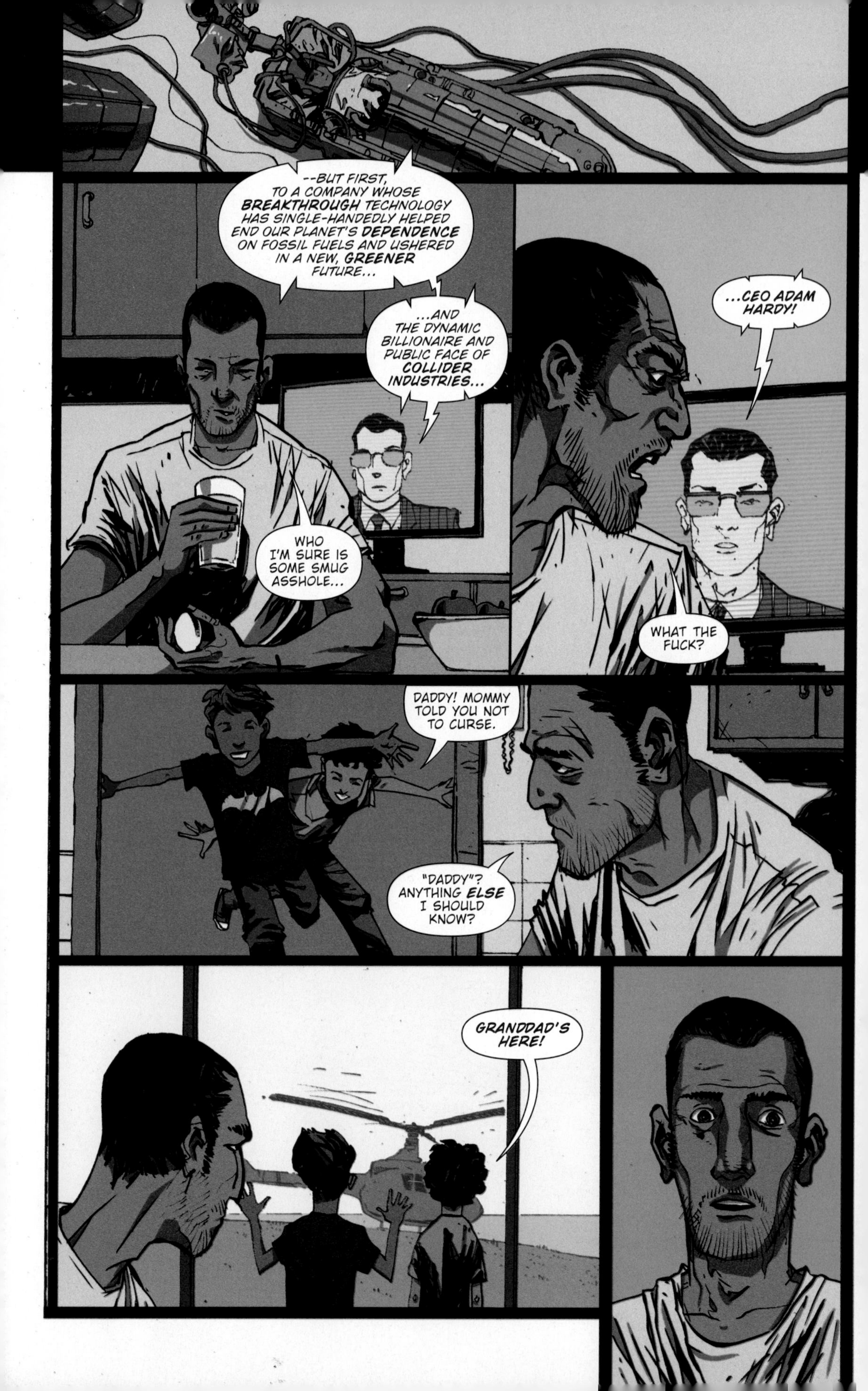
--BUT FIRST, TO A COMPANY WHOSE BREAKTHROUGH TECHNOLOGY HAS SINGLE-HANDEDLY HELPED END OUR PLANET'S DEPENDENCE ON FOSSIL FUELS AND USHERED IN A NEW, GREENER FUTURE...
...AND THE DYNAMIC BILLIONAIRE AND PUBLIC FACE OF COLLIDER INDUSTRIES...
WHO I'M SURE IS SOME SMUG ASSHOLE...
...CEO ADAM HARDY!
WHAT THE FUCK?
DADDY! MOMMY TOLD YOU NOT TO CURSE.
"DADDY"? ANYTHING ELSE I SHOULD KNOW?
GRANDDAD'S HERE!

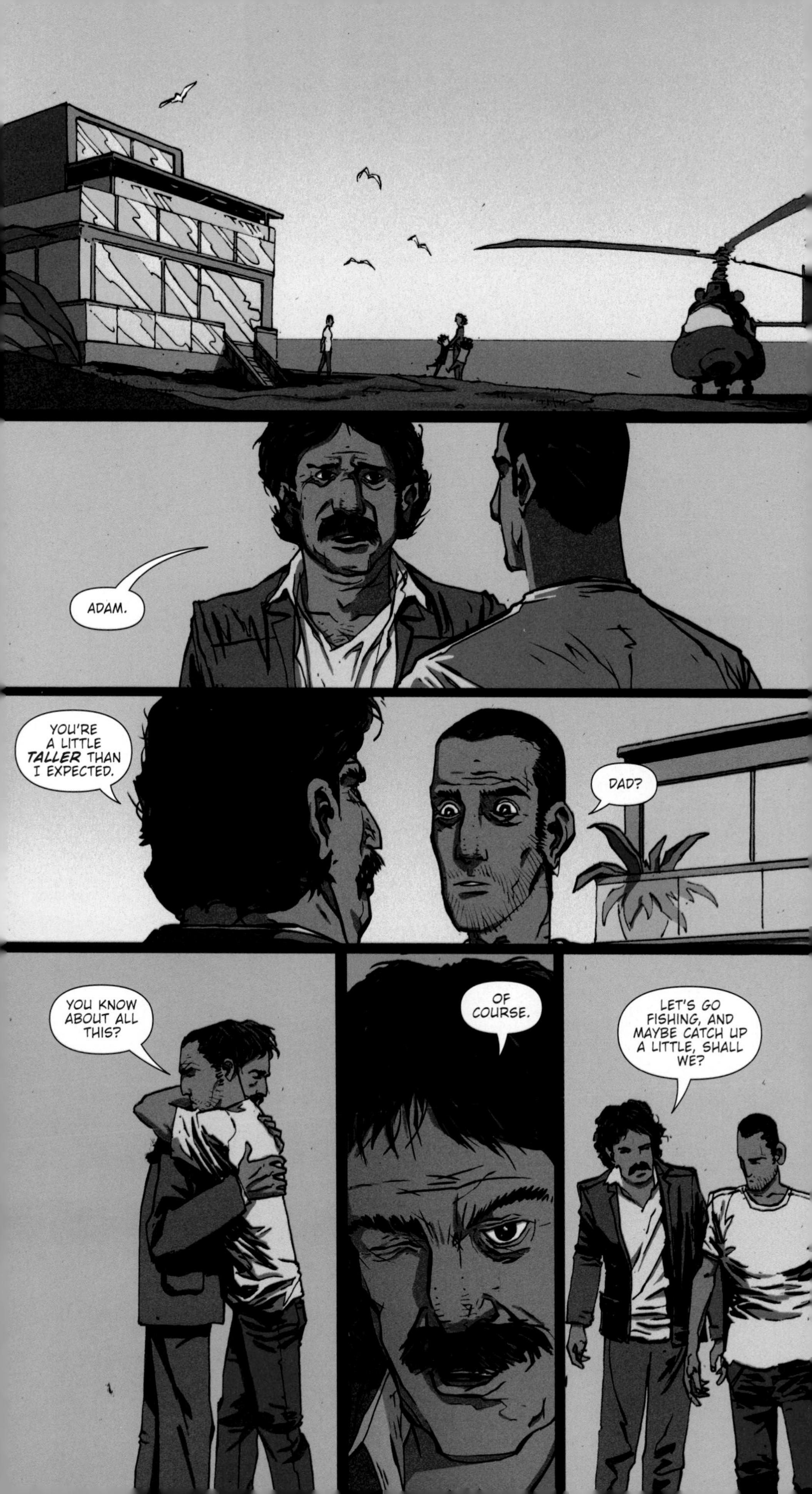
ADAM.
YOU'RE A LITTLE TALLER THAN I EXPECTED.
DAD?
YOU KNOW ABOUT ALL THIS?
OF COURSE.
LET'S GO FISHING, AND MAYBE CATCH UP A LITTLE, SHALL WE?

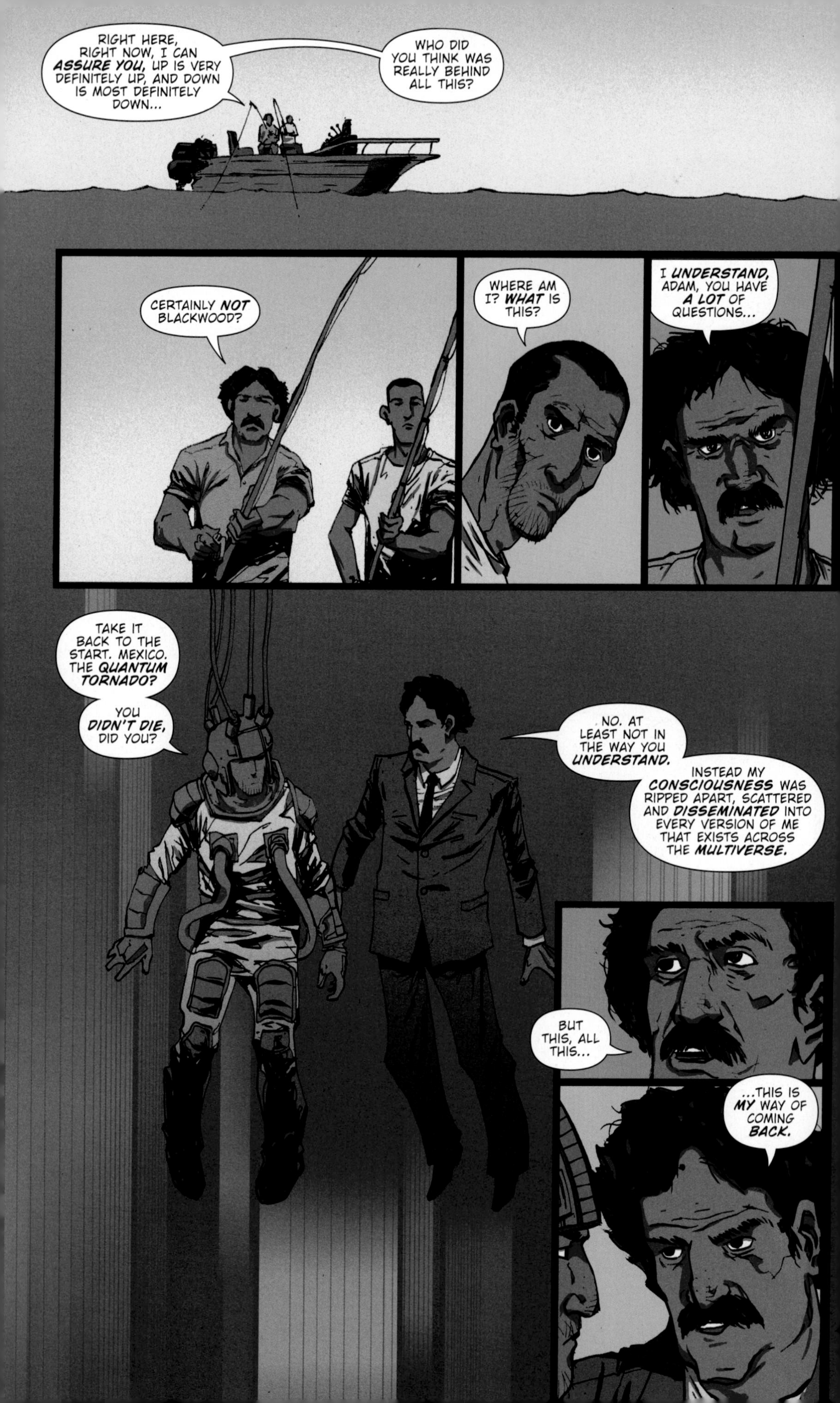
RIGHT HERE, RIGHT NOW, I CAN ASSURE YOU, UP IS VERY DEFINITELY UP, AND DOWN IS MOST DEFINITELY DOWN...
WHO DID YOU THINK WAS REALLY BEHIND ALL THIS?
CERTAINLY NOT BLACKWOOD?
WHERE AM I? WHAT IS THIS?
I UNDERSTAND, ADAM, YOU HAVE A LOT OF QUESTIONS...
TAKE IT BACK TO THE START. MEXICO. THE QUANTUM TORNADO?
YOU DIDN'T DIE, DID YOU?
NO. AT LEAST NOT IN THE WAY YOU UNDERSTAND.
INSTEAD MY CONSCIOUSNESS WAS RIPPED APART, SCATTERED AND DISSEMINATED INTO EVERY VERSION OF ME THAT EXISTS ACROSS THE MULTIVERSE.
BUT THIS, ALL THIS...
...THIS IS MY WAY OF COMING BACK.

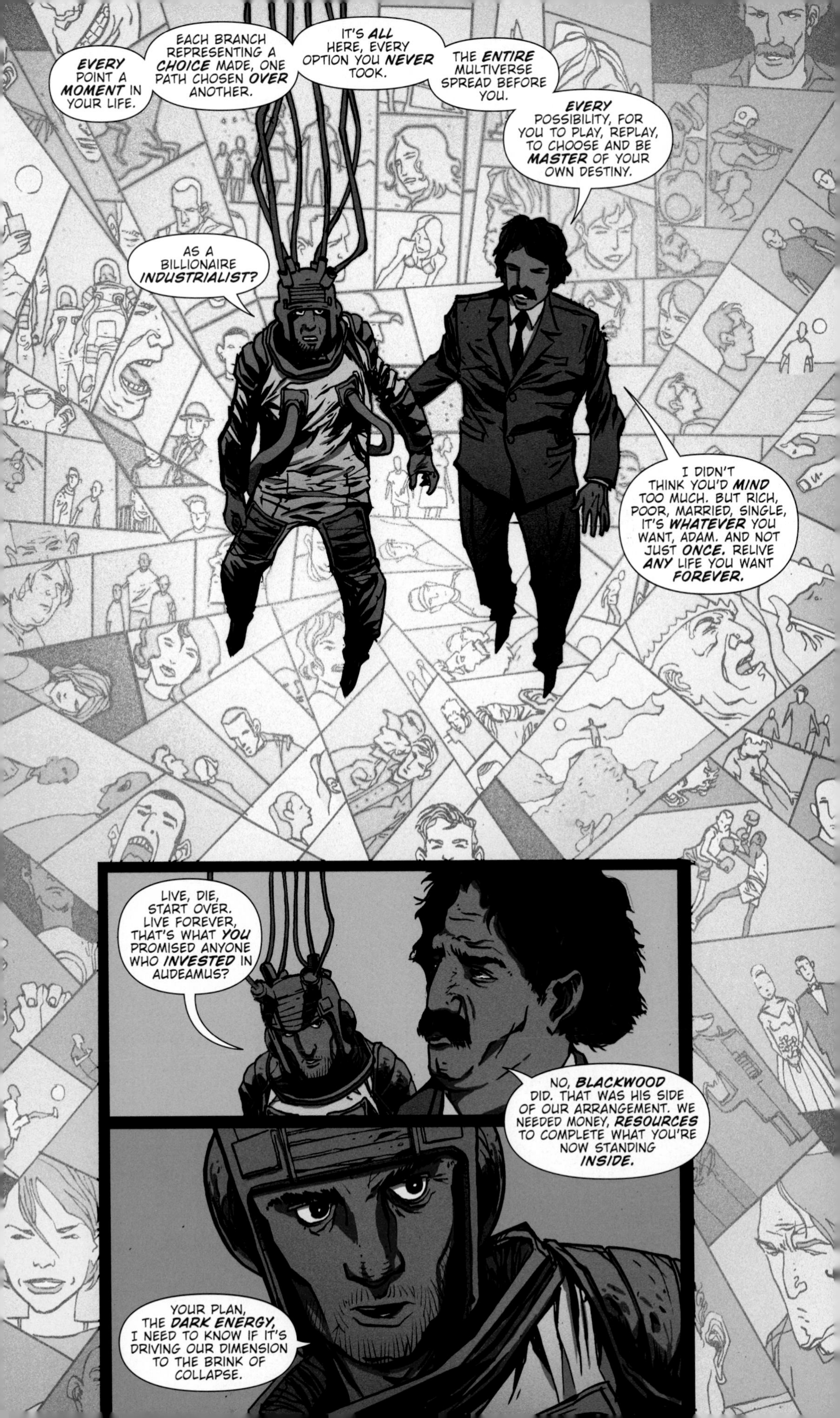
EVERY POINT A MOMENT IN YOUR LIFE.
EACH BRANCH REPRESENTING A CHOICE MADE, ONE PATH CHOSEN OVER ANOTHER.
IT'S ALL HERE, EVERY OPTION YOU NEVER TOOK.
THE ENTIRE MULTIVERSE SPREAD BEFORE YOU.
EVERY POSSIBILITY, FOR YOU TO PLAY, REPLAY, TO CHOOSE AND BE MASTER OF YOUR OWN DESTINY.
AS A BILLIONAIRE INDUSTRIALIST?
I DIDN'T THINK YOU'D MIND TOO MUCH. BUT RICH, POOR, MARRIED, SINGLE, IT'S WHATEVER YOU WANT, ADAM. AND NOT JUST ONCE. RELIVE ANY LIFE YOU WANT FOREVER.
LIVE, DIE, START OVER. LIVE FOREVER, THAT'S WHAT YOU PROMISED ANYONE WHO INVESTED IN AUDEAMUS?
NO, BLACKWOOD DID. THAT WAS HIS SIDE OF OUR ARRANGEMENT. WE NEEDED MONEY, RESOURCES TO COMPLETE WHAT YOU'RE NOW STANDING INSIDE.
YOUR PLAN, THE DARK ENERGY, I NEED TO KNOW IF IT'S DRIVING OUR DIMENSION TO THE BRINK OF COLLAPSE.

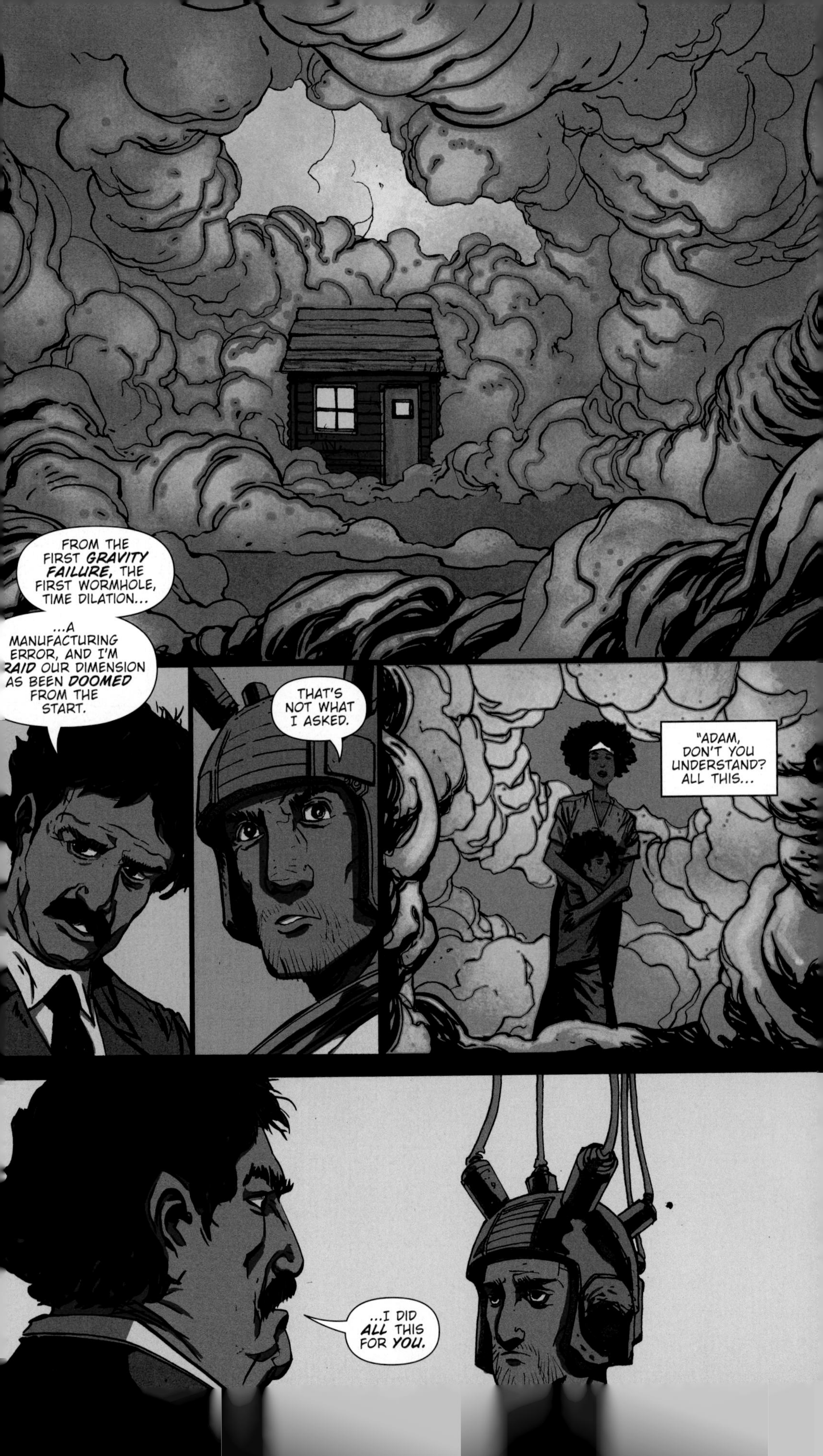
FROM THE FIRST GRAVITY FAILURE, THE FIRST WORMHOLE, TIME DILATION...
...A MANUFACTURING ERROR, AND I'M RAID OUR DIMENSION AS BEEN DOOMED FROM THE START.
THAT'S NOT WHAT I ASKED.
"ADAM, DON'T YOU UNDERSTAND? ALL THIS...
...I DID ALL THIS FOR YOU.

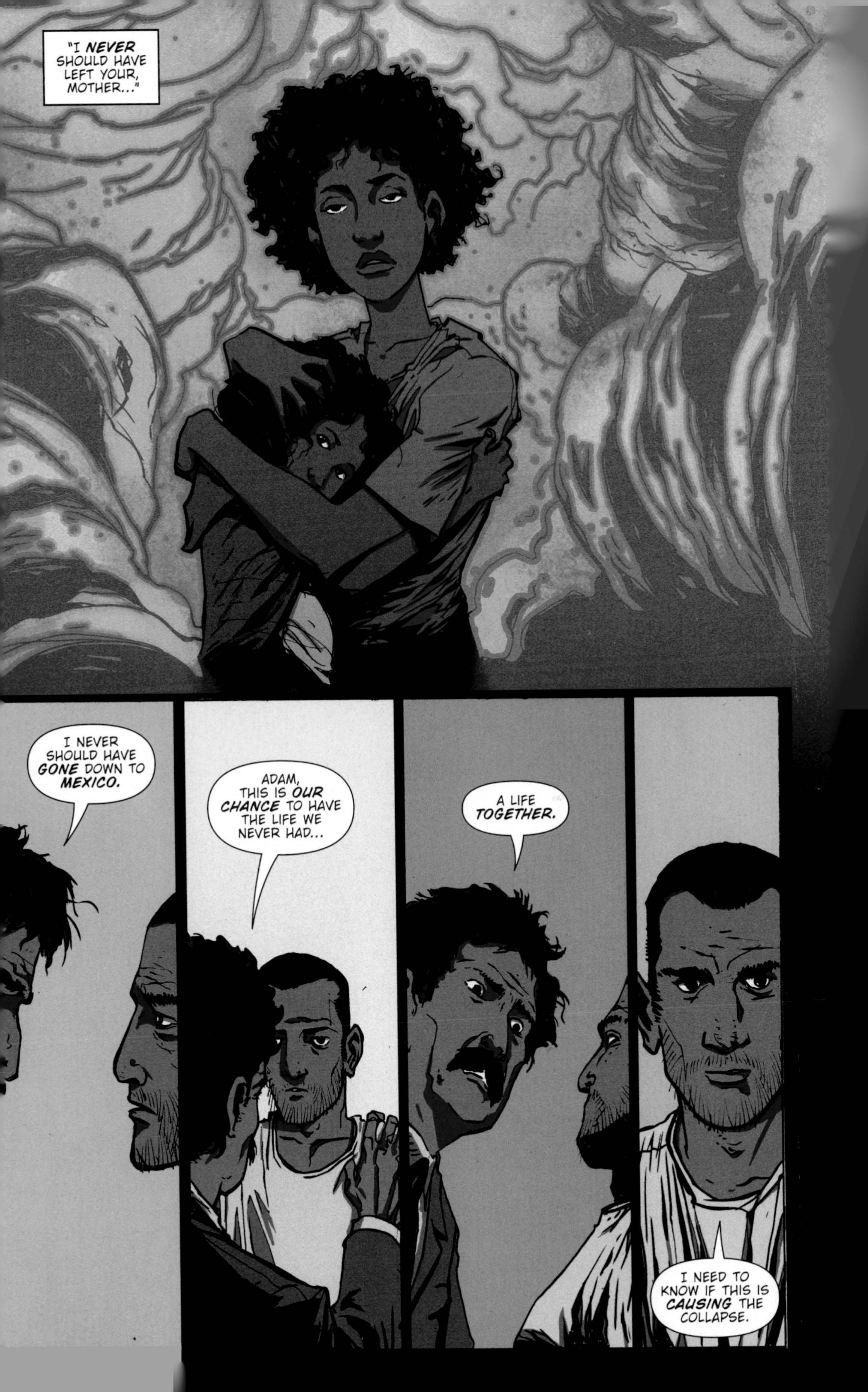
"I NEVER SHOULD HAVE LEFT YOUR, MOTHER..."
I NEVER SHOULD HAVE GONE DOWN TO MEXICO.
ADAM, THIS IS OUR CHANCE TO HAVE THE LIFE WE NEVER HAD...
A LIFE TOGETHER.
I NEED TO KNOW IF THIS IS CAUSING THE COLLAPSE.

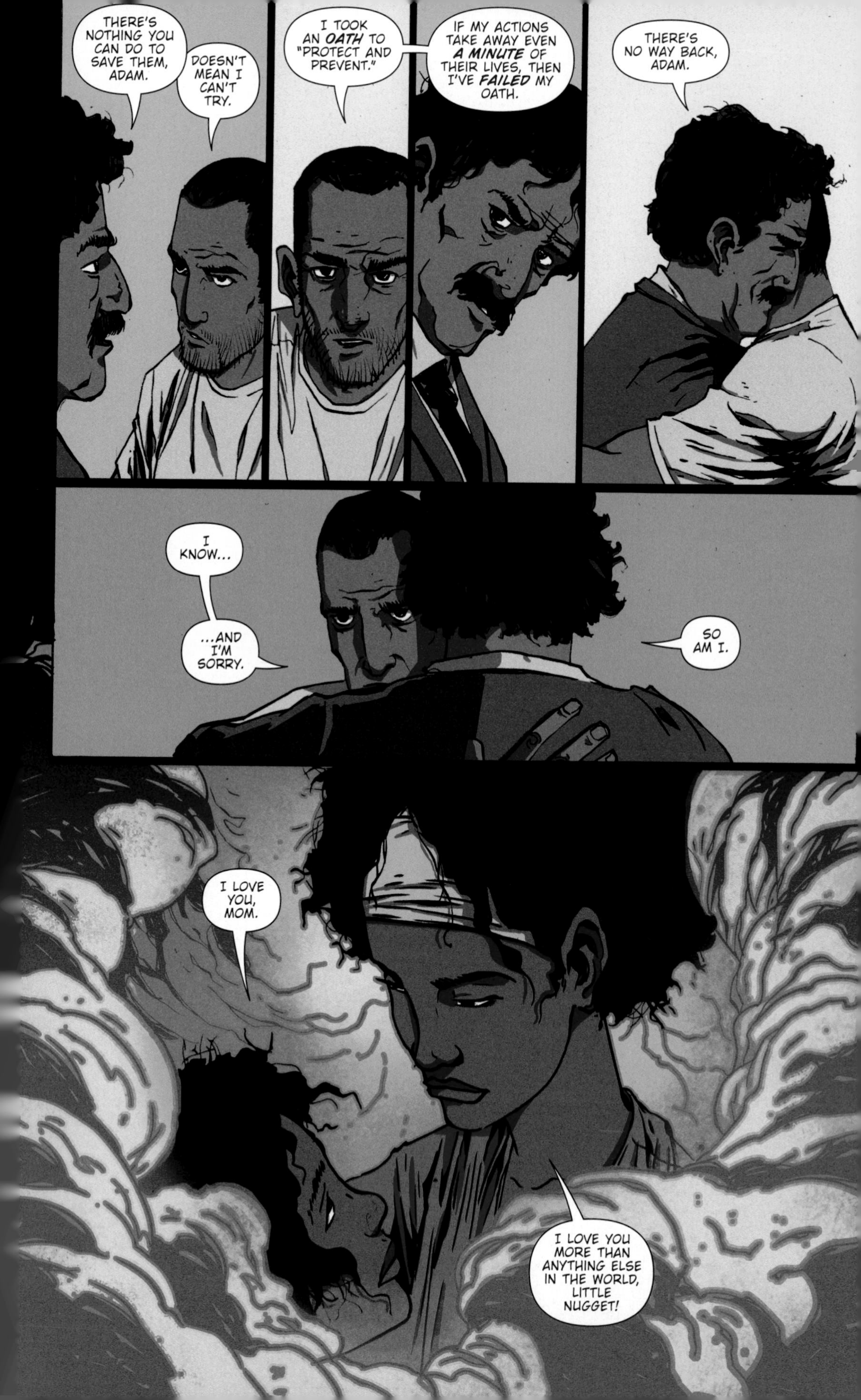
THERE'S NOTHING YOU CAN DO TO SAVE THEM, ADAM.
DOESN'T MEAN I CAN'T TRY.
I TOOK AN OATH TO "PROTECT AND PREVENT."
IF MY ACTIONS TAKE AWAY EVEN A MINUTE OF THEIR LIVES, THEN I'VE FAILED MY OATH.
THERE'S NO WAY BACK, ADAM.
I KNOW...
...AND I'M SORRY.
SO AM I.
I LOVE YOU, MOM.
I LOVE YOU MORE THAN ANYTHING ELSE IN THE WORLD, LITTLE NUGGET!

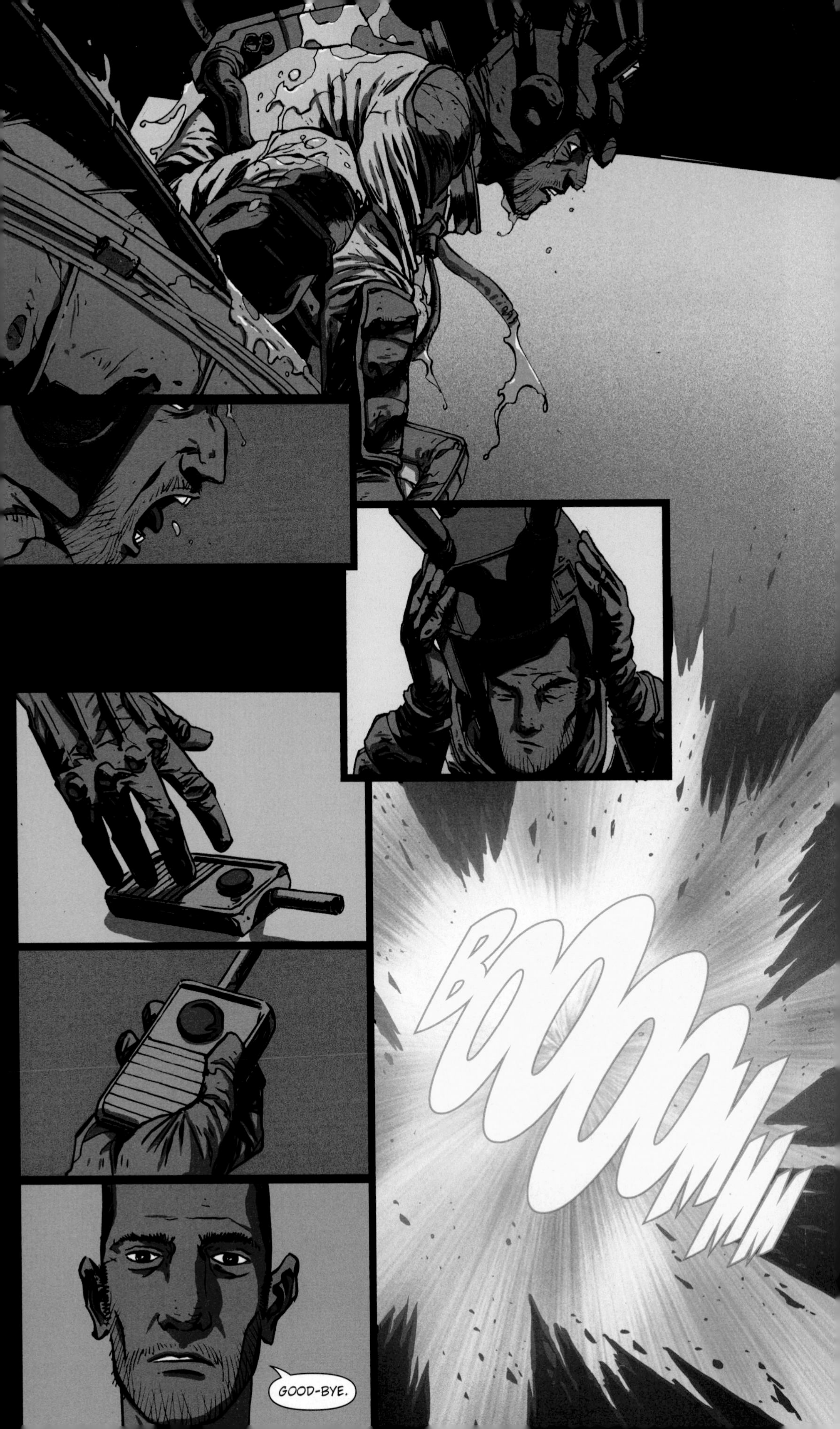
BOOOOMMM
GOOD-BYE.

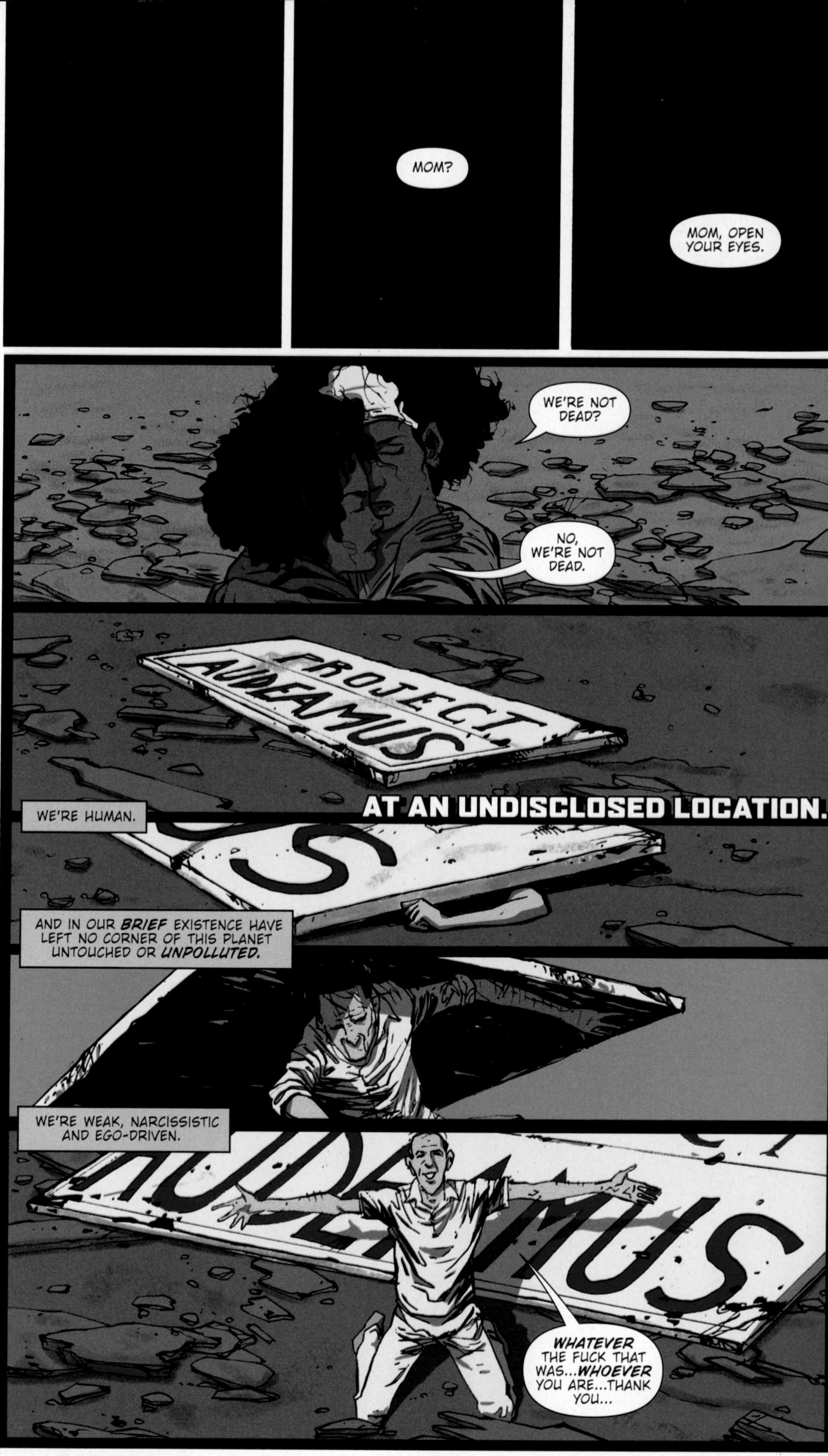
MOM?
MOM, OPEN YOUR EYES.
WE'RE NOT DEAD?
NO, WE'RE NOT DEAD.
PROJECT AUDEAMUS
WE'RE HUMAN.
AT AN UNDISCLOSED LOCATION.
AND IN OUR BRIEF EXISTENCE HAVE LEFT NO CORNER OF THIS PLANET UNTOUCHED OR UNPOLLUTED.
WE'RE WEAK, NARCISSISTIC AND EGO-DRIVEN.
WHATEVER THE FUCK THAT WAS...WHOEVER YOU ARE...THANK YOU...

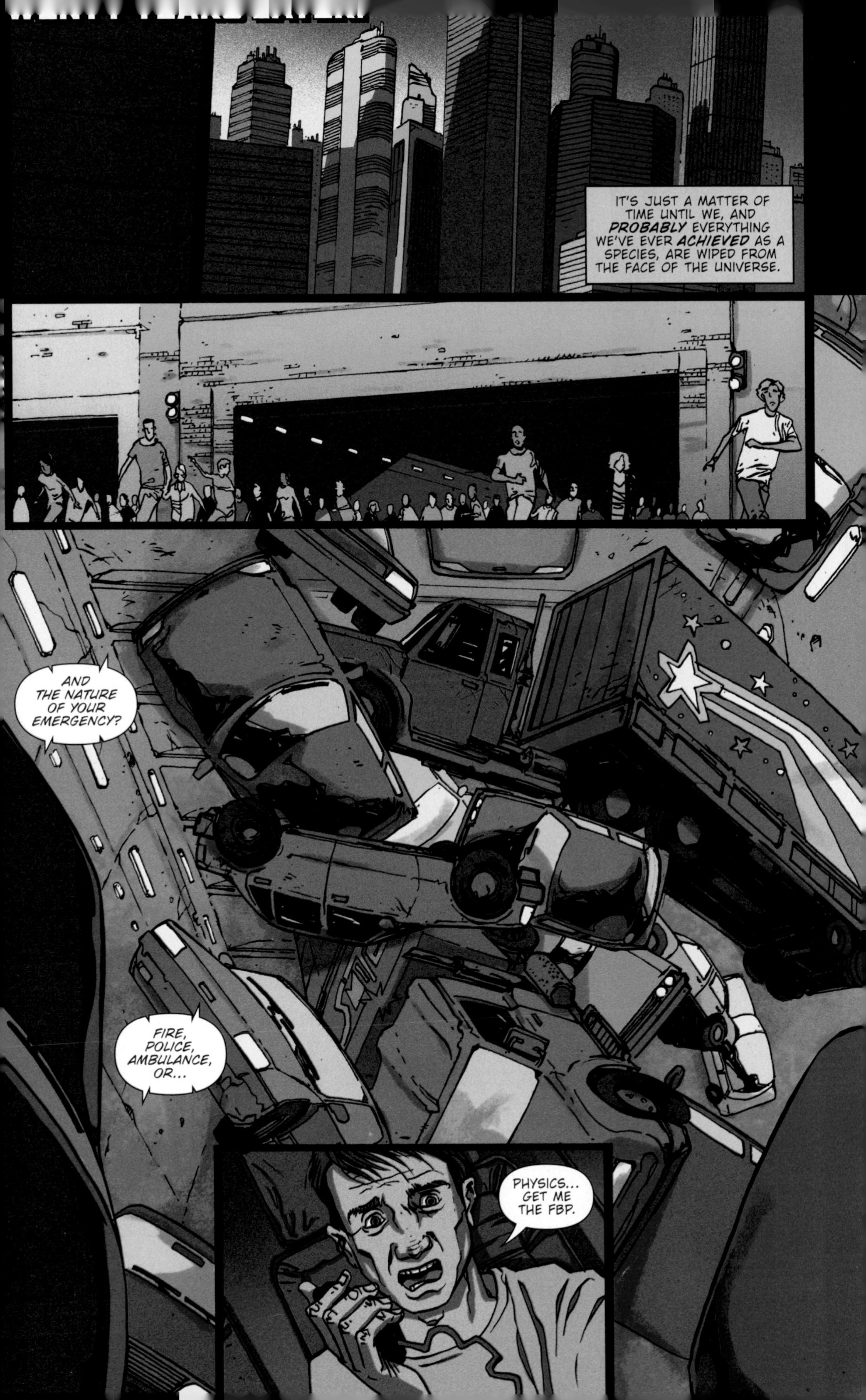
IT'S JUST A MATTER OF TIME UNTIL WE, AND PROBABLY EVERYTHING WE'VE EVER ACHIEVED AS A SPECIES, ARE WIPED FROM THE FACE OF THE UNIVERSE.
AND THE NATURE OF YOUR EMERGENCY?
FIRE, POLICE, AMBULANCE, OR...
PHYSICS... GET ME THE FBP.

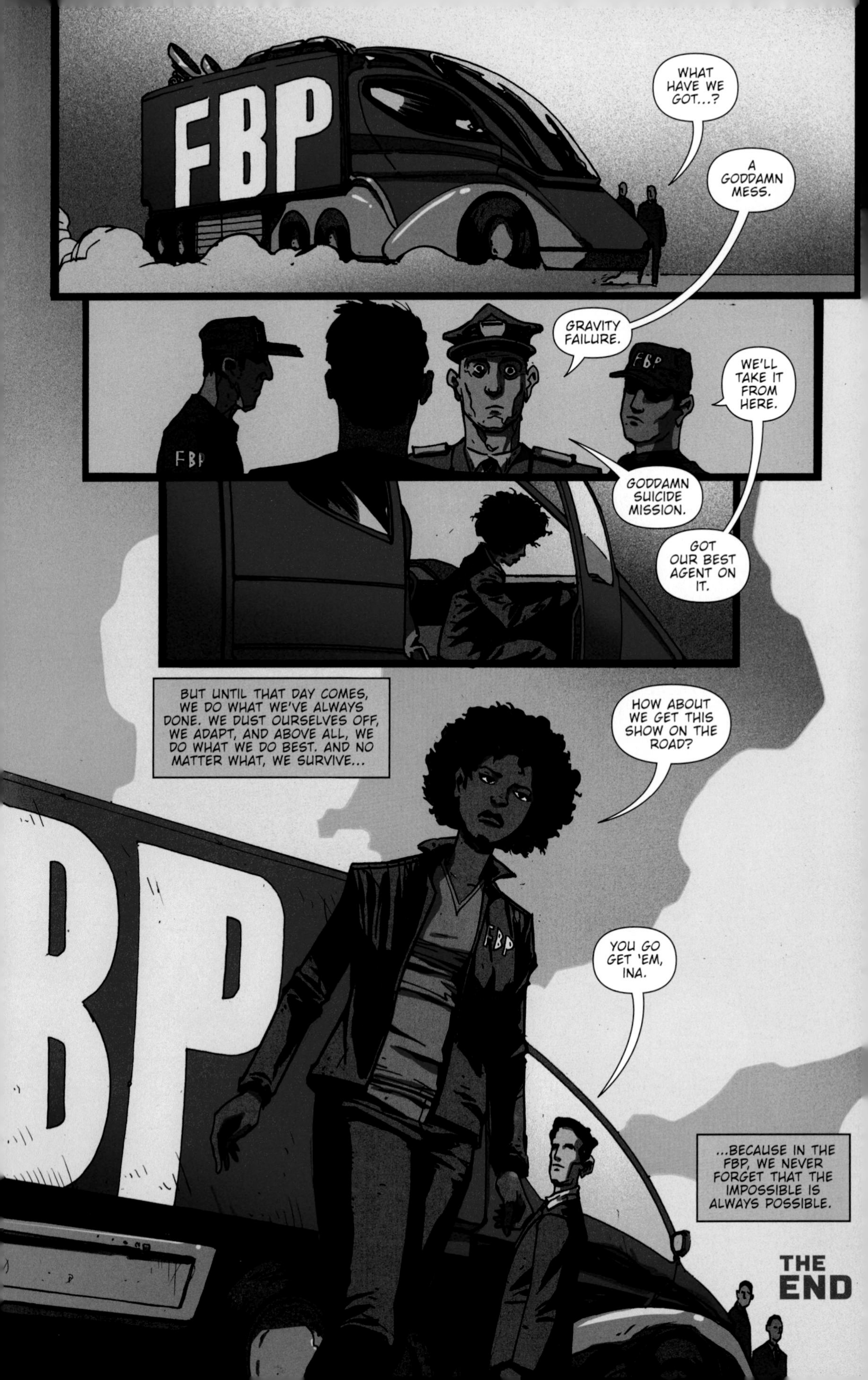
FBP
WHAT HAVE WE GOT...?
A GODDAMN MESS.
GRAVITY FAILURE.
WE'LL TAKE IT FROM HERE.
GODDAMN SUICIDE MISSION.
GOT OUR BEST AGENT ON IT.
BUT UNTIL THAT DAY COMES, WE DO WHAT WE'VE ALWAYS DONE. WE DUST OURSELVES OFF, WE ADAPT, AND ABOVE ALL, WE DO WHAT WE DO BEST. AND NO MATTER WHAT, WE SURVIVE...
HOW ABOUT WE GET THIS SHOW ON THE ROAD?
YOU GO GET 'EM, INA.
...BECAUSE IN THE FBP, WE NEVER FORGET THAT THE IMPOSSIBLE IS ALWAYS POSSIBLE.
THE END

Afterword by Simon Oliver

Not so many years ago (but many more than I'd care to remember), back when I was writing what would become the very first issue of my very first comic book, a comic book artist told me, "If you're doing what you really love, then it's something that you'd be doing even if you weren't being paid for it."

At the time I wasn't too sure; I was, for the first time, caught in a Möbius strip of endlessly writing and rewriting the same pages, repeatedly trying and repeatedly failing miserably to come up with twenty-two pages that carried something that even half resembled a story. Every time I thought I had cracked it, the very next morning, in the cold light of day, far from the witty brilliance I'd been so sure I'd achieved when I downed keyboard, it suddenly seemed more like a series of haphazard scenes written by a dribbling idiot and bolted together by an imbecile on a moron's conveyer belt. The only light I saw at the end of the tunnel was probably the premature end of a mistaken career barreling down at me.

A few years later and a few issues under my belt, I was stuck in Los Angeles traffic flicking through radio stations, and somewhere between the God-botherers and some crazy-ass Korean gangster rap I caught a scratchy report about tornadoes tearing through the Midwest. Now I admit (and no offense, Kansas, and your square-shaped state friends), it was something I didn't usually pay that much attention to, but somewhere deep in my caffeine-addled brain a switch had been flipped. And, as any writer will tell you, once that switch is flipped, it can't easily be unflipped.

I spent all that night bouncing ideas around, and the next day, at the crack of dawn (probably more like midday, if I'm honest), I frantically called Mark Doyle at Vertigo—"Hey, wouldn't it be great if we took tornadoes and weather-based phenomena (which if you think about it are kind of crazy in themselves) and replaced them with physics..." Many lesser men would have hung up, but thankfully, tall Mark D, somewhere in the midst of my half-formed ramblings, "got it."

Writing a monthly ongoing comic is something like being on a runaway train, and I mean that in the nicest possible way. Once they suck you onboard, it's very hard to get off. From issue number one, every month you go screaming through another station, and you'd better be ready to toss another issue off to appease the comic book gods or there will be hell to pay.

It's a very hands-on, very personal experience, one that I think is almost unique among all the other visual storytelling media. Yes, an editor's there holding your hand to make sure you don't totally embarrass yourself in print and keeping the train on the tracks (thanks Mark, Greg, Molly, and everyone at Vertigo), but month-in, month-out, what you, the reader, get in your hands is by and large the undiluted, fever-dreamt vision of what the writer and art team have come up with, usually only weeks, days or sometimes, dare I say it, hours before.

And once it's out there, it's out there. There is no turning back. Remember that fight you had with the class bully in fifth grade? The one where you came up with the perfect witty response that you should have said, only it's two days and one black eye too late? Well, I wake in a cold sweat, my mind swirling with a three-month-old issue and suddenly, from nowhere, I come up with the greatest line of dialogue I should have used, but didn't. The should haves and could haves, they become part and parcel of the job and the speed and the "no regrets," "no crying in comics" attitude you have to take on to hit twelve issues a year, but hopefully those moments get fewer and fewer with each issue and each book.

I've grown to love the constraints and limits of writing comics— the printed page, the precision of depicting action in strange, static, flat, two-dimensional panels, the unlimited special effects and locations budgets, the haiku-like restrictions of the twenty/ twenty-two page format and, probably most important, the creative freedom to tell the kind of story I want to tell.

For me, that's the real joy of writing comic books and working on a book like FBP. Over two years and twenty-four issues I've had the freedom to do pretty much anything I wanted to do. I've literally taken my storytelling to places I'd never taken it before, created and explored new worlds, come up with new characters, breathed some life into them and dragged them to hell and back. The fact that I get to do that every day and make a living from it is crazy. But even crazier is the idea that people out there are interested enough to buy (beg, borrow or steal) it.

So really, thank you. As you're holding a copy of the fourth volume of FBP, I'm guessing you might have read the other three (or not, but if you liked it, you can double back and read the rest now that you know how it ends). We all have busy lives and there are a million things out there competing for your attention, so thank you for making time to read this book, and I hope that you get as much enjoyment from reading it as I have from writing it.

Simon Oliver
Los Angeles, CA
2015

Behind the Scenes
FBP: FEDERAL BUREAU OF PHYSICS #24
Script by Simon Oliver • Art by Alberto Ponticelli

FBP #24 - SECOND DRAFT NOTES
There are going to be quite a few call backs to scenes and characters from earlier in the book, particularly the first few issues, so you might want to have them close by for reference.

PAGE ONE
These first two pages are open to some nice flowing panels to go with the Lord Byron poem I'm ~~stealing~~ quoting to play out over them.

So I'll give you a gist of the images and ideas and you have fun Alberto, go with a traditional panel layout, or something else, up to you.

The end of the world is upon us, let's start big.

Panel 1.x
BIG IMAGE - Start out with view of the Earth from space. A similar image to the one we used in the last issue, but maybe wider to make our Earth smaller.

Only now the earth should be even more fun house, bent out of shape, the pink antimatter haze/ cloud is denser and has covered the entire galaxy (remember this is about the complete destruction of our dimension, not just our Earth), and what we see of the Earth is poking out through the pink clouds —<we'll repeat a similar image on page 8, so give yourself room to increase the amount of pink haze later on>

Note - and this is really just for background, and won't come up in the script, but because the cloud isn't uniform across the world different parts of the world will be affected to different degrees. This will explain why the levels of destruction differ and how Ina and Liz will survive and other parts of the world are wiped out.

Now I'll start the Byron poem quotes here, I'm using "Darkness", but I won't go line by line, I'll pull what I need in line pairings (and the lines will play in tight pairs and fours across the pages) and of course I will adjust and trim and edit to the art later on, this is to give everyone an idea of where we're going with this...

BYRON POEM
I had a dream, which was not at all a dream.
The bright sun was extinguish'd, and the stars
Did wander darkling in the eternal space,
Rayless, and pathless, and the icy earth.

The palaces of crowned kings—the huts,
The habitations of all things which dwell,
Were burnt for beacons; cities were consum'd,
And men were gather'd round their blazing homes.

Their funeral piles with fuel, and look'd up
With mad disquietude on the dull sky,
The pall of a past world; and then again
With curses cast them down upon the dust.

Gorging himself in gloom: no love was left;
All earth was but one thought – and that was death
Died, and their bones were tombless as their flesh;
The meagre by the meagre were devour'd.

And the clouds perish'd; Darkness had no need
Of aid from them – She was the Universe. (*)

And an asterisk on the last line should direct the reader down to the Byron shout out at the bottom of the page.

(*) - "DARKNESS" - LORD BYRON - b.1788 - d.1824

Panel 1.x
Now once we've shown our galaxy and Earth, we should come into the planet and that traditional disaster movie trope—destroying famous landmarks.

Mix up the angles...Maybe wide on some, like the Great Wall China and the Pyramids, and them tight and ground level for to show destruction playing out, people getting enveloped and killed at ground level for the Eiffel Tower and Piccadilly Circus.

The deaths should be visually similar to how we played out Bailey's death in the last issue, but because we're down on Earth and not in I/D space feel free to change it up a little with that in mind.
Here's a list. Feel free to add or subtract...
- Great Wall of China.
- Egyptian Pyramids.
- Eiffel Tower–it should crashing down in a cloud of pink haze.
- Statue of Liberty–Time Square.
- Piccadilly Circus–chaos and death as the pink cloud wafts through.
- Angkor Wat–Buddhist Monks in orange robes running away would be a good visual.
- the Colosseum in Rome–(hey Alberto, feel free to destroy your own country).

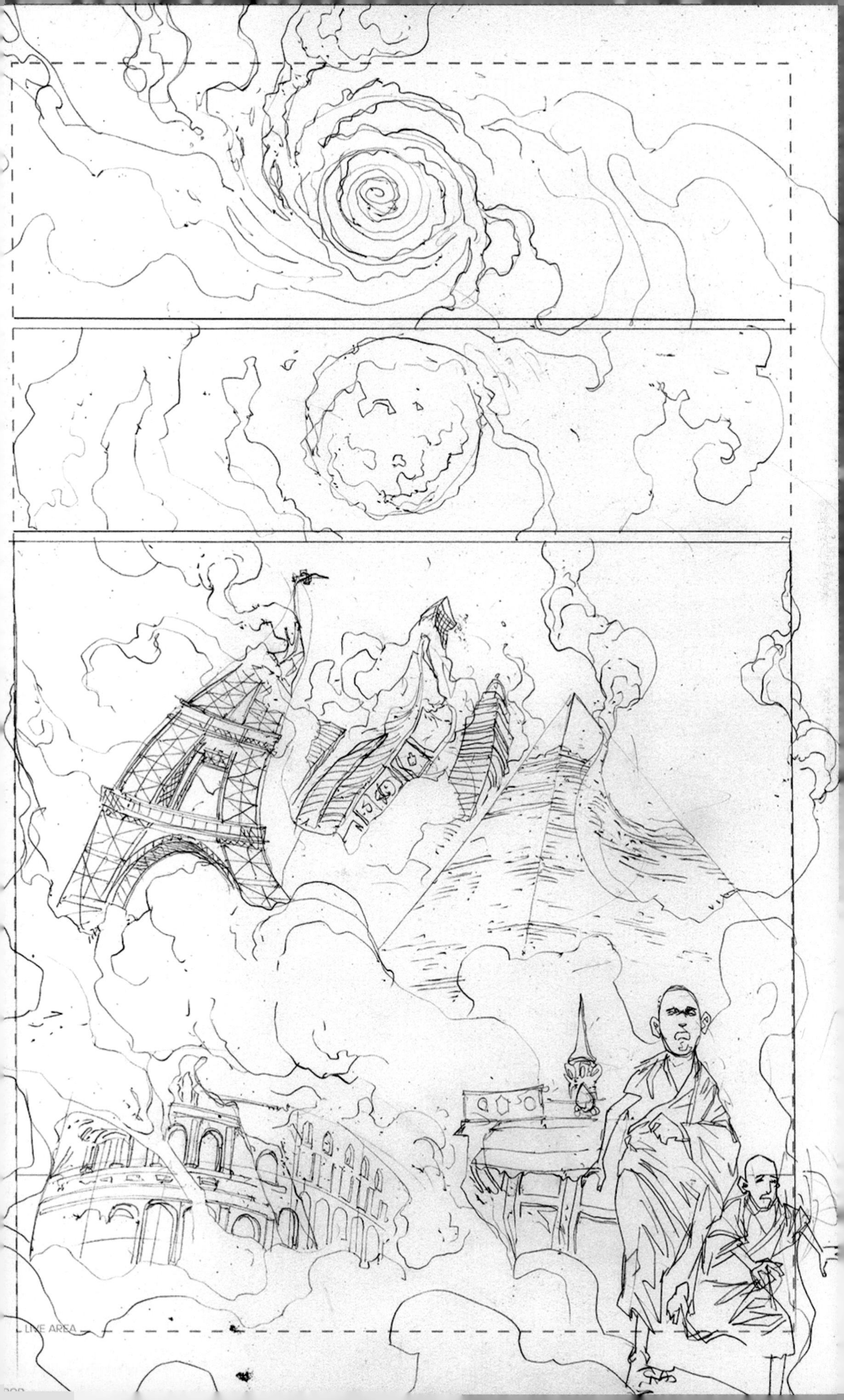
LIVE AREA

PAGE TWO

Panel 2.x

Start out the first half of the page with more destruction, accompanied by the verbal stylings of Lord Byron.

Panel 2.x

Then come down into the second half to the familiar forest in the pacific northwest to find the bucolic cabin we left Ina and Liz in.

Start wide... trees and a clearing, no sign of the pink cloud or any of the destruction or chaos of the previous panels.

Panel 2.x

Come in tighter, the cabin, an open fire that Ina and Liz fell asleep in-front off, still smouldering.

They can be stirring, or rather Liz is, waking Ina, show her rubbing the sleep from her eyes.

LIZ

Ina, what is it...?

INA

This...

Panel 2.x

Now punch in on Ina, and despite the peace and quiet, Ina knows a storm is coming.

INA

....This is it...

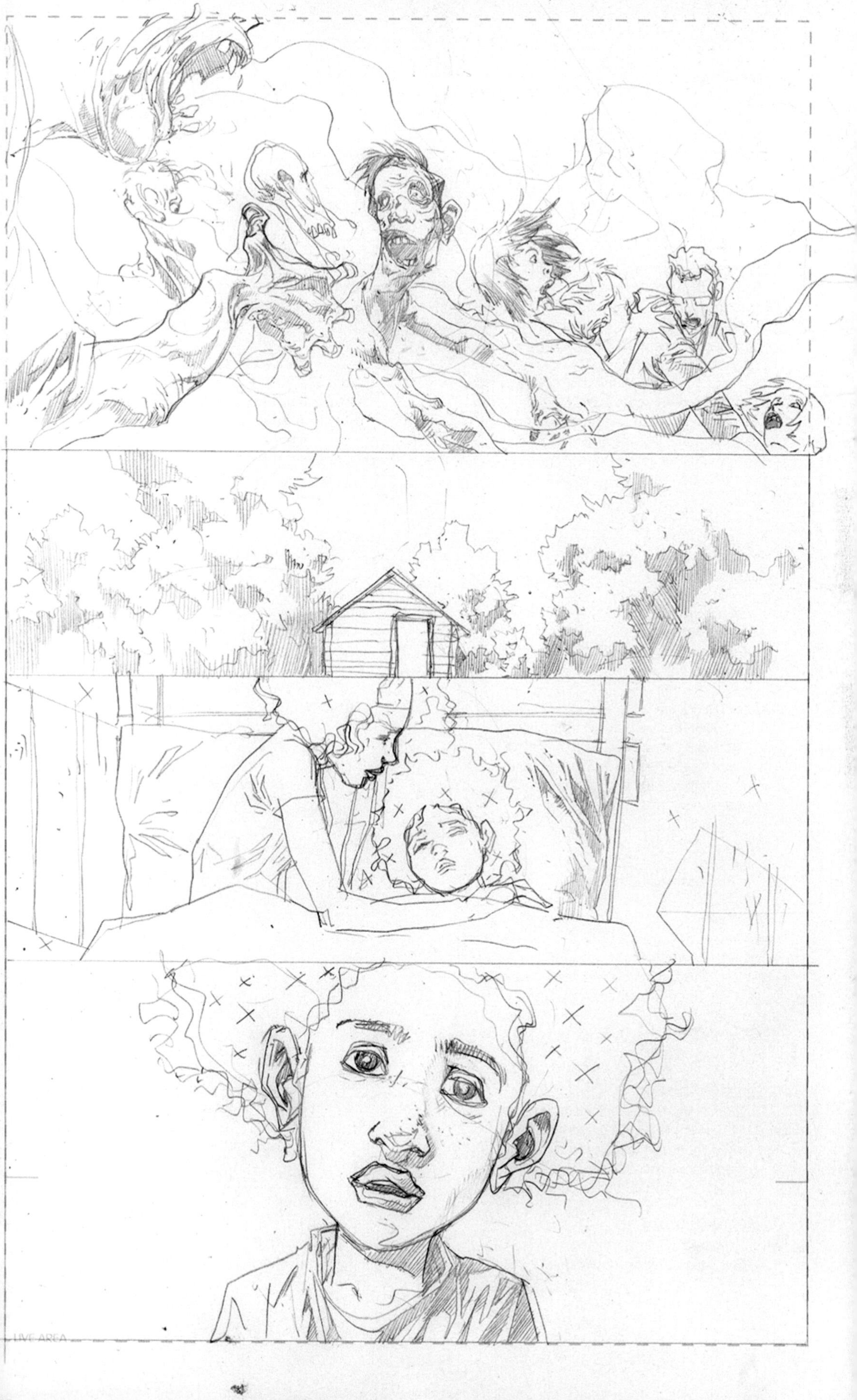

FBP FEDERAL BUREAU OF PHYSICS #20
Script by Simon Oliver • Art by Alberto Ponticelli

PAGE ONE
Lets start out with a few pages to catch us up with Liz and Ina in the hours and days after they left the stadium and went their own way after issue 19.

The idea is that the world beyond the stadium is really Fucked, order and civilization has broken down, and we're taking the first steps into a post-apocalypse, "the Road" type world, where only the strongest will survive.

Now with Ina, and it will start here, a lot of the voice over style narration in this arc will be coming from her, and from a future version of Ina. She going to be talking from a time when she's all grown up, that's going to the very end point of the book, revealed at the last issue.

Panel 1.1
Start off in the remains of a small suburban North Western town, the stores have been looted, cars block the streets.

But in the main square a small platform/stage has been erected for a preacher, and a lot of people have taken time away from survival to listen to what he has to say.

HELLFIRE PREACHER
...For years we trusted them. We trusted that they would make the world a better place, trusted them when they told us that "knowledge" was everything...

INA
(voice over)
Physics was failing us...

Panel 1.2
and now onto the stage they lead out a "scientist"— well it's probably the local middle school science teacher, glasses, and a white lab coat - but at its heart it's all very medieval looking.

The crowd booing and hissing and throwing rotten food at him.

HELLFIRE PREACHER
But when the flock begins to question the word of the shepherd, the shepherd is left no choice, the flock must be thinned, the liars must be singled out and punished.

SCIENCE TEACHER
(to the crowd)
But I taught your children...

CROWD
...you taught them nothing but lies.

CROWD
Booo... Hiss...

INA
(voice over)
Quantum tornadoes had ripped through our dimension spreading chaos, destruction and death...

Panel 1.3
they put a noose around his neck and haul him up to hang from lamp posts.

SCIENCE TEACHER
Help me... someone help me...

INA
(voice over)
Civilization stood on the brink.

Panel 1.4
and end on a wide shot showing all the white coated scientists hanging from lamp posts as the birds peck out their eyes.

And in the hard foreground Liz is pulling Ina away by the hand... We need to get them in, establish them before taking us to the next page.

LIZ
Ina, don't look back...

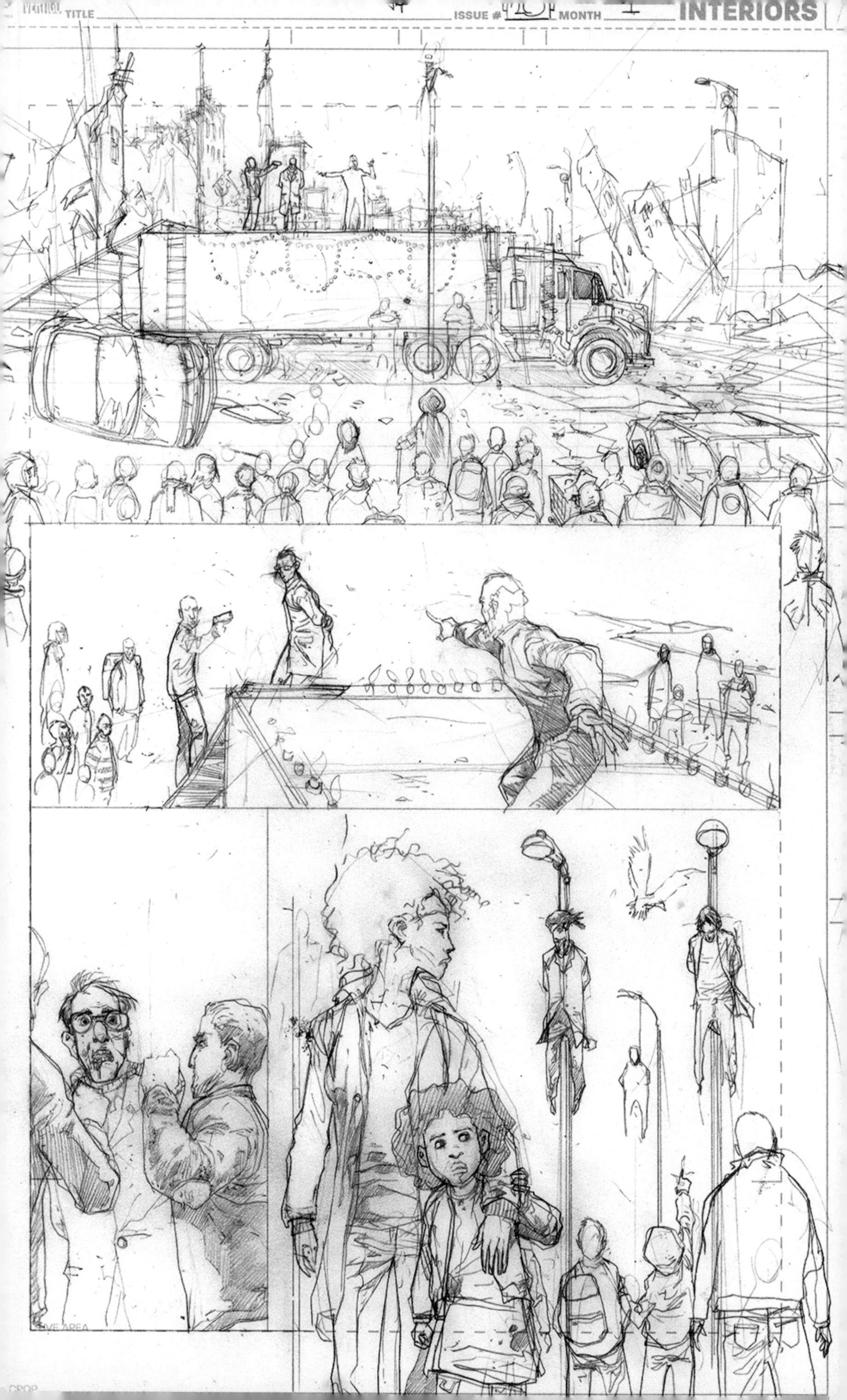
TITLE
ISSUE #
MONTH
INTERIORS

PAGE ONE

#1 — these first two are the preacher's bubbles — connected to one another — "WE BELIEVED THEM... WE TRUSTED THEM... TRUSTED THEM WHEN THEY TOLD US KNOWLEDGE WAS EVERYTHING..."

#2 — "..... AND THAT SCIENCE WOULD BE OUR SALVATION."

#3 — Ina's VO — "PHYSICS WAS FAILING US."

#4 — once again the preacher, and this is one sentence broken in two — "WHEN THE FLOCK BEGINS TO QUESTION THE WORD OF THE SHEPHERD, HE IS LEFT NO CHOICE..."

#5 - ".....THE LIARS MUST BE SINGLED OUT FROM THE FLOCK AND PUNISHED."

#6 — Teacher —"BUT I TAUGHT ALL YOUR CHILDREN..."

#7 — Preacher from off panel — "YOU TAUGHT THEM NOTHING BUT LIES...."

#8 — Liz — "INA, DON'T LOOK BACK..."

#9 — more of Ina's VO — "QUANTUM TORNADOES HAD BROUGHT US CHAOS, DESTRUCTION AND DEATH..."

#10 - Ina's VO — "CIVILIZATION STOOD ON THE BRINK."

#11 — Ina — "MOM?"

FBP #20 – Lettering Placement

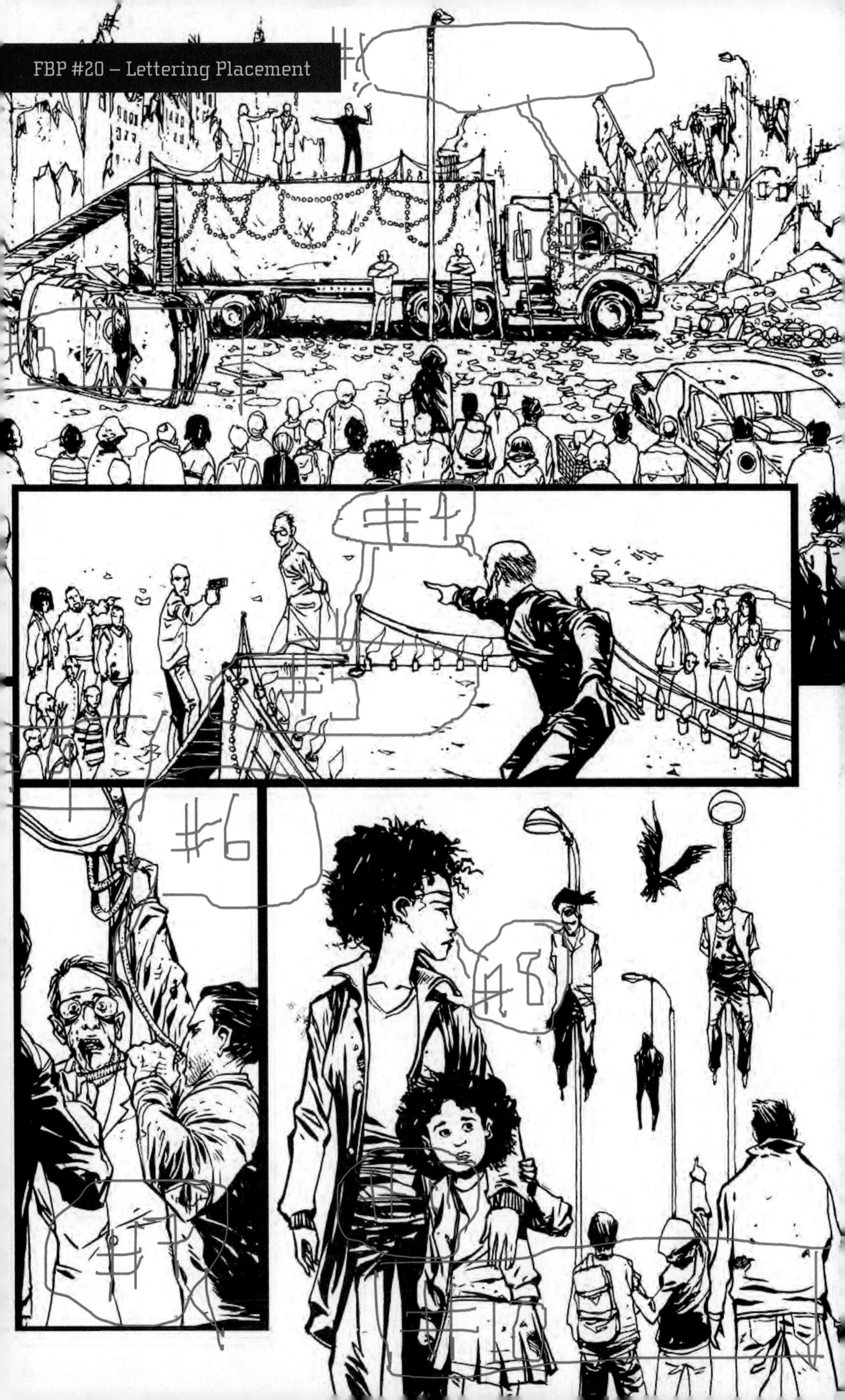
#4
#5
#6

FBP FINAL ARC BREAKDOWN

I'm going to be running three fairly distinct story lines each to show a different angle of how the big story is unfolding.

ADAM, CICERO, ROSA AND BAILEY -

- in inter-dimensional space.

- Cicero knows that something is really wrong, that Blackwood lied and his machine doesn't generate dark energy it simply sucks it up and moves it somewhere else.

- as he's figuring this out, up in I/D space the fuel hose has broken and Adam's ship is stranded, turns out the suits with the good seals are in the space station the ship is heading to, the ones they have are the shit ones, and Adam being deemed expendable has been preselected to undertake any suicide missions.

- But to everyone's shock, being the hero he is Adam volunteers, he really is the only one on board with the "right stuff". A roll of duct tape later and he's in space doing what needs to be done.

- Bailey is relieved and happy that Adam is okay, (we have to play it back and forth with her allegiances, never knowing exactly where they are).

- but played out from Adam's pov "gravity" style, while she was in space something else has gone wrong, but ground control won't tell him what they think has happened, Adam reenters the space ship to discover the leak has killed all his fellow D-nauts and he's now alone.

- meanwhile the geek that Cicero stole the pass from is getting questioned about it being used to access the files in Blackwood's house. Security is soon on his tail. Cicero grabs Rosa, they take Bailey hostage and barricade up in the second launch room, where Rosa's portal is ready and waiting for blast off.

- Cicero doesn't know exactly what Blackwood's plan is, or why they were lied to, all he knows they have to escape. Bailey is the only one who knows how to launch the portal carrying ship from inside the actual ship, so they have no choice but take her with them... and follow Adam into I/D space.

- when Bailey is dragged along with them (Rosa for one is not happy about her inclusion) that's when we reveal that she is Blackwood's secret daughter.

- Blackwood wants to send a unit into I/D space to get them but the third space craft isn't finished yet - so we set a ticking clock - counting down to the launch of armed goons sent to the space station.

- Blackwood wanted and hoped Adam would die somewhere along the way, because he doesn't want to share him with Adam's father - more on that in a minute.

- the effect the launch has on the planet below gives Cicero the spark to what's going on. Once they are all reunited at the portal space station Cicero works on proving his hunch - that Blackwood's dark energy "mover" is destabilizing the universe and actually causing the deterioration.

- Bailey's kept tied up to a chair by Rosa, and throwing her proverbial spanner in the works. She knows about the TV snow gag, she knows that her father has been talking to Adam's father, and tells Adam this.

- Adam sets up an intercom with his father, only here in I/D space he's able to create a more 3d hologram type image of his father, who's just the other side of the divide that Rosa's portal is going to open.

- it's like having his father right there, Adam and his father reconnect, well really meet for the first time. Only what Adam doesn't know, and does think to ask is how deeply his father is involved. The reality is his father is the mastermind behind the plan. Destabilize the planet, sacrifice the many, so the few can be saved on Blackwood's "life boat," because once the portal is open it's a matter of minutes before our dimension collapses behind it.

- on board the space station sides are being carved, Adam is being influenced by his father and Bailey while Cicero's findings are dismissed, and he and Rosa are sidelined.

- the clock is ticking -

- both side of the argument have to be fleshed out. Professor Hardy has to make a strong argument, that it's now or never "that the survival of mankind is more important than any one individual, even if it's billions of individuals. Whereas Cicero argues that mankind is inventive, and that given time, and cooperation humans can come up with a better plan.

- Blackwood's extraction unit arrives and storms the space station, it needs to come down to the wire - Adam's indecision nearly costs everything right up to the end we're not sure what he's going to do - BUT -

- finally, won over Adam sides with Cicero and decides to destroy the portal and the dark energy tunnel, turning his back on and betraying his own father, who has loomed so large for all of them, not just Adam.

- Adam rigs it so he's the only one who stays behind, while the others escape, sacrificing his life to blow the portal up... dying a hero, while the rest return safely to Earth.

- an Earth that will one day collapse, but because Blackwood's dark energy machine has been destroyed, it won't be tomorrow. And hopefully by the time that day comes mankind will have come up with a solution that won't necessarily mean the deaths of billions.

INA AND LIZ

- the single mom and daughter, going on a "The Road" type trip across the country as the physics situation gets worse and civilization crumbles around them.

- Liz wants to take Ina back to the place where she was conceived, when Liz was truly happy, when the best part of her life, Ina, was created.

- all kinds of shit, physics and human will get thrown at them along the way, Liz doesn't even tell Ina where they're heading until she absolutely has to, but by the final episode they've reached a small cabin in the woods, a million miles from anyone, where Liz is happy to let the world end.

- a lot of emotional meat in this thread, and a good contrast to what's going on in the space station.

AND MISTER CREST.

- yeah, the guy, the embezzling banker from the first arc is coming back to help us with part of Blackwood's plan - to save only the wealthy or well connected.

- after his near death experience in the bubbleverse Crest has been on a spiritual quest, we can pick up his story in a Buddhist monastery in Thailand, where Crest is meditating (and screwing Norwegian hippies - his scenes have to have an air of fun fuck up about them).

- an Atomcraft heli-transporter arrives to take Crest to the secure assembly point.

- years before, Crest signed up for Blackwood's life boat program, too coked-up to really know what it was all about - and now it's in full effect.

- Crest gets taken to the luxury assembly compound, where like Davos all the rich and powerful are assembling. Without a clue as to why he's there, Crest has to figure out what's really going on, without drawing attention to himself.

- he helps us out by piecing that part of the puzzle together, ends up getting caught and killed before the final issue, but along the way has achieved what the meditation could never do - redeem his past sleazy actions.

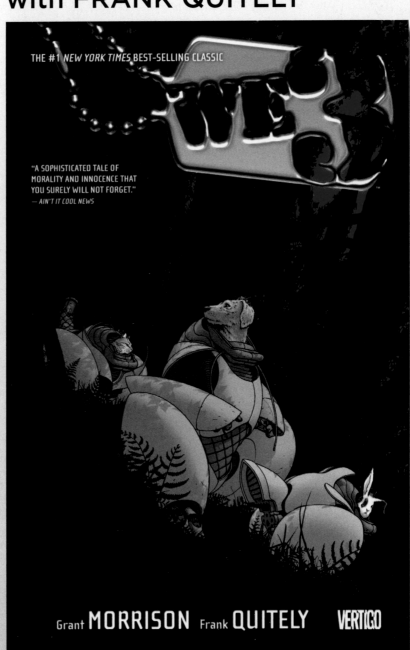